D0425040

THE MAKING OF
THE ROMAN ARMY

THE MAKING OF THE ROMAN ARMY

From Republic to Empire

Lawrence Keppie

BARNES
&NOBLE
BOOKS
NEW YORK

This edition published by Barnes & Noble, Inc.,
by arrangement with B.T. Batsford, Ltd.

1994 Barnes & Noble Books

ISBN 1-56619-359-1

Printed and bound in the United States of America

M 9 8 7 6 5 4 3

Contents

Acknowledgments

The author and publisher wish to thank the following for making photographs available and for permission to reproduce them:
The Mansell Collection, pl. 1, 6, 11, 15, 20; École Française d'Archéologie, Athens, pl. 2; Bildarchiv Foto Marburg, pl. 3; British Museum, Dept. of Coins and Medals, pl. 4a, 4b, 4e; Hunter Coin Cabinet, University of Glasgow, pl. 4c, 4d, 12a–d, 16a–d, 17a–d; John Patterson, pl. 5c, 14a; Museum of Fine Arts, Boston, pl. 5d; Museo Campano, Capua, pl. 10; Dr D. Baatz, pl. 13; M.H. Crawford, pl. 14b; Rheinishes Landesmuseum, Bonn, pl. 18; Mittelrheinishes Museum, Mainz, pl. 19a–d.
The author and publisher also wish to thank the following for permission to reproduce line-illustrations: Society for the Promotion of Roman Studies, fig. 9; The Librarian, Ashmolean Library, Oxford, fig. 47.

The Plates

List of Plates

8

Line Illustrations

INTRODUCTION

Not *another* book on the Roman army? Can there be *anything* new to say? Certainly the Roman army has attracted many writers, but the present book is not yet one more descriptive account of the army of the Roman Empire, familiar to students of Roman Britain from its frontier works and forts. Rather the theme here is of the army's growth, and of its developing institutions and traditions, all of which lie behind the familiar imperial army. The present work carries the story of Rome's army from a militia guarding a village on the Tiber down to the mid-first century AD. In a sense the following pages should constitute prolegomena to Graham Webster's *The Roman Imperial Army*, the most useful introduction to the armed forces of the Empire itself. The legions which lay encamped on the northern coast of Gaul in the summer of AD 43, ready to embark for the Claudian invasion of Britain, were the heirs to eight centuries of growth and development. The four individual legions—*II Augusta, IX Hispana, XIV Gemina* and *XX* (soon to be *Valeria Victrix*)—all carried with them to Britain the memory of campaigns waged, and battle-honours acquired over many years, since these particular units had come into being during the Civil Wars at the end of the Roman Republic.

My own interest in the Roman army before the Empire developed during preparation of a doctoral thesis, now published by the British School at Rome, under the title *Colonisation and Veteran Settlement in Italy, 47–14 BC* (London 1983), which documented the establishment on land in Italy of time-served soldiers of the armies of Julius Caesar, the Triumvirs and Augustus. The lack of a book on the army, bridging the gap between Republic and Empire, was immediately apparent. Our knowledge of the Republican army is based largely on literary references in ancient authors, which have been studied principally by historians. The army of the Empire is known mainly through inscriptions and its archaeological remains, and its exponents are often archaeologists working in the frontier provinces of the Empire where these categories of evidence survive in quantity. Yet archaeological remains *do* exist for the Republic; the volume of such material is bound to increase as more Roman camps and fortifications are identified by fieldwork and aerial photography. In recent years the work of Peter Connolly, in searching out and illustrating in inimitable style the armour and weaponry of the Republic has opened the eyes of many to the army before the Empire. The period between Marius and Caesar has been studied in detail by Jacques Harmand whose *L'Armée et le Soldat à Rome* (see Bibliography) remains indispensable. It will doubtless surprise the reader to know that not a single Roman camp has yet been found in Italy itself, to testify (for example) to operations against Hannibal, or the Celtic tribes in the Po Valley. In past generations study of the Roman army was taken up by many distinguished military men – serving or retired regular officers—to whom fieldcraft was a way of life. Their special expertise should not be overlooked. Foremost among them were Generalmajor Von Göler, Colonel Stoffel, Hauptmann Veith, and (in more recent times) Major-General Fuller and Captain Sir Basil Liddell Hart. For any reader who wishes to deepen his understanding of the psychology of the fighting man of any age in the face of the enemy, John Keegan's *The Face of Battle* (London 1976) must be essential reading.

Wherever possible the illustrations and line-drawings accompanying each chapter are of material and sites strictly contemporary with the period under discussion. Thus the reader will find here no scenes from Trajan's Column, the space-fillers of many modern coffee-table productions, nor will Caesar's legionaries be shown marching in uniforms which would have seemed to them futuristic. In fact the only conscious concessions to evidence outside the period under review will be the ground plan (fig. 47) of the legionary fortress at Inchtuthil (built AD c. 84–86), which remains crucial evidence for the internal organisation of a legion in the Early Empire, and a sculptured relief of Praetorian Guardsmen from Rome (pl. 20), which seems to date from the close of the first or the beginning of the second century AD (but see below, p. 234).

In accordance with the criteria laid down for this series, I have kept notes to a minimum, citing for the most part only the basic ancient literary or epigraphic evidence. The notes should be consulted in conjunction with the Bibliography, which is designed to direct the reader to earlier work on each topic discussed. Place-names are a problem, as always. In general I have preferred the Latin form, usually accompanied by the modern name; occasionally I have used the latter alone, where it will be more familiar. All dates are BC, except where specified as AD.

I am glad here to record a deep debt of gratitude to Dr Graham Webster, who encouraged me to submit my ideas to Batsford, and kept a benevolent eye on the progress of the present book. He has read the complete text in draft form, as have Mr Michael Crawford and Dr Brian Dobson. Miss Elizabeth Rawson read a draft of Chapters 1 and 2, and Dr Edith Wightman a draft of Chapter 3. It is also a pleasure to thank participants in the Fregellae excavation of 1982, where half-formed theories were subjected to close examination, especially by John Patterson, Jon Edmondson, and Michael Vercnocke. John Patterson readily agreed to take photographs for me in the course of fieldwork in Campania and around Benevento. Much of what follows was drafted in Italy, on trains or in the garden of the British School at Rome, on two separate visits in July and September 1982; Amanda Claridge and her colleagues always made me welcome at the School and smoothed my path. An invitation from Brian Dobson to participate in the 'Roman Army' course at Durham in April 1983 gave me the opportunity to argue my views before an informed audience which included Peter Connolly, Frank Walbank and Jim Summerly; what I have to say about the growth of professionalism in the army owes much to Professor Walbank's own assessments of the Roman attitudes to warfare under the Republic. Peter Connolly was kind enough to lend me his slides of Roman weaponry from Numantia, which form the basis of fig. 18. Among other friends who offered advice or help, I am happy to mention John Drinkwater, David Kennedy, Brigitte Galsterer-Kröll, Donal Bateson, Andrew Burnett, Jane Jakeman and Helen Whitehouse. Peter Kemmis Betty's close scrutiny of the finished typescript did much to improve the final presentation.

The line illustrations were drawn by the author, except where acknowledged to the contrary. Details of the sources of all photographs will be found in the 'Notes on the Plates'. To all the individuals and institutions involved, I am deeply grateful for their co-operation.

Finally it is important to place on record my thanks to Michael Crawford for his hospitality and generosity, and ever-willing offers of transportation over the years in search of inscriptions and sculptured reliefs in far corners of Italy.

Hunterian Museum
University of Glasgow

1 The Army of the Roman Republic

Rome naturally had an army from its earliest days as a village on the Tiber bank. At first it consisted of the king, his bodyguard and retainers, and members of clan-groups living in the city and its meagre territory. The army included both infantry and cavalry. Archaeological finds from Rome and the vicinity would suggest circular or oval shields, leather corslets with metal pectorals protecting the heart and chest, and conical bronze helmets. It must, however, be emphasised at the outset that we have very little solid evidence for the *organisation* of the early Roman army.

The wars between Rome and her neighbours were little more than scuffles between armed raiding bands of a few hundred men at most. It is salutary to recall that Fidenae (Fidene), against which the Romans were fighting in 499, lies now within the motorway circuit round modern Rome, and is all but swallowed up in its northern suburbs. Veii, the Etruscan city that was Rome's chief rival for supremacy in the Tiber plain, is a mere 10 miles to the north-west (fig. 1).

In appearance Rome's army can have differed little from those of the other small towns of Latium, the flat land south of the Tiber mouth. All were influenced in their equipment, and in military tactics, by their powerful northern neighbours, the Etruscans, whose loose confederation of Twelve Cities was the dominant power-grouping in central Italy in the middle of the first millennium BC. Roman antiquarian authors have preserved a few details about the institutions of the early army, and it is perhaps just possible to establish some sequence of development. It was believed that the first military structure was based on the three 'tribes' of the regal period—the *Ramnes*, the *Tities* and the *Luceres*—all Etruscan names and so a product of the period of strong Etruscan influence. Each tribe provided 1000 men towards the army, under the command of a *tribunus* (lit. tribal officer). The subdivisions of each tribe supplied 100

1 Italy, c.400 BC, showing major tribes and Greek colonies. Inset: Rome and vicinity

men (a century) towards this total. The resulting force—some 3000 men in all—was known as the *legio*, the levy (or the 'levying'). The nobility and their sons made up a small body of cavalry, about 300 men, drawn in equal proportion from the three tribes. These were the *equites*, the knights; all men who had sufficient means to equip themselves for service as cavalry belonged to the *Ordo Equester*, the mounted contingent (usually known now as the Equestrian Order).

SERVIUS TULLIUS AND THE FIVE CLASSES

For the student of the early Roman army, it might seem that a fixed

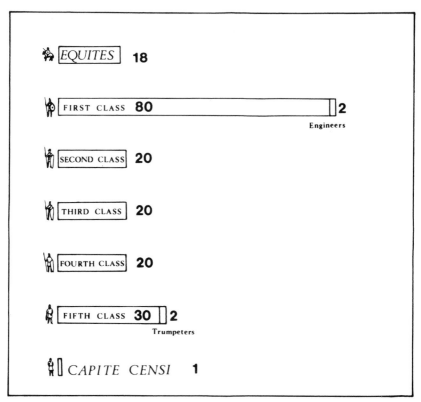

2   The 'Servian Constitution'

point exists in the reign of the sixth king of Rome, Servius Tullius, about 580–530. Servius is credited with establishing many of the early institutions of the Roman state. In particular he is said to have conducted the first census of the Roman people, and to have divided the population into 'classes', according to their wealth (see fig. 2). This Servian 'constitution' had a double purpose, political and military. In the first place, it organised the populace into centuries (hundreds) for voting purposes in the Assembly. The groupings were linked to the financial status of the individual, and his corresponding ability to provide his own arms and equipment for military service. Thus the resources of the State were harnessed to the needs of its defence. The *equites*, the richest section of the community, were formed into 18 centuries. Below them came the bulk of the population, who served as infantry, divided into five 'classes'. Members of the 'first class' were to be armed with a bronze cuirass, spear, sword, shield and greaves to protect the legs; the 'second class', with much the same panoply minus the cuirass; the 'third', the same but lacking the greaves; the 'fourth' had spear and shield only, and the 'fifth' was armed only with slings or stones. In each class those men who were over 46 (the *seniores*) were assigned to defend the city against possible attack, while the remainder (the *iuniores*) formed the field army. Below the five classes was a group called the *capite censi*, i.e. men 'registered by a head-count', with no property to their name, who were thereby disqualified from military service.[1]

The Servian reforms, it is clear, signalled the introduction at Rome of a Greek-style 'hoplite' army in which close-knit lines of heavily-armed infantry formed the fighting force. The Romans were later to claim that they had borrowed hoplite tactics from the Etruscans. This statement, which highlights the native Italic tradition, obscures the fact that the hoplites were an importation from Greece, where heavily-armed infantrymen had become the staple component of the battle-line by about 675. The hoplite (the word means a man armed with the *hoplon*, the circular shield that was the most distinctive element in his defensive equipment) was the standard fighting man at the time of the Persian and Peloponnesian Wars in the fifth century and of the armies of Athens and Sparta when Greek civilisation was at its height. The hoplites fought in close order, with shields overlapping, and spears jabbing forwards, in a *phalanx* (lit. a roller), which could be of any length, but usually eight (later 12 or 16) rows deep (pl. 1). Casualties in the front line were made good by the stepping forward of the second man in the same file, and so on. The phalanx was made up of companies of some 96 men, with a width of 12 men and a depth of eight.

However, it has been doubted whether a system of the complexity of the Servian Constitution could have been devised at Rome at such an early date. The first stage was more probably the establishment of a single *classis*, encompassing all those capable of providing the necessary equipment for themselves, so as to be able to take their place in the line of hoplites. All other citizens were designated as *infra classem*, i.e. their property was less than the prescribed level. In origin the word *classis* meant a call to arms—its more familiar meanings in Latin and English are a later development.[2] The antiquarian writers report the strength of the new hoplite 'legion' as 4000, and the accompanying cavalry as 600. It should be remembered that throughout the Roman Republic the soldiers fighting for Rome were her own citizens for whom defence of the state was a duty, a responsibility and a privilege.

VEII AND THE GALLIC INVASION

In the last years of the sixth century, the ruling family of Tarquins was expelled from Rome, and a Republic established. A century of small-scale warfare against adjacent communities brought Rome primacy over Latium. The Etruscans meanwhile had declined in strength, faced by the hostility of the Greek colonies of southern Italy, their trading rivals, and by the onward surge of migrating Gallic (i.e. Celtic) tribes, who by the fifth century had penetrated the Alps, were pushing against Etruscan outposts in the Po valley, and were pressing southwards against the heartland of Etruria itself. In the long-term it can be seen that the Etruscans provided a buffer for the towns of central and southern Italy against the Gallic advance, which consumed much of their remaining strength. At the height of this crisis, in 406, Rome entered into a final round of conflict with her neighbour and arch-rival, Veii. Fighting continued in desultory fashion over a ten-year period, and was brought to a successful conclusion with the capture of Veii in 396 by the *dictator* M. Furius Camillus. The ten-year duration of the war prompted a patriotic comparison with the Trojan War. In order to prepare for the struggle against Veii the Roman army was apparently expanded from 4000 to 6000 men, probably by the creation of the 'second' and 'third' classes of the Servian system. Men of the second class had to appear for service with sword, shield, spear, greaves and helmet, but were not expected to provide a cuirass; men of the third class were to have spear, shield and helmet, but not the greaves. To balance the absence of protective armour, the new groups used the long Italic shield, the *scutum*, in place of the traditional circular shield of the hoplite. The *scutum* allowed better protection of the body and legs. A further sign of the changing conditions of service was the payment of a daily cash allowance to soldiers—-the *stipendium*—which helped to meet the individual man's living expenses while away from home for an increasingly lengthy period. The cavalry force of the legion was also enlarged, from six centuries to 18 centuries (1800 men). The members of the new centuries were provided with a mount at public expense (*equites equo publico*). Help from the public treasury was given towards the maintenance of the horse while on campaign.

The fall of Veii all but coincided with a further push southwards by the Gauls, who now penetrated into the Tiber valley, and in 390 threatened Rome itself. The new, enlarged army was swept aside on a stream called the Allia, north-east of Rome, and the town was captured and looted. Camillus was recalled to office, the floodtide of the Gallic advance soon ebbed to the far side of the Apennines, and Rome was saved.

ARMY REFORMS

The open-order fighting at which the Gauls excelled had shown up weaknesses in the Roman phalanx, and in the next half-century the army underwent substantial changes. The phalanx-legion ceased to manoeuvre and fight as a single compact body, but adopted a looser formation, by which distinct sub-sections became capable of limited independent action. These sub-units were given the name maniples (*manipuli*, 'handfuls').[3] Moreover, there took place at the same time, or at least within the same half-century, a significant change in the equipment carried by many of the individual soldiers. The oval Italic *scutum* became the standard shield of the legionary—some were indeed using it already (above, p. 18).The circular hoplite shield was discarded. Furthermore, the majority of legionaries were now equipped with a throwing javelin in place of the thrusting spear. But, as we shall see, some men continued to be armed with the latter for two centuries or more. These changes in equipment are sometimes ascribed to Camillus himself, but they were probably introduced more gradually than the sources allow.

The new flexibility of battle-order and equipment, combined with a shift to offensive armament, were to be cardinal factors in the Romans' eventual conquest of the Mediterranean world. The hoplites had worked in close order at short range, but the new legionaries were mostly equipped to engage with the javelin at long range, then to charge forward into already disorganised enemy ranks, before setting to with sword and shield. The Macedonians and Greeks, who maintained the traditional system, and later carried the phalanx to extremes of regimentation and automation, fossilised the very instrument of their former success, to their eventual downfall.

By 362 at the latest the army was split into two 'legions', and by 311 into four, which becomes the standard total. The word 'legion' now acquires its more familiar meaning, of a 'division' of troops. Command of the army rested with the consuls, the two supreme magistrates of the state, who held civil and military power for a single year and were replaced by their successors in office. Each consul usually commanded two of the legions. Sometimes, if a single legion was despatched to a trouble-spot, command could be held by a praetor. Each legion also had six Military Tribunes, likewise elected in the Assembly (see below, p. 39).

WAR AGAINST THE SAMNITES

During the fourth century Rome expanded her area of control southwards along the coastline towards the mouth of the Liris

(Garigliano) river and inland across the mountains of southern Latium. This expansion soon brought her into conflict with the Samnites, whose confederation of tribes bestrode the highlands of the central Apennines. Conflict was almost inevitable in the wake of Roman expansion. The struggle lasted half a century, and ended with the complete subjugation of the Samnites. Rome's army was not always successful, and the nadir of her fortunes was the entrapping in 321 of the entire army in the Caudine Forks.

In his account of the year 340, after the close of the First Samnite War, and as a preamble to a battle against the Latin allies, the historian Livy (who wrote much later, at the time of the emperor Augustus) offers a brief description of Roman military organisation, which was designed to help his readers follow the ensuing battle descriptions.[4] He notes that the legions had formerly fought in hoplite style in a phalanx, but that later they had adopted manipular tactics. More recently (and he gives this as a separate development) the legion had been split into distinct battle lines (fig. 4). Behind a screen of light-armed (*leves*), the first main line contained maniples of *hastati* (spearmen); the second line was made up of maniples of *principes* (chief men), and the third line, made up of the oldest and most mature men, consisted of maniples of *triarii* (third rank men). We shall meet with these three groupings again. All the soldiers in the three lines carried the oblong *scutum*, and the first and third (and perhaps also the second, but this is not specifically stated) had the *hasta* or short spear, as the name *hastati* implies. There is no reference to the *pilum*, which (if Livy's account is accepted) may not yet have been introduced.[5] Other groups, whom Livy calls *rorarii* and *accensi*, were lightly equipped and formed a final reserve in the rear.

Livy's account must be largely derived from much later sources, especially Polybius (below, p. 33), so that its independent value is not great. Yet its very incongruities may lend it a certain measure of authority. Livy may have been attempting to reconcile patchy and discordant source-material; but it is difficult to suppose that the legion he describes ever existed as a reality. The *rorarii* and *accensi* could be held to represent the Fourth and Fifth Servian classes, now added to the other three and equipped in simple fashion. But *accensi*, in the normal meaning of the word, should be servants rather than fighting soldiers.[6] For the organisation of a Roman legion solid ground is reached only with Polybius himself (below, p. 33).

The defeat of the Samnites left Rome the undisputed mistress of the Italian peninsula. The Etruscans and other tribes of central Italy had already succumbed, and Rome was soon poised on the southern edge of the Po Valley, eager for further expansion northwards. Of decisive

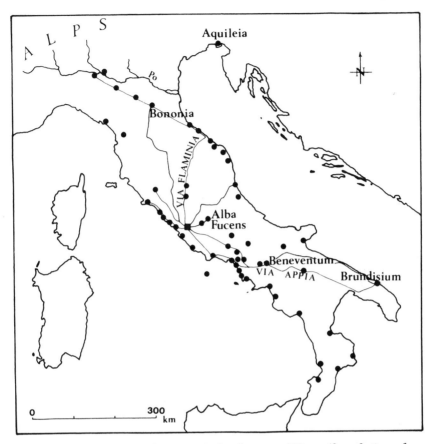

3   Roman roads and colonies in Italy, down to 171 BC (foundation of Aquileia)

value towards establishing and consolidating her control was colonisation: i.e. the setting down of bodies of her own citizens or her Latin allies, with a primarily agricultural role, to dominate import-ant land routes and to secure the coasts. The establishment of colonies also served to satisfy the land hunger of a growing population (fig. 3). Against the Samnites, the Romans used colonies to close off exits from the upland valleys, and to split up the constituent tribes of the Samnite group. The planting of colonies went hand in hand with the construction of a road system throughout Italy, which linked these outposts to the capital.

ROMANS, LATINS AND ALLIES

It is easily forgotten in accounts of warfare under the Republic that

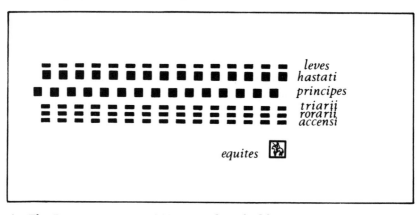

leves
hastati
principes
triarii
rorarii
accensi

equites

4   The Roman Legion, c. 340 BC, as described by Livy

the legions, drawn from Roman citizens, were accompanied on campaign and in battle by contingents drawn from the towns of Latium, Latin colonies and the Italian allies. These contingents known collectively as the *Socii* (Allies) served in accordance with treaty obligations incurred at the time of their surrender to Rome or acceptance within her alliance. As far as can be determined, they were organised and equipped in a more or less identical fashion to the Romans, with their own distinctive arms and tactics being gradually subsumed. At the beginning of a normal year, the consuls summoned the chief magistrates of the towns which were to provide troops, agreed the total to be furnished, and the date and place of assembly. The contingents from individual towns came to be about 500 men strong, together with cavalry, in one or more squadrons called *turmae*. Each contingent, which was later termed a *cohors* (cohort—the precise derivation of this word is unclear),[7] served under a local magistrate as *praefectus*. How long the Latins and Allies had to serve is not clear. The burdens were much disliked, and led to rumblings of discontent from time to time. Those allies whose towns lay on the coast (e.g. Naples) were required to furnish ships, oarsmen and marines, when a fleet was required for war service. Groups of cohort-contingents, usually 10 in number, were placed together to form an *ala sociorum*, equivalent in size to a legion of Romans. A consular army of two legions was normally accompanied on campaign by two such legion-equivalents. In addition there was a sizeable élite group, drawn from all the allied communities, called the *extraordinarii*. The term *ala* (lit. a wing) reflects the position of the Allied troops on each flank of the two-legion army; later of course, under the Empire, the term *ala* was used exclusively for cavalry. As far as we are able to build up a picture, each cohort contingent contained maniples of *hastati, principes* and *triarii*, and so was a miniature version of the legion itself. The cohorts were of course drawn from different communities, and retained their identities on campaign; Livy mentions many individually by name. The *ala sociorum* (i.e. the legion-equivalent) was commanded by a number of Prefects of the Allies (*praefecti sociorum*), who were Romans of equestrian rank, nominated by the consuls. Most probably there were six *praefecti sociorum* to each *ala*, so that they matched the six tribunes of the legion itself; the cavalry, massed separately in battle, was commanded by Roman *praefecti equitum* (Cavalry Prefects), often of senatorial rank. To be carefully distinguished from the Latins and Allies are foreign mercenaries, most notably Cretan archers, a familiar feature of the Hellenistic military scene.

PYRRHUS

Rome's expansion towards the southern limits of the Italian peninsula brought her into contact with the Greek cities along the seaboard of Lucania, Calabria and Apulia, cities which had been established over the previous three centuries from the mainland of Greece (fig. 1). For the most part the Romans were given a cordial welcome, as offering protection against the native tribesmen of the interior. One city, Tarentum (Taranto) remained aloof, and, fearing the end result of the onward Roman advance, called to her aid King Pyrrhus of Epirus (on the west coast of Greece), who eagerly responded, seeing in southern Italy a stepping stone to the fulfilment of his own larger ambitions in Sicily. Pyrrhus arrived in Italy in 280 with a substantial army, said to have consisted of 20,000 hoplite mercenaries, 3000 cavalry and a corps of elephants, now seen by the Romans for the first time. The subsequent encounters with Pyrrhus were a test-bed for the developing manipular tactics against the phalanx, now at the peak of its development in the wake of Alexander's world conquests. Individual soldiers in the Macedonian phalanx carried pikes 16 feet (5 m), or more, in length, which they needed both hands to support. The phalanx now presented to its opponents a bristling hedge of overlapping spear-points. Pyrrhus had fought in the wars of Alexander's successors and was familiar with the latest refinements of military thinking. The first encounter at Heraclea (Policoro on the instep of Italy) showed the worth of his phalanx. The Roman legions and their Allies could not break through, and were driven back; the elephants completed the rout. Roman sources stressed the bravery of their men, to hide the reality of the defeat. Nevertheless, Pyrrhus' losses were far from negligible, and after a ferocious two-day battle at Ausculum (Ascoli Satriano) in 279, he commented that one more such victory over the Romans would be the ruination of his whole army.[8] Pyrrhus now departed for Sicily, but failing to find any lasting success, he returned to Italy in 275. Advancing north-west along the line of the Via Appia towards Capua, he clashed with a Roman army near Malventum (later Beneventum) and was forced to withdraw. Soon he left Italy for good.

CARTHAGE AND HANNIBAL

The remainder of the century was overshadowed by conflict with Carthage, the powerful merchant city on the Bay of Tunis. Carthage had viewed Rome's development with increasing alarm. The first clash centred on Sicily, uncomfortably sandwiched between the two powers. What began in 264 as a dispute over control of one city (Messana) quickly escalated into open war. Roman efforts were stupendous. Her hitherto insignificant naval forces were rapidly expanded, and inexperience in ship design and seamanship was compensated by the invention of a boarding-bridge, known as a *corvus* (raven) from the sharp beak-like hook at one end. The *corvus*, pivoting on the mainmast, could be dropped on to the deck of an adjacent enemy ship, where it stuck fast, allowing legionaries placed on board the Roman vessel to rush across the bridge, and swamp the more lightly armed defenders. This early success prompted the transportation of a substantial expeditionary force to Africa. But the initiative was lost, advantageous peace terms over-hastily rejected, the Roman force humiliatingly defeated. A long drawn-out, desultory struggle ensued, with the two sides increasingly exhausted, and occasional victories never conclusive, or not followed up. A final effort by Rome in 241 brought a decisive naval victory off the west coast of Sicily. Carthage agreed to evacuate Sicily, which became Rome's first overseas province.

The intervening years between this and the second Carthaginian (or Punic) War saw further Roman advances: the addition of Sardinia and Corsica to her domains, and the gaining of a toe-hold beyond the Apennines in the Po Valley, an area which, because of the presence of Gallic tribes, the Romans had termed *Gallia Cisalpina*, Gaul 'this side of the Alps'. Meanwhile the Carthaginians had turned their energies towards Spain, and under the energetic leadership of Hamilcar soon created an even richer empire than hitherto. Roman anxiety led to an agreement in 228 by which a limit

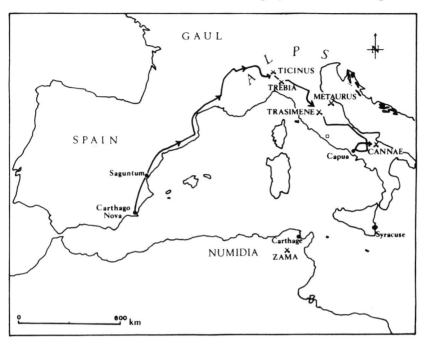

5   Italy and the western Mediterranean, c. 220 BC, showing Hannibal's
route to Italy, and major battle-sites of the Second Punic War

to Carthaginian advance was set at the Ebro river, but a further
collision was almost inevitable.

In 219 the Carthaginians, now under Hamilcar's son, Hannibal,
moved against Saguntum (Sagunto), friendly to Rome though lying
south of the Ebro, which fell after months of bitter street fighting.
(fig. 5). War was declared. Hannibal's swift offensive through southern Gaul caught the Romans off-guard by its very speed (though it
seems clear from troop-dispositions for 218 that the Senate had not
discounted an attack from the north). The consul P. Cornelius Scipio,
charged with confronting Hannibal in Spain itself, arrived in southern
Gaul too late to intercept Hannibal there, but with remarkable fore-
thought sent on his army of two legions to Spain, with a view to
preventing reinforcement from that source, and himself returned to
northern Italy.

Crossing the Alps Hannibal descended into Cisalpina; the Gauls
flooded at once to join him. Roman attempts at resistance on the line
of the Po led to a skirmish on the Ticinus river, and a more decisive
defeat on the Trebia, which brought substantial Roman losses. Scipio
himself withdrew to join his own legions in Spain, while Hannibal

25

pushed on rapidly into Italy, across the Apennines into the Arno valley near Florence. Moving south-eastwards now to reach the Tiber valley, he outflanked Flaminius, consul for 217, and turned to wait for him on high ground beside the Lago di Trasimeno (Lake Trasimene), where on a misty morning the Roman force was entrapped and cut down; Flaminius was killed.

Hannibal now recrossed the Apennines, avoiding a direct attack on Rome itself, and moved south into Apulia, where more towns joined him and he could await reinforcement and news from home, as well as treat with a potential ally, King Philip V of Macedon. A period of successful Roman manoeuvring under Q. Fabius Maximus *Cunctator* (the Delayer) restricted his movements and checked his impetus, but an impatient Roman public transferred command to the consuls of 216, Varro and Paullus, who were authorised to seek an early battle.

DISASTER AT CANNAE

The two armies clashed near the small town of Cannae in the valley of the Ofanto river in Apulia (fig. 6A). The consuls, with an army of 16 legions including Allies (a total of about 75,000) had a substantial numerical advantage over Hannibal, who had about 40,000 men. Hannibal, familiar by now with standard Roman tactics—the placing of the legions in the centre and cavalry on the wings—drew up his chief infantry force, the Africans (now largely equipped in Roman fashion with captured arms) at either end of his line (see fig. 6A, 1), and stationed his less-reliable troops, Celts and Spaniards, between them in a crescentic formation, ballooning out towards the Roman lines. This whole disposition was screened from Roman eyes by lightly-armed skirmishers. The consuls meanwhile, expecting to fight a conventional battle, hoped that the very weight of numbers would win the battle and planned a frontal attack to break Hannibal's line. The gaps between the maniples were reduced, and the overall frontage of each legion further narrowed by a reduction in the number of front rankers. This compact mass—the traditional phalanx of old—forced back Hannibal's centre, but found itself hemmed in to left and right by the Africans. The Roman cavalry on the left had already been driven off by the opposing Spanish and Celtic horse, which galloped across the rear of the infantry and fell upon the Allied cavalry still grappling with the Numidian horsemen on the right wing (2). Hannibal's centre, though by now pushed back a substantial distance, held on, the Africans turned inwards to face the ends of the advancing legions, and the now victorious Spanish

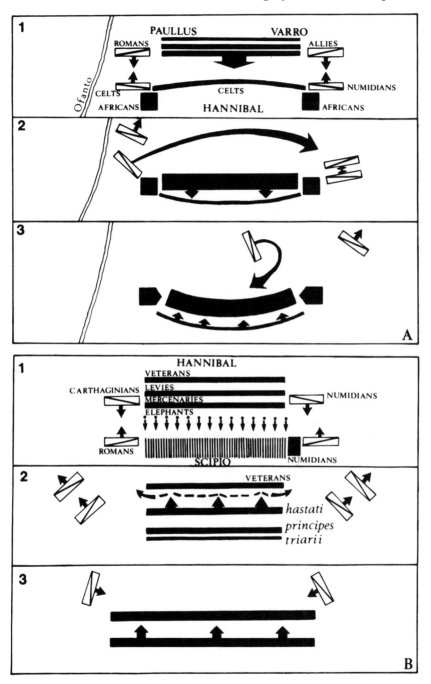

6 a: The battle of Cannae, 216 BC (see p. 26) **b:** The battle of Zama, 202 BC (see p. 31)

and Celtic cavalry returned to close off the only avenue of escape (3). The disaster was complete: over 50,000 Romans and Allies were killed, with no opportunity for proper deployment. Many more communities in the South now went over to Hannibal, including the important city of Capua.

Hannibal must have hoped that Rome would now sue for peace, and his own aims—a complete break-up of the Roman confederacy, or the establishment of a Carthaginian province in southern Italy— would be brought to fruition. But there was no weakening of resolve at Rome. Efforts to replace the fallen led to the enlistment of the *capite censi* (above, p. 17) who were normally exempt from service, and of two legions of slaves, and the emptying of the prisons. Hannibal was contained in southern Italy; the Macedonian king, his ally, was occupied by a revolt in Greece and Roman diversions in the Adriatic; and further assistance was sent to Spain where all the while a detached Roman force under P. Scipio and his elder brother (Cnaeus Scipio) had been successfully preoccupying the attentions of the Carthaginian armies in Spain, so preventing any reinforcement reaching Italy. An army was despatched to recover Sicilian towns which had revolted, and siegelines were drawn round Capua. In 211 the chief Sicilian city, Syracuse, was taken after a long siege; Capua too fell, despite desperate attempts by the Capuans to break the lines of encirclement from within and the Carthaginians to relieve them.

THE WAR IN SPAIN

However, these successes were offset by a reverse in Spain, where in 211 the two Scipios, over-ambitiously advancing in separate columns into the far south of the peninsula, and deserted by fickle local allies, were defeated and killed – Cnaeus after a desperate last resistance behind an improvised rampart of piled mule-loads and soldiers' packs.

In the following year command in Spain was voted by the Assembly to P. Scipio's son, of the same name. Young Scipio had served with his father at the Ticinus and Trebia battles, and was among the survivors of the Cannae debacle, but he was only 24 years old, and had held none of the more senior magistracies; yet he had an engaging and forceful personality and was heir to a name which symbolised for the Spanish tribes and their chieftains the honour of Rome.

Early in 209 he made a sudden dash of over 300 miles from N Spain to reach Carthage's chief outpost, Carthago Nova (Cartagena), which he took by a frontal attack combined with a sudden assault across the shallow waters of an adjacent lagoon. The initiative was now his, and many wavering tribes came over to the Roman side. Scipio spent the rest of the year toughening up his troops for the land battles he knew must come.

'He devised the following scheme for the Tribunes, for the training of the infantry. He bade them on the first day do a run of nearly four miles in full kit, on the second to rub down, clean and generally make a close examination of their equipment; on the next day to rest and do nothing; and on the following, some men to fight with wooden swords sheathed in leather with a button at the end, and others to throw javelins similarly fitted with buttons; on the fifth day to revert to the marching they had done on the first, and so on.'[9]

Scipio now took the offensive, and confronted Hannibal's brother Hasdrubal, who had taken up a strong position at Baecula. Firstly he engaged Hasdrubal's attention by a frontal attack using only auxiliary troops, and while the Carthaginian's attention was preoccupied, sent in the legionaries on both flanks. But Hasdrubal himself escaped, and gathering a sizeable force, crossed the Alps in his brother's footsteps. Finally he was halted at Sena Gallica on the Adriatic coast; Roman reinforcements were rushed north in an epic march, and Hasdrubal was defeated and killed on the Metaurus river.

In Spain itself the fighting continued, and in early 206 Scipio faced the remaining Carthaginian forces under Hasdrubal Gisgo (unrelated to the other Hasdrubal, or to Hannibal) at Ilipa near modern Seville (fig. 7). Some days passed, with each commander drawing up his troops for battle, but neither side was prepared to launch an attack. Each day Hasdrubal placed his Africans in the centre and his Spanish allies on the wings; Scipio followed the normal Roman practice, putting the legions in the centre and his own Spanish allies on either side. One morning, however, Scipio formed up his troops at daybreak, placing the legions on the wings and the Spaniards in the centre (1). Hasdrubal had to deploy for battle in great haste. There was no time for his men to get something to eat as they hurried to take up their normal positions. By the time Hasdrubal realised that the Romans had changed their accustomed dispositions, it was too late. Scipio ordered a general advance. Next, in what seems a very complicated manoeuvre, Scipio marched the legions off in column away from the centre, which was ordered to advance very slowly towards the enemy (2). Scipio then had the two columns of legionaries turn at right angles towards the Carthaginians, and

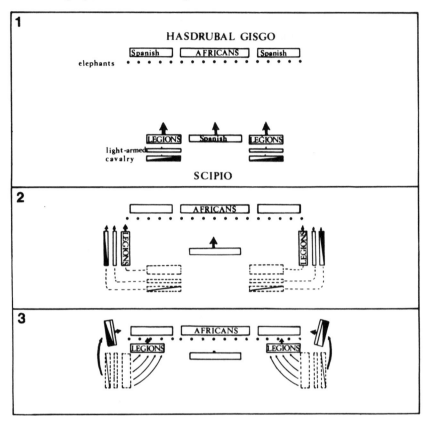

7   The battle of Ilipa, 206 BC (see p. 29)

finally to deploy obliquely to cover the gaps between them and the still advancing centre (3). The whole manoeuvre recalls the elaborate parade-ground movements of London's Trooping the Colour ceremony. The Roman cavalry and light-armed troops had remained on the outer flanks of the legions throughout the manoeuvre, and now emerged to fall on the flanks of the Carthaginian army, while the legions assaulted Hasdrubal's Spanish allies. His Africans, facing the Roman centre, which had contrived never quite to come within range, could only watch while the legions did their work. The whole Carthaginian line broke up as individuals raced for the safety of their camp. A sudden thunderstorm put an end to this most bizarre of encounters before Scipio's inspired tactics brought their full reward. But a moral ascendancy had been established: Hasdrubal thought it prudent to abandon his camp, and his army soon melted away. The Carthaginian interlude in Spanish history was over, and the Romans had found an intelligent and imaginative commander, who was to prove a match for Hannibal himself.[10]

THE CLIMAX OF THE WAR

Scipio returned to Rome and secured a consulship for 205, though against all precedent (he had not yet been praetor). He was given Sicily as his province with its garrison of two legions, survivors of the Cannae battle seemingly so long ago. Scipio was empowered to cross to Africa if he could, but the Senate declined to authorise an increase in his army, fearing perhaps that its loss would leave them again at Hannibal's mercy. But Scipio was permitted to call for volunteers and some 7000 came forward, making his force (including Italian Allies) up to some 30,000 in all.

First he was able to defeat, by an outflanking movement (now becoming his hallmark), the Carthaginian home forces under Hasdrubal Gisgo, who had escaped from the Spanish debacle, and their ally, King Syphax of Numidia, in a battle in the south-west of the country. At this Hannibal was summoned home; he landed near modern Sousse, on the east coast of Tunisia, with such remnants of his forces as he had been able to ferry across from southern Italy. He moved westward in search of reinforcements, and Scipio followed. The two armies came face to face near Zama (fig. 6B). Hannibal, perhaps adopting the scheme from his opponents, formed a triple battle-line, with his Celts and Moroccans in the first line, to take the brunt of the attack, newly raised Libyan and Carthaginian levies forming the second line, and the veterans of his Italian campaigns held back in a third. In front were his elephants, 80 or more. Scipio meanwhile, capitalising on the inherent flexibility of the legions' structure, left gaps in his own lines, with a view to providing avenues of escape for the elephants, which might thus pass through with a minimum of damage. The gaps were masked by the light-armed *velites* (below, p. 33). On both wings cavalry forces faced one another, the Roman force greatly augmented by a contingent brought by Scipio's new ally, the Numidian prince Masinissa.

The battle began with a charge by the elephants, which were harassed by the *velites* and encouraged to rush through the waiting gaps in the Roman lines (1). Meanwhile, the Roman and Numidian horsemen put to flight the opposing squadrons, whom they out-numbered, and pursued them across the horizon. Battle was now joined between the infantry (2). Hannibal seems to have hoped that his first two lines would blunt the impetus of all three Roman lines (*hastati, principes* and *triarii*), but in the event we are told that the *hastati* completed their destruction almost alone, so that in the final phase Hannibal's veterans had to face all three Roman lines (3), which Scipio now marshalled to form a single battle front, presumably intended to turn Hannibal's flanks. Nevertheless, the struggle was fierce and long, until the Roman cavalry appeared in Hannibal's rear, and flung themselves upon it. The victory was complete, and Carthage sued for peace at once. Rome owed much to Scipio who had proved himself a master tactician, learning much from Hannibal himself; the latter, after a whirlwind start, seemed to lose his initial sparkle, and became the slave of events rather than their master. Scipio adopted the extra surname *Africanus* by virtue of his great achievement.

EFFECTS OF THE WAR

Obviously, such a serious and prolonged bout of warfare strained Rome's military system to the utmost, and all but exhausted the country's reserves of manpower for a generation. In normal times (above, p. 19) an army of four legions would be maintained, against any eventuality, together with an equivalent force of Latins and Allies (above, p. 21). Livy provides details of the numbers of legions raised and kept in service during the two Punic Wars. Surprisingly, during the first war, the total remained at four or five, but during a threatened Gallic invasion in 225, and then over a long succession of years from 218 onwards, the total number in service jumped sharply. An additional seven legions were raised in 217, and the same extra number in 216 (partly to replace losses at Trasimene and Cannae). Continuing recruitment in the following years resulted in upwards of 20 legions being in service in the period 214–203. Several *legiones urbanae*, a sort of Home Guard, were formed from the old, the unfit and the under-aged, for the defence of the city (*Urbs Roma*). When the war ended the number stood at 16, a figure soon to be reduced (in 199) to a peacetime complement of six. Livy is sometimes able to give the numerals of legions involved in specific campaigns. The long period of war brought Roman troops to a fresh peak of training and efficiency, especially under the young Scipio; but the Roman legion as a fighting instrument was far from uniformly successful in these years. In so far as can be ascertained, Hannibal employed a phalanx, but his adoption of Roman equipment in 217, and the three-line structure at Zama could indicate a growing assimilation of Roman fighting techniques within his own composite forces. For the individual Roman, the long drawn-out war meant that more men were called up for military service and kept under arms over the winters too. Some six or seven years' continuous service was a regular total. The system of annually changing command proved a crippling drawback, though commonsense in the end dictated the prolongation in command of the most competent and successful leaders.

Under the year 211, at the height of the war, Livy reports the formal creation of a force of *velites* (cloak-wearers—they lacked any defensive armour), to serve in the van of the legion as skirmishers.[11] It may be that the reform in 211 (if a genuine record) should be linked to a reduction in the minimum census requirement for service, which we know took place about 214. Doubtless this brought into the legion a new body of men who could afford only a minimum of offensive weaponry, cheaply produced, and who yet required to be accommodated within the legion's framework.

POLYBIUS AND THE ROMAN ARMY

In the sixth book of his *Histories* the Greek author Polybius breaks off his narrative of the Second Punic War (at the end of 216), and turns to a lengthy description of the Roman constitution and the Roman army.[12] The account of the army is of inestimable value, not least in that the picture is written by a contemporary, himself an officer of cavalry, who had seen the Roman army in action against his own countrymen, the Greeks. Polybius wrote in or about 160, but seems to have used a Roman source of somewhat earlier, if ill-defined, date. It is reasonable to take his account as reflecting the organisation of the Roman army as it emerged from the struggle against Hannibal.

Polybius begins with a detailed picture of the procedure for raising an army of four legions in a typical year. The strength of the legion is given at 4200, but it could be filled out in an emergency to a full complement of 5000. All men of military age (i.e. between 17 and 46) were required to attend each year on the Capitol in Rome for the selection process—by this time it was common also for levies to be held outside Rome, as the body of citizens became more scattered throughout Italy. The selection process was called *dilectus*, 'the choosing' of the best candidates from among those who presented themselves. In Polybius' day all those with property valued at over 400 Greek *drachmae* (=400 *denarii*) were liable for service. In a slightly defective passage he gives the length of service as 16 years for a footsoldier and 10 years for an *eques*, but it seems clear that these figures represent the maximum that a man could be called upon to serve, not the norm. In normal circumstances a man could, in the second century BC, expect to serve up to six years in a continuous posting, after which it was expected that he would be released. Thereafter he was liable for call-out, as an *evocatus*, up to the maximum of 16.[13] Some men might serve for a single year at a time, and be obliged to come forward again at the next *dilectus*, until their full six-year period was completed. Where men came forward voluntarily, they would presumably be accepted gladly, but there was always a measure of compulsion; service in the legions of the Republic can be likened to 'national service' in many European countries in the twentieth century: an obligation on every fit male as his contribution to a country's defence. A general of known worth and reputation, embarking on a fresh campaign, might draw into his legions numerous volunteers who had already completed their six-year stint, perhaps under his personal command. They provided a valuable stiffening to his forces. The legionary received an allowance at the daily rate of one third of a *denarius*, the principal silver coin of the Roman world. If he was retained for an entire calendar year, this amounted to an annual sum of about 120 *denarii*. The payment, whose modern value is difficult to assess, went towards the cost of his equipment and living expenses. The *equites* serving in the cavalry received more: one *denarius* per day, from which to meet the cost of maintaining their horses.

Once the recruits had been selected, the youngest and poorest were assigned as *velites* (fig. 8); the next group in age and property became *hastati*; those in the prime of life were to be the *principes*, and those remaining—the oldest and most mature among those selected for service—became the *triarii*. The *hastati* and *principes* each totalled 1200 men in all; the *triarii* numbered 600, and by a process of subtraction from the total figure of 4200, it can be assumed that there

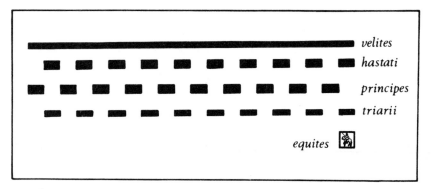

8   The Roman legion, c. 160 BC, according to Polybius

were 1200 *velites*. Next, Polybius offers a detailed description of the equipment and weaponry of each group. The *velites* had swords, javelins, and a small circular shield (the *parma*). The *hastati* and *principes* carried the oval *scutum*, the short Spanish sword (*gladius*), and two *pila* (one heavy and one light-weight). The date of the introduction of the *gladius* is not clear, but it seems likely to have been adopted from Spanish auxiliaries serving with Hannibal's forces rather than be the result of later Roman campaigns in Spain itself. All the soldiers wore a bronze pectoral to protect the heart and chest, a bronze helmet and a pair of greaves. The *triarii* were similarly dressed and equipped, except that they carried a thrusting spear (the *hasta*) instead of the *pilum*. In order to be distinguished from a distance, the *velites* covered their helmets with wolfskin, and the *hastati* wore tall upright feathers in their helmets, so exaggerating their height.

The decision on whether to place a man in the *hastati, principes* or *triarii* was based largely on age and experience not on financial status, though some remnants of the old class structure are visible: the poorest of the soldiers were assigned to the *velites*—they simply could not afford the weaponry of their better-off comrades. Polybius also reports that those soldiers among the *hastati, principes* and *triarii* who belonged, by virtue of the censors' assessment of their property, to the First Class (above, p. 16), wore a shirt of mail, so preserving some degree of exclusiveness and identity.

The *hastati* and *principes* of each legion were each divided into 10 maniples of 120 men, and the *triarii* into 10 maniples of 60. The *velites* were assigned, for administrative purposes, to the maniples in proportion. Each maniple had two centurions, of which the senior held the command. All the centurions were men who had served in the ranks, probably for several years, before elevation. The senior centurion of the legion, who commanded the extreme right-hand maniple of the *triarii* (the *centurio primi pili*, later called *primus pilus*)[14], was included *ex officio* along with the tribunes, in the general's war-council. The legion's cavalry, 300 strong, was divided into 10 *turmae*, each under three decurions; the senior decurion ('leader of 10 men') in each group of three commanded the *turma*. Polybius notes that the cavalry were armed in his day in 'Greek fashion' (i.e. with linen corslets, strong circular shields and long spears), but he observes that formerly (perhaps up to the Macedonian Wars of the 190s) they had lacked body armour and had carried only a short thrusting spear and a light shield.

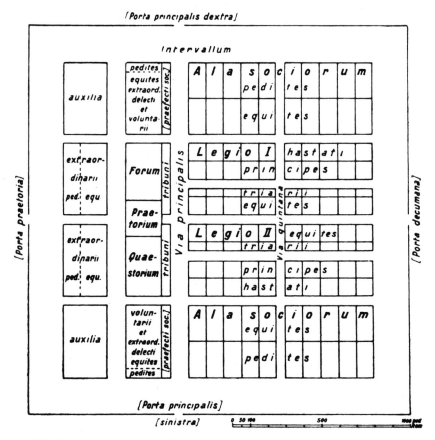

9   The Roman camp according to Polybius. Scale in Roman feet.
Reproduced from *The Journal of Roman Studies* xxii (1932), by permission
of the Society for the Promotion of Roman Studies

THE ROMAN CAMP

Polybius now proceeds to describe the Roman camp and shows how
a consular army of two legions and an equivalent number of Allies
would be accommodated within it. The tent belonging to the
magistrate in command (the *praetorium*) occupied a central position
and was flanked by the *forum* (an open market place) and by the
quaestorium, the tent of the quaestor, a junior magistrate who
managed the financial affairs of the army in the field. In front of the
praetorium were set orderly lines of tents housing the legions and the
Alae Sociorum, and behind were local auxiliaries and the *extraordinarii*. The accompanying illustration (fig. 9) shows the camp

as envisaged by Ernst Fabricius, following General William Roy; it may be said that other versions have been drawn up over the years, and certain points of major difficulty remain. Scholars have more recently divined that Polybius was in effect describing *half* of a four-legion camp (i.e. when both consular armies were encamped together), in which two encampments of the type just described would be placed together, with the *praetorium, quaestorium* and *forum* of each set back-to-back. Later in his account Polybius seems to imply that when two legions rather than the four were camped together, the administrative buildings were placed *between* the two legions rather than to one side of both! Certainly under the Empire, when two legions shared a single base (fig. 52), the administrative buildings lay between the two. The ground-plan of one of the camps at Renieblas (below, p. 46), which may date to about 150, was thought by its excavator to follow just this layout (fig. 13).

The names of streets and gates in the Roman camp must excite a certain interest. The main street was termed the *via principalis* (Principal Street) because it went past the *principia*, a general name under the Republic for the area in the camp where senior officers, including the Tribunes, had their tents. The *via principalis* led to the *porta principalis sinistra* and the *porta principalis dextra*. Polybius notes that there was a street parallel to the main thoroughfare which was called the *via quintana* (Fifth Street) because it bisected the maniples of the legions: the first to fifth maniples lay on one side and the sixth to tenth on the other. From later sources we know that the other two major streets in the camp, lying at right angles to the *via principalis*, were termed the *via praetoria* (Praetorian Street) and the *via decumana* (Tenth Street), leading respectively to the *porta praetoria* and the *porta decumana*. We could suppose that in origin the *via praetoria* was adjacent to the *praetorium*, and that the *porta decumana* was next to the 'tenth' maniples (i.e. at the far end of the camp). Yet it may be observed that the term *decumanus* was employed by Roman land-surveyors from an early date to designate any major east–west line in a grid of land-squares. Perhaps, then, military surveyors adopted the term from their civilian counterparts, and it may be wrong to seek a purely military derivation for the term. At any rate the abolition of the *Alae Sociorum* in the early first century BC presumably resulted in alterations to the camp-layout, which may help to explain some of the discrepancies between Polybius' camp and the ground-plans of forts and fortresses under the Empire (cf. below, figs 47, 48, 52).

The legions and the Allies all contributed to the essential work of constructing the camp's defences—the digging out of the ditch, piling up of the soil to form a low rampart, and the setting into the top of the rampart of the palisade-stakes which the soldiers carried as an essential element of their kit. The soldiers lived in tents, placed in neat rows, according to a precise plan, so that all knew their station within the camp. The Roman emphasis on camp-building, and the skill with which the camp itself was laid out, particularly impressed Polybius. The Greeks had never devoted much energy and planning to the selection or laying out of a camp. They often concentrated on seizing a natural defensive position, where the labour of entrenchment was minimised. The story was told that when Pyrrhus first beheld, at Heraclea, a Roman army entrenching for the night, the realisation came to him that he was not fighting (as he had thought) some barbarian tribe.[15] Pyrrhus of course was familiar with the precepts of camp-building as practised (or at least laid down) in the Greek lands. He had never expected to see such a regularly laid-out camp in the lands of the West. Precisely when—or from whom—the Romans learnt the art of camp building is not clear: another story has it that the Romans learnt by watching Pyrrhus![16] More probably the military engineers adopted the layout from contemporary town-planners. The earliest *secure* archaeological evidence for Roman camps belongs to the mid to late second century (below, p. 44).

Of particular interest is Polybius' account of the routine procedures of camp life by day and night: guard rotas, sentry duties and watchwords. He notes the harsh, but totally effective, punishments inflicted on those who had failed in their duty, in the camp or in battle, and on those convicted of theft, perjury, or sodomy. Entire maniples, which had given ground without due cause, exposing their neighbours in battle, could be decimated, i.e. a tenth part of their number, selected by lot, would be clubbed to death by their comrades. More positively, there existed a system of military decorations, by which valour and bravery received a conspicuous reward. Finally Polybius describes the process of striking camp, and the order of march as the army moved out of its encampment to resume its advance.

THE LEGION IN BATTLE

Polybius does not offer here an account of the legion in battle, but there are a number of combat descriptions both in his own work and in Livy's writings, which might seem able to fill the gap. However, very few accounts describe tactics in detail: a Roman (or Greek) audience would take much for granted. Certainly the legion approached the enemy in its triple line of *hastati, principes* and *triarii,* with the *velites* forming a light screen in front. Each of the three lines consisted of 10 maniples. The maniples were not drawn up side by side, but gaps were left equal in width to their own frontage (which can be estimated at about 120 ft or 35 m). The gaps in the line of *hastati* were masked in the second line by the maniples of the *principes*; similarly the maniples of the *triarii* masked gaps in the line of *principes*. This much seems clear (fig. 8). But the tactical disposition at the onset of the battle is less well reported. Some have supposed that the legion joined battle with wide gaps in each line (the *quincunx* is a favourite modern description, from the five dots on a dice-cube). Yet this could allow an enemy to penetrate deep into the Roman formation, and get behind the maniples of the first line. (This would matter less against a phalanx of the Macedonian type, which was required to maintain its own rigidity.) However, it is much more likely that the gaps, or at least some of them, were filled before the armies clashed. (The main battle sequence in the film *Spartacus* shows this happening.) There were two ways in which the gaps could have been filled: either each maniple simply extended its frontage, thus giving individuals more room in which to deploy their weapons; or if the maniple was drawn up two centuries deep, the rear century may have run out (almost certainly to the left) and formed up alongside the century in the line itself. On balance this seems the more likely method of deployment.

Battle would be opened by the *velites* who attempted to disorganise and unsettle enemy formations with a hail of light javelins. This done, they retired through the gaps in the maniples of the *hastati* and made their way to the rear. The maniples of the *hastati* now reformed to close the gaps. If the *hastati* were rebuffed, or lost momentum, they retired through the gaps in the line of *principes*, who would now extend their own maniples and advance to the attack. If the enemy was still undefeated, or had gained ground, the *principes* retired through the gaps in the line of the *triarii*, and the process was repeated. Obviously the survivors of the *hastati* and the *principes* now reinforced the *triarii* in this final trial of strength.

TRIBUNES AND LEGATES

Throughout the middle Republic the most senior officers serving within the legion itself (excluding the consul or praetor who had charge of the army as a whole) were the military tribunes. The office of tribune had considerable prestige. All tribunes were required to have served at least five years in the army as a qualification for office, and 10 of their number (out of the 24 tribunes of the four consular legions) had to have served 10 years. Presumably they gained this experience as *equites*, or even in the ranks. By birth tribunes had to be members of the Equestrian Order—the Knights. Some tribunes would be the sons of Senators, destined for a public career and the highest magistracies. Such was the prestige of the tribunate, that distinguished men, even ex-consuls, would serve. Tribunes of the first four legions formed each year (i.e. the consular legions, numbered *I–IV*) were elected in the Assembly, but tribunes for any legions above this total were chosen directly by the magistrate in command. The duties of the tribunes were not purely, or even principally, military; they had a remit, as elected magistrates, to protect the interest, health and welfare of the soldiers. As the size of the army expanded, they did come to exercise general command over the individual legions, by rotation in pairs, for two months at a time during the campaigning season.

However, from the time of the Second Punic War, or at least from the Macedonian Wars of the 190s, it became customary for the magistrate to take with him to his province one or more legates (*legati*), senators of mature years, appointed by the Senate on the magistrate's advice, to whom he 'delegated' part of his forces and duties. This new delegation of command was a result, it is clear, of campaigning outside Italy over wide geographical areas, where the magistrate could not hope to exercise immediate control. The legates could be given, over a short or extended period, semi-independent commissions, with control of a portion of the troops or ships at the magistrate's disposal. The tribunes, closely tied to the individual legion, were evidently unsuited to this role. Over much the same period, and perhaps as a direct consequence, the tribunate ceased to be sought after by senators, so that the quality of the individual holders declined. Often the men who served as legates were in the course of a senatorial career, and 'between' offices; sometimes they were already ex-Praetors, but more often ex-Plebeian Tribunes, ex-Aediles, or ex-Quaestors. Thus for the most part they were of good birth but little military experience. Of course their duties would call for expertise which was as much administrative and juridical as military. At any rate, for the ambitious young senator, anxious to show his military—and political—talent, under a successful commander very much in the public eye, the route to promotion and fame came to be as a legate, not as a tribune.

ROME IN THE EAST

After the defeat of Carthage, Rome turned against Philip V of

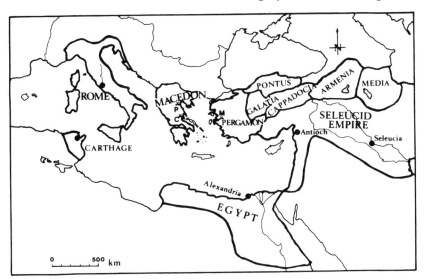

10   The eastern Mediterranean world, c. 200 BC. Note:
C = Cynoscephalae, M = Magnesia, P = Pydna

Macedon, and sent a force of two legions (and an equivalent number
of Allies), across the Adriatic (fig. 10). At first, indifferent and
changing leadership effected nothing, though the army contained
many veterans of the Hannibalic war and Zama. In 198 a force of ten
elephants was sent by Masinissa, his gift to the war effort. The arrival
of the consul for 198, T. Quinctius Flamininus, injected a new sense
of purpose. Roman and Macedonian forces came into contact
unexpectedly in the range of hills called Cynoscephalae ('Dog's
Heads', from their distinctive profile), where the Romans found
Philip's men guarding the pass between the town of Pharsalus (see
below, p. 108) and the plains of northern Thessaly (fig. 11).
Skirmishing brought up more sizeable forces to contend for the
east–west ridge that controlled the pass itself. The Roman legions
were able to deploy fairly quickly, before Philip's phalanx, at a
considerable disadvantage on the uneven ground, arrived in full
strength. The Macedonian phalanx was about 16,000 strong.

When the battle began, Philip had only about half the phalanx on
the ridge, along with some peltasts and other light forces (1).
Flamininus immediately attacked with his own left wing; the
phalanx responded, and drove the legionaries down the slope.
Flamininus now used his right wing to attack the Macedonian left,
which was still in the process of deploying, and with the aid of the

41

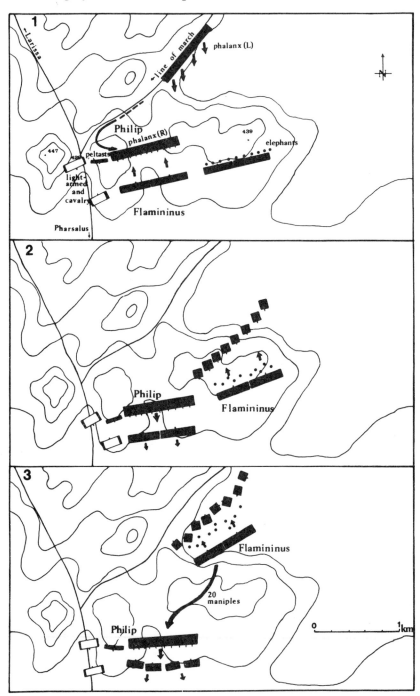

elephants destroyed its structure (2). The battle now seemed to consist of two quite separate encounters. Clearly, whichever of the two commanders could react more quickly to the situation would win. An unnamed tribune, of one of the two legions on the Roman right, detached twenty maniples of legionaries (probably the *triarii* and *principes* of his own legion—or the *triarii* of his own and the accompanying 'legion' of Allies). Apparently on his own initiative, he led them back up the slope, over the crest and charged into the rear of the Macedonian right wing, which was still advancing slowly down the other flank (3). The ranks of Macedonian spearmen, with their long pikes (*sarissae*) pointing forward, were unable to turn, and were cut down where they stood. As Polybius observed, the superiority of the flexible manipular structure over the regimented phalanx is nowhere more apparent than in the Cynoscephalae battle, which ended the war and the supremacy of Macedon in the eastern Mediterranean.[17]

The eclipse of Macedon encouraged the Seleucid king Antiochus to invade Europe: he landed in Greece, and in 191 took up a position at the Pass of Thermopylae against a Roman army advancing southwards. The Romans outflanked the position, just as the Persians had done in the more famous battle against Leonidas' Spartans in 480, and Antiochus evacuated his forces from Greece. In the following year the war was carried into Asia Minor, under Scipio's brother (but with *Africanus* himself serving as a legate). Antiochus had assembled a great army, comprising a phalanx of the Macedonian type, together with mounted archers, elephants, a camel corps and scythe-wheeled chariots. The Roman forces, four legions (including Allies) and substantial contingents from friendly states in Greece and Asia Minor, made contact with Antiochus' army at Magnesia (Manissa). His polyglot assemblage fell into confusion with hardly a blow struck, the legionaries added to the turmoil with volleys of *pila*, and Roman losses were minimal. In a final clash with Macedon from 171 onwards, Roman mismanagement again almost led to disaster, but the appointment of L. Aemilius Paullus restored confidence and discipline: in a hard-fought battle at Pydna on the flanks of Mount Olympus the phalanx was initially successful but again fell into disarray; skilful use of the maniples by Paullus hastened its total destruction (pl. 2). Rome at this time was uninterested in establishing a permanent military presence east of the Adriatic, and the army

---

11   The battle of Cynoscephalae, 197 BC (see p. 41)
(*after Kromayer*)

withdrew. But in 149 Macedonia was finally made into a province. Three years later Carthage was stormed after a fierce struggle, and its territory transformed into a province, which the Romans called Africa. The boundary between the new province and the native kingdom of Numidia to the west was marked by a ditch, the *Fossa Regia*, which may constitute the earliest frontier work of the Roman world.[18]

SPAIN AND THE WEST

If Roman interference in the eastern Mediterranean against the declining power of the Hellenistic kingdoms was largely crowned with success, the progress of her endeavours in the west—in Spain— was marked by frequent reverses; everywhere there was evidence of greed, cruelty, and insensitivity towards the half-conquered tribes. It was indeed not until the time of Augustus that Spain was entirely brought within Roman control. An army of two (later four) legions was kept permanently in Spain from the end of the Second Punic War, and the need to maintain its numbers proved a constant drain on manpower. Roman citizens, Latins and Allies, alike demurred at being despatched to Spain—an ancient equivalent of the Russian front—where hard fighting in an inhospitable terrain might bring little reward. Roman ineptitude encouraged further revolts from 154 onwards: the Lusitanians of the far West inflicted defeats on successive Roman commanders, and a treacherous massacre of their chief warriors in 150 only fuelled the revolt further, and called up a formidable foe, Viriathus, who had commanded a native force in the Roman service, and so knew something of their methods. Almost simultaneously the Celtiberians of the northern highlands broke into open revolt, and a succession of commanders struggled to control them. By 141 a single strongpoint remained in rebel hands: the hilltop fortress of Numantia, near modern Soria.

Not far away to the east, on high ground at Renieblas, is a series of superimposed Roman camps, probably the bases of successive Roman commanders of the 150s and 140s in their attempts to overawe the Numantians and capture the town (fig. 12). The camps at Renieblas, with their walls and internal buildings in stone, and short traverse ditches masking the gateways, stand comparison for their regularity with any matching sequence from Britain or Germany (figs 13, 14). The camps seem likely to have held a force of two legions, together with a corresponding number of Allies. The consul of 137, with a remit to bring the war to a prompt close, was

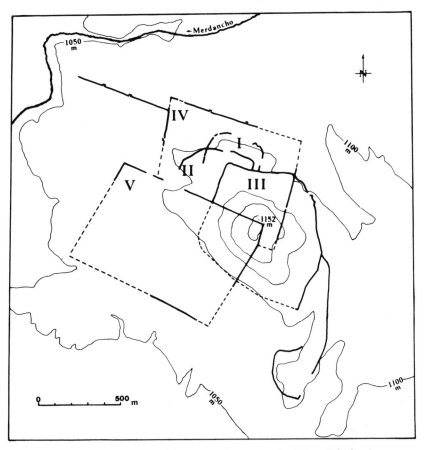

12 Roman camps at Renieblas east of Numantia (*after Schulten*).
Camps I–II date from the early to mid second century BC, Camp III
probably to 153–152, and Camps IV and V perhaps to the 80s

surrounded by the Celtiberians in his camp (presumably at Renieblas) and compelled to surrender his entire force. The shame was
sufficient for the Senate to despatch to Spain the state's most reliable
and proven commander, P. Cornelius Scipio Aemilianus, a son of
Aemilius Paullus and a grandson (by adoption) of the conqueror of
Hannibal. Aemilianus restored order in the army, reduced the
enemy's subsidiary strongholds, and laid siege to Numantia which
fell after a siege of many months. The defences were razed and the
surviving inhabitants sold into slavery.

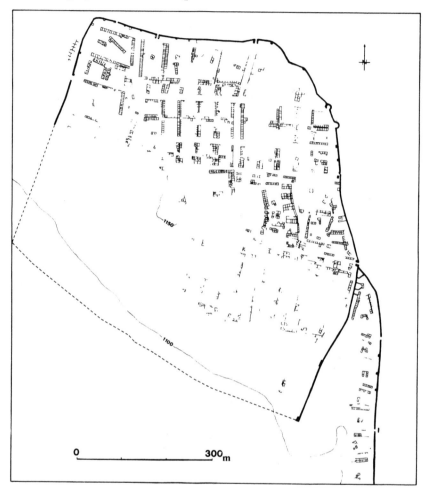

13 Camp III at Renieblas (*after Schulten*); 111 acres (45 hectares). Schulten identified this camp, with some plausibility, as the winter-quarters of the consul Q. Fulvius Nobilior in 153–152 BC

THE SIEGE OF NUMANTIA

A detailed account of Aemilianus' campaign and the siege is preserved in Appian's *Iberica* (Spanish History) which catalogued Roman military endeavours in Spain from the Second Punic War to the final conquest under Augustus. Appian tells us that a stone wall, 8 feet (2.5 m) wide and 10 feet (3 m) high, and accompanying ditch, were built round Numantia, a total distance of 48 stades (6

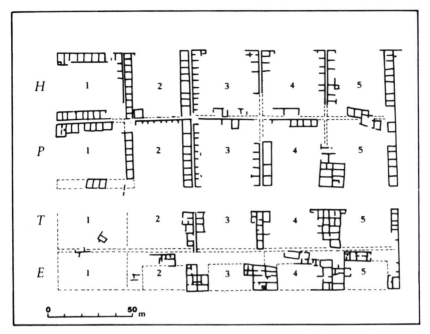

14 Camp III at Renieblas: plan of barracks (*after Schulten*) for five maniples each of *hastati* (H), *principes* (P), and *triarii* (T); and five *turmae* of *equites* (E)

miles/10 km), with wooden towers at intervals of 100 feet (30 m). Seven forts were placed round the perimeter (fig. 15). The nearby river was blocked by a boom consisting of tree-trunks bristling with blades and spearpoints.[19]

Aemilianus had prepared his troops for the siege by hard training, as reported by Appian:

> He did not dare to engage in active warfare before he had trained his men by hard exertion. He went over all the low-lying ground in the vicinity, and had one new camp after another fortified and then demolished each day, very deep trenches dug and then backfilled, high walls built up and then pulled down, while he himself watched the work from dawn until dusk.[20]

Appian's account of the siege is interesting in itself—Numantia is the Masada of Spain. We learn much of the Romans' capacity for siegecraft, as well as their dogged perseverance. But more important his account can be complemented and illustrated by archaeological remains of the Roman fortifications surviving as upstanding field-

47

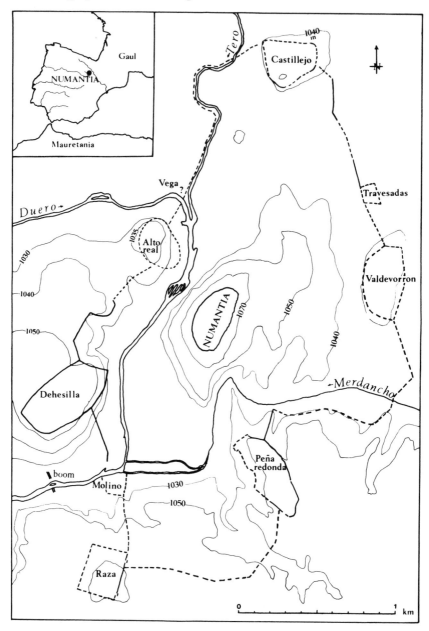

15 Siegeworks around Numantia (134–133 BC): general plan (*after Schulten*)

16 Siegecamp at Peña Redonda (Numantia); 27 acres (11.2 hectares).
After Schulten

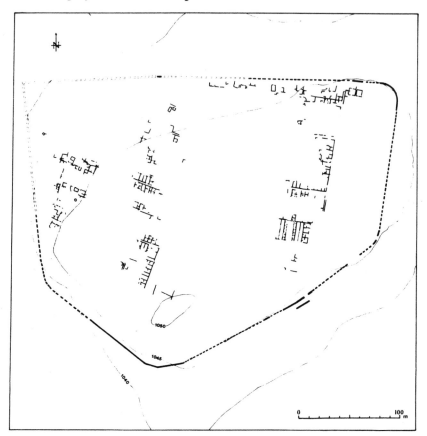

17 Siegecamp at Castillejo (Numantia); 18 acres (7.35 hectares). *After Schulten*. The site had already been used on two occasions by Roman troops encamped by Numantia; substantial traces of earlier structures were found below the Scipionic buildings

works on the bleak hillsides round Numantia, which were examined in a classic sequence of excavations by Adolf Schulten in 1903–12. The excavations revealed the enclosing wall and a section of ditch and the two piers of the 'boom' across the Duero. The ground-plans of the largest perimeter forts, at Peña Redonda (fig. 16) and Castillejo (where Aemilianus may well have had his headquarters; fig. 17), provide a vivid commentary on the camp-layout as described by Polybius; the irregular shapes correspond to convenient land-contours. Schulten's reconstruction of the ground-plans are perhaps over-ambitious and in the accompanying Figures attention is directed towards the actual remains. Internal buildings were of stone, or set on stone sills, and many structures can be individually identified: administrative buildings, tribunes' houses and barracks. That these and the Renieblas series have not been the subject of more intense study must in part be due to a narrow preoccupation, in this country and beyond, with the army of the Empire. (Other Roman camps are known on approach routes to Numantia from the south, but cannot be shown to date to the period of the siege.)[21] The excavations also produced a large quantity of weaponry, useful to an appreciation of the evolution of the legionary's equipment (fig. 18).

THE ROMAN DEBT TO GREECE

The Romans always acknowledged that they had learnt much from others. The hoplite had been introduced from Greece (above, p. 17), and we can find much in the Roman military system which had an origin there. The use of passwords, religious rituals before battle, trumpet calls—all this is familiar from Greek and Hellenistic armies. Similarly the Greeks had brought siegecraft to a fine art, and engineering projects were commonplace. Much therefore that we might regard as particularly Roman had solid Greek antecedents. But the Roman genius for organisation and perseverance is everywhere apparent, in camp-building, in field-fortification and even bridge construction. For the aspiring Roman Alexander, help was available in the form of handbooks on strategy, fieldcraft and generalship in the Hellenistic manner. Cato himself, the epitome of the nationalistic Roman outlook in the mid-second century, wrote a treatise *On Military Affairs*, and some form of handbook for military tribunes is thought to have formed the basis of Polybius' description of the camp. For the young Roman anxious to become the very model of a Hellenistic major-general, all this was prescribed reading.

THE GROWTH OF PROFESSIONALISM

At first, military service in the Roman army entailed a man being away from his home—usually a farmstead in a country district—for a few weeks or months over the summer. The campaign season opened in March and closed in October, as official festivals in the Roman calendar make clear. But the need to fight overseas and to leave troops to form garrisons in the newly-won provinces meant

---

18 Roman weaponry from Numantia. Daggers (1–3) from Castillejo, and *pila* (4–8) from Renieblas. Drawn by John Callan. Scale approx. $\frac{1}{4}$
OVERLEAF

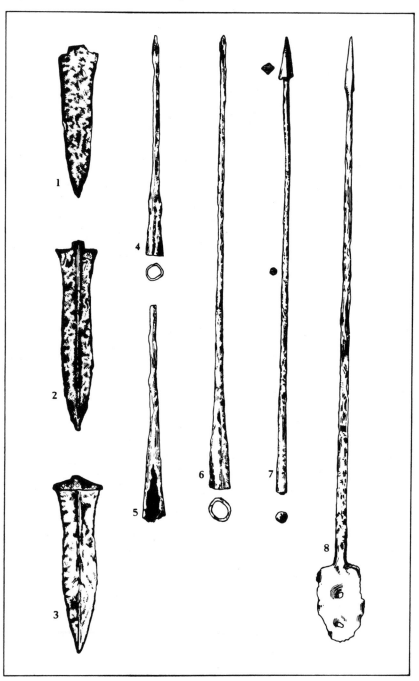

that men were away from home for longer periods. Inevitably what had been seen as a duty and voluntary obligation took on a somewhat different character.

There clearly existed from about 200 onwards, and perhaps earlier, a core of near professionals, men who liked the adventure and the risks, or who had few if any home ties, and who were glad to volunteer over a number of years, up to the prescribed maximum of 16 years, or more. A splendid example from this period must be the centurion Spurius Ligustinus, an account of whose career, given before the consul of 171, is presented by Livy:

> 'I became a soldier in the consulship of P. Sulpicius and C. Aurelius (200 BC). In the army which was taken over to Macedonia I served two years in the ranks against King Philip; in the third year because of my bravery T. Quinctius Flamininus gave me a post as centurion in the tenth maniple of the *hastati*. After Philip's defeat, when we had been brought back to Italy and released, I immediately set out for Spain as a volunteer with the consul M. Porcius (195 BC). This commander judged me worthy to be assigned as centurion of the first century of the *hastati*. For the third time I enlisted again as a volunteer in that army which was sent against the Aetolians and King Antiochus (191 BC). By Manius Acilius I was made centurion of the first century of the *principes*. When Antiochus had been driven out and the Aetolians subdued, we were brought back to Italy. And twice after that I served in campaigns where the legions were in commission for a year. Then I campaigned twice in Spain (181 and 180 BC), first under Q. Fulvius Flaccus, and then under the praetor Ti. Sempronius Gracchus. I was brought home by Flaccus along with the others whom he brought with him from the province to take part in his Triumph because of their bravery. Four times within a few years I held the rank of *primus pilus* (i.e. centurion of the first century of the *triarii*). Four and thirty times I was rewarded for bravery by my commanders. I have received six civic crowns. I have served out twenty two years in the army and am more than fifty years old'.[22]

After his initial six years of service in Macedonia, Ligustinus had re-enlisted as a volunteer, and served in Greece, Spain, Asia Minor, and perhaps elsewhere for a further 16 years, being showered by military decorations by a succession of admiring generals. His plea was designed to ensure that he received an appointment appropriate to his experience and status. In fact he was adjudged most worthy of all the applicants for the centurionate, and made *primus pilus* in the

19 A frieze from the Altar of Domitius Ahenobarbus (see p. 223 for description). Drawn by John Callan

First legion. It may be observed that he had not lost all contact with his home: he was a married man with six sons, of whom four were 'grown up', and two married daughters!

At the end of the campaign (perhaps a year or less, or the full term of six years—or more in an emergency), the soldier was released from his military oath, and returned to take up the threads of a civilian life, enriched with whatever booty he had been able to acquire in the course of his service. The possibility of booty was seen as an incentive, or at the very least a financial compensation, for military service. It was rare for the Senate to offer any form of gratuity to the time-served veteran, though participation in a major victory, which brought a war to a successful conclusion, could result in a donative being paid by the general from the proceeds of the war, often at the time of his Triumph. On a few occasions soldiers might be given a plot of land in recognition of their service: after the end of the Second Punic War, territory confiscated from disaffected communities in southern Italy was distributed to Scipio's veterans, with two *iugera* (1.25 acres) being given in recognition of each year spent under arms. Some of the colonies founded in northern Italy in the early second century included, or were reserved for, veterans, and plots were distributed according to the 'military rank held: the ordinary soldier could receive up to 50 *iugera* (about 30 acres), where his whole family could make a fresh start in a new community.

A CITIZEN ARMY

In essence, the Roman army of the early and middle Republic was its citizenry under arms led into battle by its elected magistrates. Yet to describe the army as a militia is to understate its capacity and misunderstand the attitude of mind of its leaders and individual members. Discipline and training were its hallmarks; the care with which the camp was laid out reveals no ordinary grouping of amateur warriors. The Romans adopted professional attitudes to warfare long before the army had professional institutions. The whole of Roman society was geared-up to expect warfare on an almost annual basis. Yet, such was Roman conservatism that, even when wars became prolonged and hostilities took place at ever greater distances from Rome itself, the essential framework of the military system did not change. After the end of the Second Punic War strong military forces had to be left in various provinces. At first the magistrate in command came home at the close of the campaign season, having seen his legion or legions safely into winter quarters, and was replaced in the spring by his successor in office. Gradually, however, the practice developed of extending the period of command, so that the same man could remain at his post for a second year as a *proconsul* or *propraetor*. Yet the link between office-holding at Rome and command of its military forces remained strong. A returning magistrate brought back to Italy those men from his legions who could be judged to have served their due time (at least six continuous years), and his successor took out a supplement of newly-enrolled recruits to fill out the ranks. The legions themselves were formally reconstituted over the winter, and a new chief centurion and tribunes appointed, just as though the legion had been newly raised at Rome. Almost certainly, though we have little reliable evidence for this period, the legions received each year a new numeral determined by the total number in service.

Little wonder perhaps that Polybius and his Greek contemporaries should be amazed at the success of the Roman army over the successors of Alexander and the well-tried phalanx. In truth of course, the Greeks were divided among themselves and their strength in decline. The vacuum was there to be filled, and this the Romans proceeded to do, with various protestations of reluctance, more or less sincere, according to circumstances.

2 Marius' Mules

Gaius Marius, who held an unprecedented series of consulships during the last decade of the second century BC, and who defeated first the Numidian kinglet Jugurtha and later the much more serious threat to Italy from migrating Celtic tribes, has often been credited with taking the decisive steps which converted the Roman army formally into the long-service professional force of which the state stood much in need. As will become apparent, this is a considerable over-estimate of the scope—and results—of his work.

Marius' background is an important factor in ancient and modern judgements on his career, so that a brief description seems worthwhile. Marius was born in 157 at Arpinum, a hilltown of Volscian origin (now Arpino), stunningly positioned on the end of a narrow ridge in the western foothills of the Apennines, some 50 miles south-east of Rome. Though his enemies claimed that he was of low birth—the 'Arpinum ploughman' in one account—he almost certainly belonged to one of the town's leading families. Marius first saw military service, probably as an *eques* serving with a legion, at Numantia, and is supposed to have attracted the attention of Scipio Aemilianus. Later he was a military tribune, and afterwards became the first member of his family to reach the Senate. A marriage in about 111 allied him with the patrician, but lately undistinguished, family of the Julii Caesares, which must mark his acceptance into the ruling circle at Rome.

POLITICAL STRIFE

The period during which Marius grew to manhood and embarked on a sequence of public offices, was marked at Rome by civil disturbance. Tiberius Gracchus, brother-in-law of Aemilianus, who had likewise served in the Numantine War, endeavoured on his return from Spain to persuade the Senate to sanction large-scale reallocation of land for the benefit of poorer citizens. He was Plebeian Tribune (a political office intended to defend the rights of ordinary citizens) in 133. His proposals, which were carried in the assembly in the teeth of the Senate's opposition, were designed in part to increase the number of citizens eligible by virtue of property-holding for service in the legions. However, Gracchus was murdered shortly after. Ten years later, his younger brother, Gaius Gracchus, was likewise elected Plebeian Tribune, and proposed a wide-ranging package of political and social reforms. Amongst his measures was a law which required the state for the first time to pay the cost of a soldier's clothing and weapons, and another which restricted the right of magistrates on campaigns to inflict punishment. He seems also to have sought to reduce the number of years spent under arms (either the 16-year maximum, or more probably the six-year norm). He also re-established 17 as the minimum age for service: evidently youths of an even more tender age were enlisting—or being conscripted—at the *dilectus*. Less certainly he insisted on the formal election of military tribunes in the assembly, a procedure which had evidently been neglected in recent years. All these measures reflect an increasing discontent at the rigours of service in the later second century, and the difficulties faced by magistrates in obtaining sufficient recruits to fill out the legions required for the defence of Rome's growing possessions. Gaius Gracchus, like his brother, soon met a violent end, along with a large number of his supporters.

JUGURTHA

Outside Italy attention turned to Africa, where the successors of the long-lived Masinissa, king of Numidia (who had fought as an ally of Scipio at Zama), contended after his death for supremacy. Jugurtha, a cousin of the leading claimants, outmanoeuvred his rivals as Rome looked on, but made the mistake in 112 of allowing the killing of some Italian traders. The Senate was forced to intervene: what had seemed at first a minor local difficulty now developed into full-scale warfare which a succession of Roman commanders were unable to control or were bribed to countenance. The catalogue of shame culminated in a total surrender of a Roman army, which was compelled to pass beneath the yoke, and withdraw within the formal bounds of the Roman province. The command now fell to one of the consuls of 109, Q. Caecilius Metellus, scion of one of the most prestigious families of the age, men whose honorific surnames (*Delmaticus, Macedonicus, Balearicus*), served as an index of Roman expansion during the second century. Additional troops were enrolled, and among experienced officers added to Metellus' staff were Gaius Marius (a sometime protégé of the Metelli) and P. Rutilius Rufus who had served as a military tribune at Numantia, and who was to gain some reputation as a military theorist and author. Metellus' first task was the stiffening of morale, and he undertook a course of sharp training on the Scipionic model. Finding the slippery Jugurtha no easy conquest, he attacked the problem in workmanlike manner, by establishing fortified strongholds throughout eastern Numidia and nibbling at the centres of the King's support. But public opinion at Rome demanded quicker results. Marius himself, returning from Numidia, was elected consul for 107 after a lightning campaign, and was clearly expected to make short work of the troublesome Jugurtha. A speech by Marius, on the morrow of the elections, as reported by the historian Sallust, emphasised his 'professionalism' in contrast with his predecessors in command. In order to increase his forces, Marius called for volunteers from the *capite censi*, i.e. those assessed in the census by a head-count (above, p. 17), and who, lacking any property, were normally excluded from service under the old Servian Constitution.[1] It is difficult to assess the total numbers of *capite censi* in the citizen body by the later second century, but they seem likely to have formed a substantial group. Marius also persuaded many time-served veterans to join him.

Transporting his forces to Africa, Marius made gradual progress, but found the same difficulty as Metellus in pinning down Jugurtha. At last, with newly arrived cavalry increasing his mobility, and Jugurtha more and more hemmed in by Roman garrisons across the country, the war was brought to a conclusion in 105, when Jugurtha was betrayed to the quaestor L. Cornelius Sulla. Transported to Rome, he was eventually paraded at Marius' well-deserved Triumph in 104.

THE THREAT FROM THE NORTH

However, public concern had already turned to a new crisis on the northern frontier of Italy, where marauding Celtic tribes—the Cimbri and Teutones—had for some time been pushing against the boundaries of Roman possessions in southern Gaul, and had already inflicted heavy and embarrassing defeats on strong Roman forces. After the most serious reverse, at Arausio (Orange) in 105, where losses equalled or even exceeded those at Cannae, Rutilius Rufus, now consul, took emergency measures in the face of a likely invasion of Italy; he improved standards of fitness and training in his army by impressing to his aid professional instructors from a gladiatorial school, and seems also to have regulated the selection of tribunes for the non-consular legions, so that they were henceforth known colloquially as *Rufuli*.

But it was to Marius that the people turned to save them from the northern threat. Already before his return from Africa, Marius had been elected—in defiance of the strict rules on repeated tenure of office—as consul for 104. He took over the army of Rutilius, which provided the nucleus for his own forces, and marched north. However the threat had passed, with the departure of the tribes towards the Pyrenees and Spain. But all could see that the respite was temporary, and Marius (who was re-elected, almost without opposition, as consul for successive years 103–101) took the opportunity to train his troops in facing the wild charges and fearless onslaught of the Celts, which had many times proved the undoing of Roman troops and their commanders. To this waiting period presumably belong a number of minor reforms generally ascribed to Marius (below, p. 66). Finally in 102 the tribes reappeared in southern Gaul, moving towards Italy. Marius calmly allowed one group—the Teutones—to pass his camp en route for the Alps, and hung upon their tail until a suitable moment arose to catch them off balance, at Aquae Sextiae (Aix-en-Provence). His training schemes were now to prove their worth.

> Marius, sending officers everywhere along the line (of Romans), exhorted them to hold their ground and stand firm, and to discharge their javelins only when the enemy had come within range, then to use their swords, and force back their opponents with their long shields. For as the enemy (who had advanced against the Romans uphill) were in a precarious position, and could put neither thrust into their blows, nor any force into their interlocking wall of shields, they would have to keep twisting and turning because of the irregularity of the ground. This was his advice, and he was the first—as they saw—to follow it.[2]

The Romans pursued the Celts back down the hill, and a small party (already placed in ambush for this moment) caught them in the rear. The entire force, said to have numbered more than 100,000, was either slain or made prisoner.

Turning then to the aid of his fellow consul, Lutatius Catulus, then holding the line of the Adige river in north-east Italy against the other main thrust—by the Cimbri—he brought them to battle at Vercellae (perhaps the modern town of Vercelli near Milan, though others place the battle in the Po delta). The Cimbri were suffering badly from the hot Italian summer. Their front rank was said to have been chained together to prevent the line breaking. But the Romans were completely victorious, and forced the Cimbri back against their wagon-laager, where the waiting womenfolk attacked and killed the fugitives before committing suicide along with their children.

THE *CAPITE CENSI*

Of all the reforms attributed to Marius, the opening of the ranks to the *capite censi* has attracted most attention, and the unanimous disapproval of ancient writers. It has been held by many in modern times, following the denunciations or asides of hostile ancient authorities, that Marius' action paved the way for the lawless, greedy soldiery whose activities were thought to have contributed largely to the disgrace and fall of the Republic a few generations later.

However, it can be pointed out at once that Marius was not the first to enrol the *capite censi*; at times of extreme crisis in the past the Senate had impressed them for service, for example, after Cannae. Moreover, and more important, Marius was merely carrying one stage further a process visible throughout the second century, by which the prescribed property qualification for service was eroded and became less meaningful. The Servian Constitution, as reported by Livy, had ordained a minimum property qualification of 11,000 *asses* for service in the legions; scholars have judged that this bar was in force at the time of the Second Punic War. However, Polybius reports that the qualification for service was 400 Greek *drachmae* (=4000 *asses*); we have seen that he wrote about 160. Finally Cicero, in a treatise whose dramatic date is 129, sets the minimum at 1500 *asses*.[3] This last reduction could be ascribed to Gaius Gracchus in 123–122, whom we know to have legislated that the state should be responsible for equipping the soldier fighting in its defence. These successive reductions in the property minimum reflect a falling away in the number of small or middling proprietors who traditionally provided the bulk of the legions' manpower. Already it would seem that by the time of Gaius Gracchus the qualification had dropped below the level at which the soldier could afford to provide all his own gear. A further reduction below the figure of 1500 *asses* (or the complete abolition of the property qualification) could have been expected within the next generation. Noticeably the sources do not say that Marius swept away the qualification (a frequent assertion by modern scholars), or changed the law on eligibility, but merely that he appealed to the *capite censi* for volunteers, whom he could equip from state funds under the Gracchan legislation. It could be argued therefore that there continued to be *in law* a property-limit below which the citizen could not be forcibly conscripted. On the other hand, nothing more is heard after Marius of any restrictions on the liability for service, and it must be likely that the financial qualification was quietly dropped, either in 107, or in the run-up to the northern war of 102–101.

An examination of the circumstances surrounding Marius' action in 107 may help to place it in a proper context. Marius had been authorised to seek a *supplementum* for the legions in Africa, which would fill out the ranks of units already serving under Metellus. This was normal practice for a magistrate taking over an army in mid-campaign. As the strength of Metellus' army was probably two legions (excluding Allies), it must be likely that Marius was seeking at most some 3000 men. He was not endeavouring to raise a fresh army, or even to add new legions to his force. The Senate authorised him to hold a *dilectus* in the normal way, in the expectation that his standing with the populace would be irretrievably damaged by the conscription of its members. Troops had probably already been enrolled that year against the threat from the northern tribes. Instead Marius called for volunteers from the *capite censi*, and attracted a force 'somewhat in excess' of the totals authorised.

It must be stressed above all that Marius' activities did not lead to any thorough overhaul or reform of the conditions of military service. As far as we can establish, the six-year norm, and the 16-year maximum, continued to operate. The compulsory enlistment of citizens continued during the first century BC, down to the time of Caesar and beyond. Yet it is probably true to say that the balance shifted further towards the near-professional army. Marius himself may well have seen the enrolment of the *capite censi* in 107 as a one-off action, to obtain at short notice the reinforcements which he could see were vital towards a speedy conclusion of the Jugurthine War. Certainly from Marius' time onwards we begin to find the aims and loyalties of the army and the state, hitherto largely the same, yawning apart, with the soldiery starting to identify with the fortunes of their commander, and giving higher priority to their personal advancement and eventual enrichment. But the process was gradual, and it is not at all clear that unbiased Roman observers of the first century would necessarily have regarded Marius and the events of 107 as particularly significant in the long-term.

One particular consequence of the Marian 'reform' of army service has been seen in the consequent offers of land which we find made to the soldiers as a reward for military service in the first century. It is true that veterans of Marius' African campaign were given land there in 103 (some may indeed have never returned, or intended to return, to Italy), and measures for the settlement of veterans of the northern wars were being canvassed, and probably brought to fruition, in 100. Presumably the land went to those who by their service with Marius now completed the legal minimum of service, rather than to all-comers. However, there is no indication (and indeed evidence to the contrary) that land or a cash gratuity became a regular feature of military service in the following century. The Senate was openly hostile to such rewards, whenever suggested, and most generals felt disinclined to press for special treatment. It was only under the stress of civil war conditions (below, p. 122) that land plots and cash gratuities were regularly offered, and obtained.

MANIPLES AND COHORTS

Changes in tactical organisation and equipment have been ascribed to Marius. In particular it is often supposed that he discarded the now time-honoured and highly successful maniples and substituted the cohort as the chief sub-unit within the Roman legion.

The cohort, as a formation of three maniples, seems to have been in use as a tactical expedient from the time of the Second Punic War. Polybius indeed, in an account of the battle of Ilipa in 206, pauses to explain the meaning of the word *cohors* to his Greek readership,[4] although it receives no mention in his detailed account of army organisation. The cohort is mentioned from time to time by Livy in his accounts of fighting in Spain during the second century; some have supposed therefore that it was a particular formation found useful by successive commanders in the Iberian peninsula long before its adoption elsewhere. The archaeological evidence for Aemilianus' camps around Numantia dating from the 130s seems to show, if the excavator's account is accepted, only the *hastati, principes* and *triarii* grouped in maniples, as before. There had evidently been no change in the way in which the encampment was laid out.

However, by the time of Caesar, the cohort, not the maniple, is the sole tactical unit of the battle line. Some have detected, in Sallust's account of the operations of Metellus against Jugurtha, the last reference to maniples manoeuvring as such.[5] Hence a belief that Marius swept them away either in 106 or during his preparations for the northern campaigns. The particular threat posed by the onrushing Cimbri and Teutones could have prompted the introduction of the cohort as the standard unit, so that the change can be placed precisely in the period 104–102. But the Romans had fought against the Celts before, and should have known their tactics. It may rather be that the two forms—maniples and cohorts—coexisted for some time as alternative tactical formations; traces of the manipular organisation continued to be reflected in the titles of legionary centurions, and in the layout of forts and camps, for centuries to come (below, figs 47, 48). As a model for the post-Marian cohort we may cite the regiments of Allies and of Latins. Individual cohorts of Latins and Allies are certainly found operating as independent entities throughout the second century.

A good argument for placing a definite decision in favour of the cohort at about the time of Marius could be that, with the lowering of the financial qualification, and its eventual abolition, the soldiers were now mostly equipped by the state (from arms factories) at public expense: variations in equipment originally linked to differing financial statuses now ceased to have any *raison d'être*. The adoption of the cohort as the standard unit probably marked also the elimination of the *velites*, who had hitherto served as a light screen in front of the *hastati*. They were, it would seem, assimilated into the regular structure of centuries, which were all made the same size (80 men under the Empire), and armed in like fashion to the other troops (fig. 20b). The last specific reference to *velites* as such occurs in Sallust's account of Metellus' campaigns in 109–108.[6] Similarly, the *triarii* now (if not much earlier) were equipped with the javelin instead of the short spear, so that their role as a final defence line in phalanx-style ceases.

Each cohort in the 'new' legion was made up—as the titles of its centurions make clear (see below, p. 174)—from a maniple drawn from each of the three old lines of *hastati, principes* and *triarii*, together with the associated *velites* (fig. 20a). The cohort was thus a microcosm of the old legionary organisation—it was not a random grouping of (say) three adjacent maniples in one of the old lines. The First Cohort of the new legion consisted of the three maniples which had stood at the extreme right of the old lines; the Second Cohort was made up of the next three maniples in order of seniority, and so on; the Tenth Cohort consisted of the maniples which had stood at the left ends of the three lines of *hastati, principes* and *triarii*.

The new legion consisted of 10 cohorts, which formed up for battle in three lines, in a four-three-three formation (fig. 20c). Most probably the cohorts were of a standard size, which we know was 480 men under the Empire (but see below, p. 174). Thus the legion had a strength of some 4800 men. Each cohort contained six centuries of 80 men (fig. 20b). Some Roman authors believed that after Marius the centuries contained, as the name *centuria* would imply (from *centum* = 100), one hundred legionaries, thus giving the whole legion

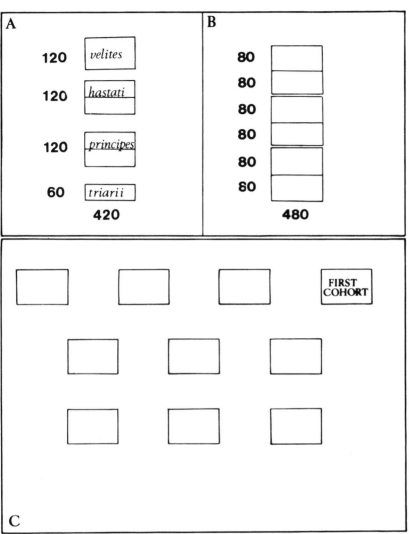

20 From maniple to cohort. **a**: single maniples (i.e. two centuries) of *hastati, principes* and *triarii* organised into a cohort (second century BC), together with *velites*. **b**: cohort of six centuries (first century BC onwards). **c**: likely battle formation of the 10 cohorts of a legion in Caesar's time

a strength of 6000. But centurions in the pre-Marian legion had commanded 60 men or less; there is no good reason to interpret the term literally in the post-Marian period. The manpower of a legion in the Late Republic is normally assessed by the Roman historians as about 5000 men; many legions were reduced well below that figure by battle-casualties, illness and natural wastage.

One difference was a new uniformity of arms and equipment. We have already seen that the *hasta* was probably discarded at this time by the *triarii*, in favour of the *pilum*, and that the *velites* probably began to be equipped like the remainder of the legionaries.

Marius is credited with a specific modification to the *pilum*, by which one of the two iron rivets, which had joined the upper (iron) to the lower (wooden) section of the shaft, was replaced by a wooden pin. The result was that when the *pilum* struck the ground, or an opponent's shield, the shaft snapped off, or the shape was so distorted that it could not be dislodged or thrown back. Doubtless *pila* (and other weaponry) could be collected up after a battle, and repaired, if so desired. Plutarch dates this modification to the eve of the battle against the Teutones in 102.[7] Archaeological evidence indicates that it was the heavy *pilum* which was modified in this way; the lighter version was socketed into its wooden shaft (fig. 18). The cohorts by their very uniformity of size and organisation were virtually interchangeable in a battle line. On the other hand the flexibility of the maniples—with troops equipped for varying functions—was lost.

The two year lull between Marius' appointment to the command in the north and the return of the Celtic tribes which it was his duty to destroy, allowed ample time for the training of his army, and measures to increase its endurance, confidence, general expertise and morale. Further exercise was provided by a public-works project, a channel subsequently known as the *fossa Mariana*, which linked the town of Arles in the Rhone delta directly to the Mediterranean. In his training of the soldiers, Marius was firm but fair, and stories abounded. He reduced the number of camp followers, making the soldier more self-reliant: the individual was required to carry his own emergency rations, and a wide range of essential hand-equipment for entrenching and cooking. This stuck in the popular imagination: the soldiers, carrying their equipment on a forked pole over their shoulders, seemed by their bowed and shambling gait to have become beasts of burden, and were henceforth known as Marius' Mules.[8] The idea that the soldier should carry a heavy load was not new: Philip II of Macedon (Alexander's father) had introduced similar regulations in his own army, and Metellus in Africa is credited by Sallust with almost identical measures. We may well suppose that the soldier was *meant* always to carry a substantial load, but like many regulations this was often ignored, and enforced only by the most determined commanders. However Marius' Mule remained in popular currency, and has epitomised for all times the heavily-laden, but determined, Roman legionary.

THE LEGIONARY EAGLE

Marius is also credited with making the eagle (*aquila*) the legion's chief standard, and a focus for loyalty and affection. Our source, the Elder Pliny, places the adoption of the eagle precisely in 104, at the start of preparations for the northern wars.[9] He notes that the legion hitherto had had a variety of standards—the eagle (which had always had the first place), the wolf, the minotaur (a man-headed bull), the horse and the boar, and that all had been carried in front of different elements in the legion. Marius is stated to have given pre-eminence to the eagle and to have abolished the others. All five standards were animal totems, reflecting the religious beliefs of an agricultural society. The boar also appears as an important battle-emblem among the Celts. We are not told which sub-units within the legion used the five standards, but we might have expected the *hastati, principes* and *triarii* to have had separate standards, and perhaps the *velites* also. Polybius notes that each maniple had two standards, one for each century.[10] We may wonder whether the increased prominence given to the eagle as the legion's emblem was linked to the increasing use of the cohort. Yet the cohort itself never seems to have had a specific standard. Moreover the old battle lines appear to have retained their own standards long after Marius. Coins of 82 and 49 (pls 4a, 4b) show an *aquila* flanked by others which bear a little square plaque or flag with the single letters H and P. These must be standards specifically of the *hastati* and *principes*. They consist of slender poles decorated with circular bosses, but bear no animal figures. Another coin issue, of about 40 shows, amongst other motifs, an *aquila* flanked by a single standard, perhaps bearing the letter P (pl. 4c). At the close of the Republic it seems likely therefore that the legion's three most important standards were the *aquila* in the care of the *primus pilus* (chief centurion of the *triarii*), and two others, presumably in the charge of the *princeps* and the *hastatus* (senior centurions of the other two groups). The retention of these standards serves as an interesting sidelight on continuity of tradition within the legion. The eagle-bearer (*aquilifer*) of the legion was thus the man who carried the standard of the senior century of the First Maniple of the *triarii*. In battle and on the march the standards were important as a rallying-point. To lose, or surrender, a standard, especially the eagle itself, was a particular disgrace.

On his return from the north, Marius was hailed as the saviour of

Rome, and held a magnificent Triumph, along with Catulus, in 101. His prestige was unrivalled, and it was expected that he would play a leading political role. As the victor of the hour, he secured election as consul, for a further year (100). Rewards for his troops were secured through the agency of radical politicians, but at the end of the year Marius retired from the city on a diplomatic mission to Asia Minor.

THE SOCIAL WAR

The following decade witnessed a heightening of tension between the Romans and the Italian communities whose increasingly strident demands for full citizenship and equality of opportunity in the state, and equalisation of the military burden, had over the previous half century been repeatedly refused or diverted, and existing barriers even reinforced. Finally, the murder in 91 of a Plebeian Tribune dedicated to their enfranchisement brought matters to a head.

The revolt of the Allies (*socii*, hence the common name for this conflict) broke into the open at Asculum (Ascoli Piceno), a hilltown in the eastern foothills of the Apennines, when a praetor and his legate, and other Romans in the town, were brutally murdered. The Senate was caught very much by surprise. Of the legions then in service, only one was accessible, in Cisalpina, but a substantial number of new formations were raised, and the state's most capable military men called to its defence. Marius was appointed a legate to the consul P. Rutilius Lupus who was entrusted with the suppression of the rebels in central and southern Italy, while Cornelius Sulla and Catulus were among those legates assigned to the other consul, L. Julius Caesar, who undertook operations in Samnium and Campania. Many of these legates appear to have operated independently, with battle-groups consisting of one legion and foreign auxiliaries.

Despite the array of talent among their commanders, the Romans (and the Latins, who had mostly remained loyal) were largely unsuccessful throughout the year. By its close the Senate had the wisdom to concede Roman citizenship to all those who had remained loyal or had desisted from the struggle. Only the most determined and recalcitrant of the rebels now persevered, with some hope of assistance from King Mithridates of Pontus in Asia Minor. But the Romans now held the initiative, and rebel towns were stormed one by one, so that resistance had all but ceased by the summer of 88.

Asculum, scene of the intitial outbreak, was besieged by Pompeius Strabo, then by his successor Sex. Julius Caesar, at first to no avail. Archaeological evidence for the siege survives in large quantities of lead slingbullets, which have come to light in and around the town. A concentration on the banks of the Castellano river east of the town may suggest that the siege was pressed hardest from that side. Some of the bullets (like those recovered later at Perugia; below, p. 123) are inscribed with abbreviated messages, a useful guide to current Latinity, propaganda, and soldiers' humour.[11] Missiles were in use on both sides: one with the message 'A gift to the *Asculani*' is obviously being fired into the town, while 'Hit Pompeius!' is clearly aimed at the besiegers. Others give the numerals of legions present, and indicate that the besieging force, comprised (or included) legions *IV, IX, X,* and *XV* (the latter is by far the most frequently attested). There were also present contingents from the nearby Latin colony of Firmum (Fermo), and from Gaul, Etruria and Spain—indeed we know from a bronze plaque that some Spanish cavalry were rewarded after the capture of the town with Roman citizenship. The siege dragged on for almost a year. Pompeius Strabo returned to draw the Roman net even tighter around the town, and it fell in November 89. Among those serving with Strabo were his son (the future Pompey the Great), the young Cicero, and a L. Sergius, very probably Sergius Catilina (Catiline), whom we shall encounter again. Unfortunately no traces have been detected of the Roman siege-lines.

CONSEQUENCES OF THE WAR

The consequences of the war for army organisation are at once apparent. The *alae sociorum* which had accompanied the legions on campaign (above, p. 22), ceased to exist, as the categories of Latin and Ally were abolished within Italy itself. All soldiers recruited in Italy south of the Po were citizens and thus served as legionaries. The Latin and Allied contingents had doubtless already been organised and equipped in all but identical fashion to the Romans themselves. The cost of keeping the army in being was now to be borne entirely by the Roman treasury. The army list was obviously now lengthened: when reliable figures next become available for the number of legions (the decade 90–80 is atypical), we can see that there were seldom fewer than 14 in the field, and major campaigns were to cause the totals to soar much higher. Given that all Italy was now the recruiting ground for the legions, the work of raising legions and of obtaining supplements for existing formations was spread across the peninsula, and carried out through the agency of officials termed *conquisitores*, of uncertain rank and status, in conjunction with local magistrates. A legion could now be raised entirely along the Adriatic coast, in the Apennines or in the south, without any input from Rome itself.

Another immediate, though less obvious consequence was that the Social War left many men embittered and homeless. Often these found a new home in the legions, adding to the increasing element of 'professionals', and infusing a spirit of callousness and indifference, which was to have serious consequences later. It may be that the Social War did more to engender the grasping, greedy soldiery of the Late Republic than any of Marius' reforms.

The half-century following the Social War saw the old Republican institutions in disarray, proving increasingly unable to cope with the task of managing a growing empire, and finally collapsing in the face of the consuming ambitions of leading politicians. The process was gradual, and its details need not concern us, except that many of the protagonists in struggles to come, relied on, or sought the support of, the army, whose attitudes and proclivities were never far from the public mind.

MITHRIDATES

While the Social War was in progress, the resourceful Mithridates, King of Pontus in Asia Minor, had been extending his power over adjacent kingdoms, massacring Roman and Italian settlers in large numbers. He invaded Greece, which welcomed him as a deliverer. All Rome's eastern possessions, and her reputation, were at stake. Cornelius Sulla, as consul for 88, was given Asia as his command, but a demagogue succeeded in transferring the task to the ageing Marius. Sulla responded by marching on the city with six legions. Deserted by all but one of his senatorial officers, he entered and occupied Rome. Later historians looked back on his action as an awesome precedent, and indicative of the new attitude of the grasping soldiery, for which Marius took much of the blame. More probably Sulla's legions, bound for Asia, contained many ne'er-do-wells from both sides in the Social War, with little affection for Rome or the Senate, and with the prospect of restoring their fortunes by the campaign in Asia uppermost in their minds, as Sulla knew well enough. The war itself, when Sulla had restored order to the city and crossed over to Greece, culminated in battles at Chaeronea and Orchomenus in Boeotia, and Mithridates thought it prudent to submit. The archaeological record of this campaign (and many others, as we shall see) is as yet quite blank, though the biographer Plutarch, himself a native of the area, was able to report that, in the early second century AD, marshy lakes around Orchomenus still yielded weaponry, the debris of the battle.[12]

But Sulla's enemies had regained control at Rome, and in 86 sent out a rival army of two legions under the consul Valerius Flaccus, to supplant Sulla in his command. However, Flaccus was killed in a mutiny, and his troops incorporated into Sulla's army. It was time for the latter to return to Italy. Despite having been long ago declared a public enemy, Sulla held his forces together and landed unopposed at Brindisi and Taranto in 83, where he was joined by young Crassus, and others of the oligarchic faction, among them Metellus Pius, son of Marius' rival, while the young Pompey (son of Pompeius Strabo), who had raised a force of three legions in his native Picenum, diverted a considerable body of the legitimate forces. Marius was already dead, but his friends, aided by the Samnites, who rose en masse for a final time, resisted strongly. In a hard fought battle at the gates of Rome, which lasted far into the night, they were completely defeated, and Marius' son, who had sought refuge in the hilltop citadel of Praeneste (Palestrina), committed suicide. Soon all Italy, Gaul, Sicily and North Africa were recovered. Sulla now attempted to buttress the old institutions of state, rather than adjust its machinery to suit current reality. His veterans received a due reward of land in colonies, which were established at some of the most recalcitrant centres of opposition to his cause, including Praeneste, and Pompeii, which was retitled *colonia Veneria Cornelia Pompeianorum*. The titles derived from the goddess Venus, to whom Sulla was particularly devoted, and his own family name, *Cornelius*. Sulla's subsequent retirement, and, more important, his early death, left the field open once again.

POMPEY AND CRASSUS

One bastion of Marian support remained in Spain, to which the praetor Q. Sertorius had retreated with other supporters of Marius in 83. Sertorius courted the Spanish nobility and chieftains, conceding a considerable measure of autonomy, and strove almost as a second Hamilcar to develop the province in the interest of Rome. Metellus Pius was despatched against him, and later Pompey, but despite the presence of an army which swelled to a dozen legions or more, neither made much progress in the face of the Spanish terrain and troops trained in the Roman manner. A winter-camp of 60 acres (24 hectares) near Cáceres on the south side of the Tagus was thought by Schulten to have been the base of Metellus Pius' forces in 80/79 BC (fig. 21). Partial excavation revealed an elongated encampment, with walls of stone, defended by two ditches. In the interior were

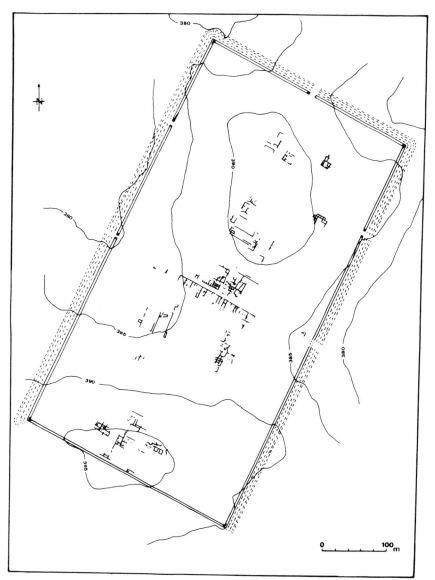

21 Winter-camp at Cáceres (*after Schulten*), probably for one legion: 60 acres (24 hectares). Early first century BC

administrative and other buildings, perhaps tribunes' houses, constructed in stone. Excavation was selective (see fig. 21), but some of the stone structures located must have been barracks. From its size the camp should have contained a single legion, but the layout differs somewhat from the Polybian model. A recent re-examination of the excavation-archive and of small finds by Dr G. Ulbert has confirmed a date of occupation in the 70s BC, and has suggested that the site was in use for up to a decade, ending in a violent destruction, perhaps at the hands of Sertorian rebels. Schulten also believed that camps IV and V at Renieblas, east of Numantia, were relics of Pompey's campaigns in 75/74 BC against the Celtiberians (figs 22–23); here again more secure dating evidence would be welcome[13]. The war was brought to a close when Sertorius was assassinated at the instigation of a fellow officer, and senatorial control was re-established.

Meanwhile in Italy itself a revolt by gladiators in a training school at Capua in 73 sparked off a general rising of the rural-based slaves of the great estates of the South, under the leadership of Spartacus, a Thracian who had earlier served as an auxiliary with a Roman army, probably in Greece. There were no troops available in Italy to resist him; the defeat of hastily raised levies served only to encourage other slaves to join his forces, until all Italy seemed at his mercy. Gradually he was able to equip his men with captured weaponry. Both the consuls of 72 were defeated in open warfare, and later in the year Crassus was given total command as pro-praetor; he decimated the survivors of two of the defeated legions, raised and trained a fresh force of six legions, and took the field in earnest. Divisions of policy among the slaves sapped the combined strength of their army, and eventually they were defeated. A small contingent, fleeing north-wards, was cut up by Pompey, returning with veterans of his army from Spain.

WAR IN THE EAST

Roman ability to respond to the Spanish War and to Spartacus was weakened by continuing warfare in the East against the renascent Mithridates. L. Licinius Lucullus, as consul for 74, had undertaken the war, and was continued in the command as pro-consul for many years. At first he enjoyed considerable success, and drove Mithridates out of his kingdom, to take refuge in Armenia. Among his forces were the remnants of the two legions of Valerius Flaccus (above, p. 71)—popularly called the Valerians—whose attempted mutiny at continued service, in 67, together with Lucullus' temporary difficulties, induced the Senate to terminate his command. Meanwhile another aspect of the continuing unrest in the eastern Mediterranean reached alarming proportions—pirate squadrons, a hazard to trade for a century or more, which the Romans had failed abysmally to

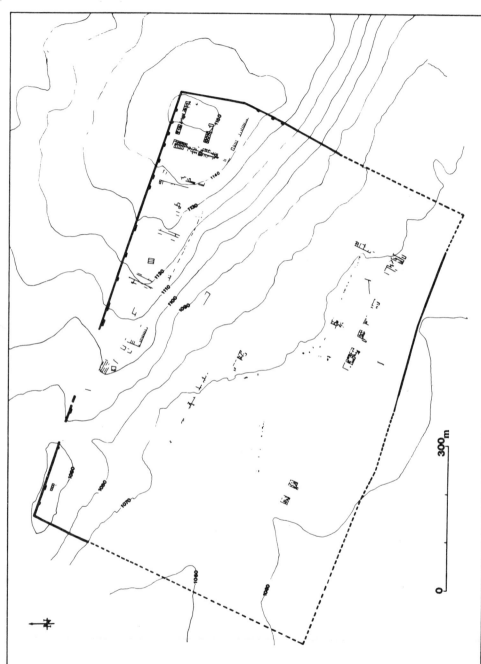

22 Camp V at Renieblas (*after Schulten*); 151 acres (61.2 hectares). Tentatively dated to the period of Pompey's campaigns against Sertorius in the later 70s BC

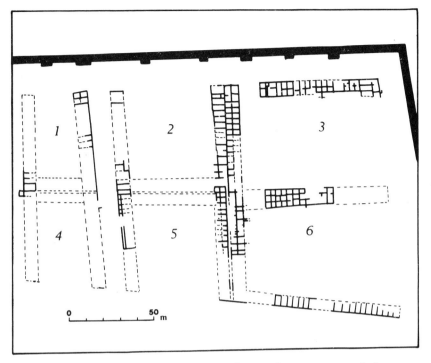

23 Camp V at Renieblas: barracks in the north-east corner of the
Camp (*after Schulten*). Schulten restored the plan to show six barracks
(1–3 and 4–6) belonging to two different cohorts, but caution is advised.
Notice the varying sizes of the barracks, which could suggest differing
manpower

contain. A final embarrassment was a raid on the Italian coastline
when two magistrates were abducted on the Appian Way. Pompey
was appointed to a special command, and given substantial funds, 24
legates, and a fleet of 200 ships. He had the right to intervene in
provinces along the Mediterranean coastline, and his powers were to
be equal to those of the governors of those provinces. In a wide-
ranging whirlwind campaign, he cleared the Mediterranean within
three months. He was now the obvious candidate to draw to an
equally speedy conclusion the Mithridatic War. He was given another
special command, this time (it may be) with powers to override other
proconsuls or propraetors, and allowed to make war or peace
without direct reference to the Senate and People at Rome itself.
Retaining his own troops, and adding to them the legions of
Lucullus, he succeeded by shrewd diplomacy and forceful action in
expelling the old king from all his possessions and compelling him to

75

flee to the Crimea, where he soon died. Meanwhile Pompey, his force now of 10 legions or more, marched southwards into Syria, which he annexed for Rome, and into Judaea where in 63 he quelled for a time the feuding between rival factions. Much inspired work of reorganisation at provincial and local level followed. Pompey resolved to establish small Roman provinces in the coastal belts of Asia Minor and the Levant, and beyond their borders to institute a ring of client states to act as buffers against attack from without, a system which was to last without serious reverse until the Civil Wars, and remained the basis of Rome's defence in the East long after.

Events at Rome had continued apace, as politicians vied for pre-eminence in Pompey's absence. A wide programme of reform, instigated by, or fronted by, L. Sergius Catilina (Catiline), failed to gather momentum, and when in October 63 Catiline failed for a second time to gain election as consul, he attempted a coup, with the backing of some of Sulla's veterans, those whom the latter had dispossessed, and disaffected elements everywhere. But his ill-equipped forces were defeated, after a stubborn contest, at Pistoria, in the Arno valley north-west of Florence, and Catiline was killed.

Pompey returned to Italy in the tense aftermath of Catiline's 'conspiracy', with the need to have his Acts in the East confirmed, and (hopefully) his troops rewarded. Those time-served men who returned with him were disbanded at once, but he found the Senate obstructive, and his proposals treated as pawns in the political game. After vain efforts to get his way, he was persuaded by the rising C. Julius Caesar to enter an informal alliance along with Crassus, which history knows as the First Triumvirate. With Caesar elected as one of the consuls for 59, Pompey's Acts were confirmed and land settlement schemes for his men and many other civilians put into effect; Crassus for his part secured more favourable terms for the tax-gathering syndicates, who were trying to restore the revenues from the exhausted Asiatic provinces. Caesar, as the junior partner, had appeared at first merely a tool of the two giants, but in the long-term he had most to gain, as will shortly become apparent.

ARMY SERVICE IN THE LATE REPUBLIC

In general terms, army service from the 80s onwards to Caesar's time remained much as it had always been. Service was for a six-year minimum period, which might be extended, but efforts by magistrates to detain men much beyond this norm could lead to discontent. Individuals could, and did, volunteer to serve longer. A good example must be the 'Valerians', who served in the East from 86 onwards.[14] Their first period of service lasted until about 75, when they were disbanded, but were reformed almost at once to fight in Lucullus' army. Roused to near mutiny in 68/67, they obtained discharge by a decree passed at Rome itself. Their case had become a political football, and they were represented by Lucullus' enemies as illegally retained by an uncaring general. However, on Pompey's arrival in the East, some re-enlisted, and it must be likely that they remained with him, to be brought home in 62. Their normal legionary framework was perhaps retained until 67, but it may well be that they were distributed individually thereafter. Precisely how many remained of the original members after some 24 years' service cannot be known; perhaps they numbered a few hundred at most. The 'Valerians' were, it is clear, an exception to the rule, worthy of report by a number of ancient sources, a group of near professionals who joined in the aftermath of the Social War, and by wish or circumstances prolonged their service. It seems clear that their service was, and continued to be, extremely profitable financially. But we should be wrong to suppose that all those serving under arms desired a long-term career.

New legions continued to be raised, and supplements found for existing formations, by means of a *dilectus*, held at Rome or in a specific area of Italy, often by a magistrate en route to his province. If sufficient men presented themselves voluntarily, well and good. Otherwise they would be chosen in the traditional way from the census rolls. On the other hand it is possible to detect a greater degree of professionalism creeping in at officer level. Here a good example is M. Petreius, who had been a tribune in a legion, then a *praefectus* (presumably of auxiliaries), then legate. He showed his worth in the final battle against Catiline. Petreius' advancement owed much to the influence of Pompey, whom he later served as legate in Spain over many years (below, p. 105).

An eminent modern historian has proposed that in the first century BC there were essentially two types of Roman army: (1) the 'standing armies' in the provinces, which formed the static garrisons, and (2) 'emergency armies' raised to meet a specific threat, and commanded by the great leaders of the time—such as Marius, Sulla, Pompey and Caesar, to whose standards men flocked eagerly in the expectation of profit, and to whose interests they became particularly attached.[15] It was argued that soldiers in the 'standing armies' could expect to serve for a long period, in one province; but in the 'emergency armies' merely for a single campaign or the duration of the war, after which they would be released and receive a special reward. But the distinction is apparent rather than real. All soldiers enlisted under the same conditions, and could not tell on enlistment how long a campaign would last, or where they might see service. Soldiers took an oath to serve their commander and not desert him until formally released; if a new commander was appointed, the oath was retaken, until the individual's due term of service was completed. Armies were kept permanently in an increasing number of overseas provinces in the first century, and these required periodic renewal.

There is one noticeable change: armies finally ceased to be commanded, and legions officered, by elected magistrates during their year of office. From the time of Sulla consuls were formally barred from leaving Italy during their term of office. Only in the year following did consuls—and praetors—proceed to a province and exercise military command. In 52 a law was passed requiring a five-year gap between office-holding at Rome and provincial command. This was an important break from the idea of the citizen army of earlier days.

The numbering system of the legions in the Late Republic is little understood. Certainly each bore a numeral, according to the sequence of their creation in a particular year. It is possible that legions sometimes—perhaps always—changed their numerals each year, as the complement of the army was adjusted to suit current needs. The numerals *I–IV* were reserved for the consuls, should they have to raise an army during their year of office. Otherwise we have little precise information, in the almost total absence of inscriptions. We happen to know that the legions based in Transalpine and Cisalpine Gaul were numbered *VII, VIII, IX,* and *X* on Caesar's arrival there in 58 BC (below, p. 81), and a chance inscription tells us that one of the legions in Cilicia in 56–54 had the numeral *XVIII*.[16] From this evidence some have discerned a clockwise numbering system, with low numerals (from *V* onwards) for Spain, and higher numerals for Macedonia and the East.[17] It may indeed be that some system was imposed; we may detect some hints of it also under Augustus (below, p. 136).

SUPPORT TROOPS

In the decades after the Social War the Romans were compelled to look more vigorously elsewhere for light infantry, and especially cavalry, which the Allies had hitherto supplied in disproportionate numbers. In successive decades we hear of those ubiquitous mercenaries, the Cretan archers, of Balearic slingers and Numidian cavalry, together with levies called out from friendly states close to the current war zone. But none of these groups was retained on any permanent footing. The Romans had realised, in fighting against the Gauls, the Numidians and later in the East and in Spain, that they could not match their opponents in the efficacy of the cavalry arm, and native levies were already being hired, or pressed into service, from the time of the Second Punic War, to remedy the deficiency. Roman cavalry fade from sight in the later second century, and we last hear of Latin and Allied cavalry at the time of the Jugurthine War.[18] In the first century BC the cavalry accompanying the legions appears to be drawn exclusively from non-Italian allies, Numidians, Gauls and later Germans. Presumably Roman cavalry ceased to be called for service. However, legionary cavalry does reappear in a different form under the Empire (below, p. 173), and respect for tradition could suggest that even in the Late Republic, the Equestrians remained liable for service, though never in fact asked to serve. Under the Empire, the legion's cavalry was drawn from the same sources as the legionaries themselves. Scholars have endeavoured to find references to Roman cavalry in the wars of Caesar and the Second Triumvirate, but none seems convincing in the face of the weight of contrary evidence. That Caesar possessed no Roman cavalry of the old style seems clear from the incident in 58 when he mounted up some soldiers of the Tenth Legion on horses vacated by Gallic auxiliaries to serve as a bodyguard (below, p. 84). None of the donatives which our sources report as given to the soldiery in the first century BC includes a category of award to *equites*, though many of those from the second century had done so. A set of regulations on office-holding in Italian towns, which dates to about 50, allows exemption from the normal minimum age-limit for local magistracies to men who had served at least three years 'on horseback' (*in equo*);[19] but such a figure may have been the theoretical norm rather than actual practice. Interestingly a tomb monument from Rome dating to about 75–50 (see pl. 5a) shows a family group, of which the central figure L. Septumius L.f. is described as *eques* and shown holding a *gladius*. Some reference to actual military service may be intended, unless the *gladius* is merely a conventional attribute of the heroic pose. Undoubtedly a few *equites* accompanied a magistrate on campaign, and served on his staff. Under the Empire the Equestrian Order continued to stress its military origin and traditions, with an annual review of its members in the city; but they were not expected to go out on active service.

3 Caesar's Conquest of Gaul

Such then was the Roman army, when Gaius Julius Caesar (pl. 6) arrived in Gaul in 58 as *proconsul*. In May of the previous year, during his consulship, Caesar had obtained by vote of the Assembly the provinces of Cisalpine Gaul (i.e. North Italy) and Illyricum (i.e. the coast of Yugoslavia), for an exceptional period of five years, with a force of three legions. Perhaps he had in mind campaigns across the Alps and towards the Danube. But soon after, the province of Transalpina (i.e. Gaul *beyond* the Alps), recently made vacant by the death of the incumbent governor, was added to Caesar's command, and with it one legion; this was to be the jumping-off point for all Caesar's Gallic conquests.

The province of Transalpina consisted of a narrow strip of land bordered by the Alps, the Cevennes and the Pyrenees, which served to secure Roman communications with her Spanish possessions, and had over the years been many times buffeted by hostile tribes to the north (fig. 24). To Caesar his command was an opportunity to enhance his own prestige and build up his own resources to match his partners in the Triumvirate. By interfering in Gallic affairs outside the boundaries of his province (at most he was authorised to 'protect' adjacent tribes, not annex their territory); by preferring aggression to negotiation, by magnifying threats to the province and raising extra forces to meet them, he amazed Rome by the brilliance of his generalship, and the swiftness and totality of his conquests. The Gauls, bogeymen in the recent and distant past, were humbled and apparently reduced to submission in a few years. When Caesar went out to Gaul, there can have been little expectation that this loquacious and unprincipled politician could achieve so much. Yet by force of personality, and the innate decisiveness of an original mind, he quickly welded an army which came to identify its own fortunes and future well-being with those of its commander, an army which with its almost uninterrupted success, and high morale, proved, when civil war came, immeasurably superior to the forces of

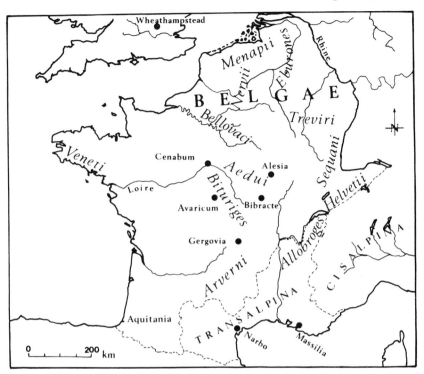

24 Gaul in 60 BC, showing major tribes, towns mentioned in the text and adjacent Roman provinces

the legitimate government, which had enjoyed none of these uplifting experiences.

The forces available to Caesar, when he arrived in northern Italy, consisted of four legions, numbered in orderly sequence from *VII* to *X*. Of these, three (perhaps *VII*, *VIII*, and *IX*) were based on Aquileia, on the eastern border of Cisalpina, to guard against attacks from the Illyrians. Only one legion, perhaps *X*, was then in Transalpina; it could well have been at the capital, Narbo (Narbonne). Caesar was fortunate throughout his years of command that the eastern borders of his provinces remained relatively quiet, and never constituted any meaningful drain on the forces at his disposal. We know nothing about the previous history of the legions, except that they were already in his provinces when Caesar reached Gaul. Under the legislation appointing him to the command, Caesar had a quaestor to handle the financial affairs of the army, and ten legates whom he personally selected.

THE HELVETII

On his arrival Caesar, claiming to be acting in defence of Rome's allies, the Aedui of the Burgundy region, took the offensive at once, against the Helvetii of modern Switzerland, who, themselves under pressure from migrating tribes, asked to pass through Roman territory on their way to a new home on the Atlantic seaboard of Gaul. Other Roman governors could easily have acceded, but Caesar refused, and barred their entry with an earthen rampart and ditch, protected by fortified posts at regular intervals, over a distance of some 19 miles between Lake Geneva and the Jura Mountains at the Pas de l'Écluse. Given the precipitous cliffs over parts of the route, it is difficult to suppose that the defence line was continuous. Some lengths of the ditch were detected by excavation in the later nineteenth century.[1] The Helvetii were compelled to follow a more difficult route to the north outside the Roman province. Caesar, who had summoned the three legions from Aquileia to join him, and raised two more (*XI* and *XII*) to meet the crisis, followed the moving column north-west for some 150 km across Central Gaul. Near Bibracte (Mont Beuvray) the Helvetii turned on Caesar, who withdrew his army of six legions and auxiliaries to a convenient hilltop (generally identified at Armecy), where he was protected on three sides by water barriers) and awaited their arrival (fig. 25). His four experienced legions (*VII–X*) were drawn up in a three-fold line of cohorts on its slopes, while the newly raised legions (*XI* and *XII*), together with the auxiliares, occupied the summit of the hill and began the construction of an entrenchment to protect the baggage.[2] A ditch system was identified on the hill by Col. Stoffel in 1886, but its date is not precisely known. Auxiliary cavalry sent to delay the Helvetii were swept aside and the latter formed up to attack. Caesar despatched all the officers' horses, including his own, to the rear of the hill—of course he had good visibility from the hilltop—but it was a useful gesture to strengthen his men's morale in their first serious battle.

The Romans had the advantage of height, and their volleys of javelins soon took effect. A general charge was ordered, and the legionaries ran down the slope driving the Helvetii before them (1). The survivors crossed a stream in front of the Roman position and gained the opposing ridge. At this point, the Helvetian rearguard, a force of 15,000 Boii and Tulingi, who only now arrived on the battlefield, launched themselves against the exposed right flank of the legions (2). Seeing them, the main body of Helvetii rallied, but Caesar had time to detach the third line from each legion (i.e. twelve cohorts

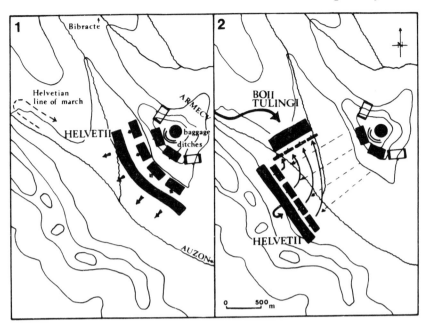

25 The battle against the Helvetii, 58 BC (see p. 82) (*after Veith and Rice Holmes*)

in all) and send them to meet the new threat. After a fiercely contested struggle, the Helvetii were beaten on both fronts. Caesar's men were too exhausted to mount an immediate pursuit. Eventually, driven by hunger to surrender, the Helvetii were ordered to return home and to rebuild their villages, where they remained cowed for a generation, until incorporated into the Gallic province by Augustus.

ARIOVISTUS

Caesar next took up an invitation from the Aedui to restrain a Suebian prince Ariovistus, whom the Roman Senate had recently recognised as 'King' and 'Friend', and whose followers had for some time been expanding west of the Rhine at the expense of the resident tribes. After an abortive parley, Caesar forced a battle somewhere near Mulhouse in the Alsace region, which resulted in a total rout of the Germans: Ariovistus escaped the slaughter but seems to have died soon after. In agreeing to the parley before the battle, Ariovistus had stipulated that no Roman infantry should be present; Caesar should come with only a cavalry escort. In order not to leave himself at a disadvantage, Caesar ordered some of the Xth legion to mount up on the horses of his Gallic cavalry, and to accompany him (above, p. 79). This prompted a wit among the soldiers to discern a further honour for this, already Caesar's favourite legion: for some time he had been treating it as a Praetorian Cohort (i.e. a governor's bodyguard). Now he was making all its members *equites*—cavalry, traditionally provided by the wealthy middle class, the Knights[3]. This incident is quite clearly the origin of the title *Equestris* which inscriptions of the middle and later first century BC attach to the legion. The epithet need mean no more than 'mounted on horse-back', but it must surely be taken in the sense of 'Knightly', reflecting the legion's special position in Caesar's esteem.

THE BELGIC TRIBES

The legions spent the winter of 58–57 among the Sequani well to the north of the formal boundary of the Roman province. Murmurings among the Belgae of north-east Gaul against this Roman advance gave Caesar the desired excuse to enlarge his forces further, by the raising of legions *XIII* and *XIV*, which he brought out from Cisalpina in the spring of 57. Caesar now advanced into the territory of the Belgic alliance, outmanoeuvred their collective forces on the Aisne, and forced them to disperse. The site of this encounter was probably at Mauchamp, where a Roman camp of 104 acres (41 hectares) was identified by Colonel Stoffel in 1862, on high ground between the Aisne and a small tributary, the Miette (fig. 26). The excavators also located ditches and ramparts linking the camp to both these water-barriers, with a fortification at the north end (and another postulated at the south), more or less as Caesar describes.[4]

Later in the same year Caesar was caught off balance by one of the Belgic tribes, the Nervii, who attacked the Roman army as it encamped on the bank of the Sambre. After desperate fighting in which the Romans suffered severely and many centurions were killed, the fortunate arrival on the scene of Caesar's senior legate, Labienus, saved the day, and the Nervii went down, allegedly almost to a man. The legions now set up winter quarters among the Belgae and in the Loire Valley, and all Gaul seemed stunned into submission. Caesar's report to the Senate called forth a Thanksgiving of unprecedented length, a great boost to his national standing.

A meeting with his fellow Triumvirs, Pompey and Crassus, at Luca (Lucca) in April 56, gave Caesar a further five years (i.e. 54–50) in Gaul, without hindrance from Rome, while Pompey was to have a similarly free hand in Spain, and Crassus in Syria. The same year (56) saw Caesar's forces at work on the western seaboard of Gaul, and

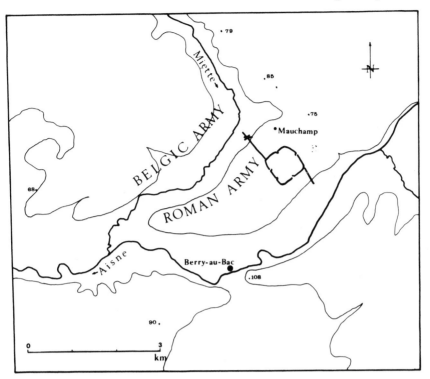

26 Caesar's encampment on the Aisne, 57 BC (*after Napoléon III*)

tribes from Aquitania to the mouth of the Rhine were reduced to submission or worsted in battle. In Brittany the Veneti retreated to their promontory forts along the coastline. Caesar was able to capture a number of these without difficulty, but he found that the defenders merely put to sea and sailed to a different stronghold. He was forced to wait while a fleet was assembled. After a hard fight in Quiberon Bay, the Veneti surrendered, to be sold as slaves. Many of these promontory forts have been identified, but archaeology as yet supplies no direct evidence for a Caesarian onslaught.

CAESAR IN BRITAIN

In the spring of 55 Caesar was active in north-east Gaul, and successfully prevented further migration by German tribesmen to the west bank of the Rhine. He followed this up by an expedition across the river, bridging it somewhere near Coblenz, demonstrating the power of Roman response, and returned safely into Gaul, breaking down the bridge behind him (pl. 7). As if this had not been a sufficiently risky undertaking for one season. Caesar followed it up in the autumn with a quick expedition into Britain: taking legions *VII* and *X*, he crossed the Channel overnight, and next morning reached the coast at or near Dover. However the landing was opposed on the beaches by strong native forces. The soldiers proved reluctant to disembark into deep water, until the unnamed *aquilifer* of *legio X* took the initiative, and plunged in, shaming his comrades into following him. Bad weather prevented Caesar's cavalry from reaching him, and he was unable to penetrate more than a few miles from his bridgehead. The opportune arrival of some envoys seeking peace enabled him to return to Gaul within a fortnight without too much loss of face and before the onset of winter. Caesar was determined to improve on this achievement, and over the winter a large fleet of suitable transports was assembled to his specifications. In July 54 he set sail again, with five legions (over half his total army), only three being left behind to hold Gaul. The size of the invasion force could suggest an intention permanently to subdue some substantial part of the island, and add it to Caesar's province. This second expedition suffered almost as badly as the first from the weather, and though he landed this time without opposition, Caesar found progress hard to achieve against British chariotry (a military vehicle long abandoned on the Continent) and skilful delaying tactics masterminded by Cassivellaunus, who had been appointed war-leader of the southern tribes. Cassivellaunus' stronghold was stormed and his forces dispersed. The siting is uncertain, though Wheathampstead near St. Albans has been advocated. Caesar now found his base-camp attacked by local Kentish forces, at the instigation of Cassivellaunus, but they were easily beaten off. Cassivellaunus now opened negotiation with Caesar, who with his mind on troubles in Gaul was happy to secure a peace settlement, by which hostages were given and an annual tribute promised, before crossing the Channel in mid September. No marching camps have as yet been located, to chart the progress of Caesar's forces.

A LEGION DESTROYED

The Gauls were now beginning to realise that the Romans were planning to stay in their territory, and that claims of acting on their behalf against mutual enemies were but a cloak for permanent subjugation. During the winter of 54–53, when Caesar was compelled because of a poor harvest to distribute his legions more widely in their winter-quarters, in order to be sure of a food supply, the Eburones of the Meuse valley made an attack on *legio XIV* (one of the newest formations) and five recently enrolled cohorts (apparently the core of another legion, otherwise unmentioned by Caesar) which were encamped together in their territory near Tongres, under the joint command of the two legates Titurius Sabinus and Aurunculeius Cotta. Weakness of resolve and divided counsels led to catastrophe: the Roman force was induced to leave the relative safety of its camp and all but annihilated in an ambush. A few men did get back to the camp, the *aquilifer* of *legio XIV* saving the eagle from immediate capture by throwing it inside the rampart, while he himself was surrounded and cut down.[5] But to no avail. The survivors in the camp all committed suicide during the night. As a result, the Nervii were emboldened to attack another legion (Caesar does not give its numeral) in its winter camp, and to enclose it with siegeworks in the Roman manner; but a resolute defence under the leadership of Q. Cicero (the brother of the distinguished orator) kept them at bay until Caesar arrived and defeated the besieging forces. At this, plans by various tribes for attacking other Roman camps came to nought. Yet it was clear to Caesar that further trouble could be expected, and by late 53 he had increased his army to ten legions with the formation of two new units: seemingly numbered *XIV* and *XV* (the former replacing the unit with this number lost with Sabinus and Cotta); and he borrowed another, numbered *I*, from Pompey (it was part of the latter's 'consular' series of 55). A second brief crossing of the Rhine served to remind the Germans of the continuing might of Rome, and Caesar's ability to enter their territory at will. At the other extremity of the Empire the same year saw the defeat of Crassus and a relatively untrained army of eight legions by the Parthians at Carrhae (a type of disaster which could easily have befallen Caesar himself, had he been less fortunate).[6] In Gaul the year drew to a close with an onslaught by marauding German cavalry on Caesar's central storage base at or near Tongres, where his wounded were recuperating, under the protection of the new *legio XIV*. This time Q. Cicero, who had charge of the base, was insufficiently strong-willed to restrain his troops within the fortifications, and allowed forage parties to wander. Only the heroism of individuals, especially centurions, enabled the Romans to hold on, until the Germans withdrew with their booty. Caesar, who arrived on the scene shortly afterwards, was not amused.

REVERSE AT GERGOVIA

Warning of renewed rumblings in the winter of 53–52 prompted fresh recruitment, and early in the year Caesar was forced to hurry back from Cisalpina across the snow-bound Cevennes. The spring of 52 was spent reducing strongholds of the Bituriges in central Gaul, fortified against him, while Caesar remained all the while fearful of a general revolt, which Vercingetorix, a young chieftain of the Arverni, was seeking to foment. In the summer of 52 Vercingetorix took the field with large forces, beginning a battle of wits with Caesar to obtain and retain the initiative. Now, if not earlier, Caesar was able to bring another legion, numbered *VI*, into active service.

Vercingetorix, with a wide measure of support from the tribes, enforced a scorched-earth policy in the path of Caesar's advance; but this was only partly successful, and Caesar found time to reduce the chief Biturigan stronghold, Avaricum (Bourges), after a short but keenly contested siege. Vercingetorix continued to harass Caesar before retiring into his own native town of Gergovia (Gergovie). Caesar's own dramatic but rather confusing account[7] of what followed is best appreciated by reference to the topography, and the results of excavations conducted below the town in 1862 by the indefatigable Colonel Stoffel: more recent work, in 1936–39, has largely confirmed Stoffel's plan but added new details (fig. 27). Caesar had placed his main camp, some 90 acres (36 hectares) in extent, on a ridge well clear of the town to the south-east, and quickly dislodged the Gauls from the summit of a nearby small hill, which cut them off from access to the Auzon river. He then linked the camps with two parallel ditches, set closely together; behind this double barrier his own soldiers could move at will, as the situation demanded. Caesar next resolved to seize another ridge just outside the town's defences, which controlled approaches to the main gate, presumably as an immediate prelude to a full-scale assault. The plan was audacious, and Caesar's ruses to delude the Gauls proved all too successful: diversionary movements to the south-east, and by allied Aeduan cavalry, confused the defenders, and a full-scale onslaught by the legions, issuing forth from the small camp (to which they had been transferred in batches from the main camp lying to the east) caught the Gauls off-guard, and the ridge was taken. But Gallic resistance stiffened, and it seems that Caesar now resolved to consolidate his existing gains, if he could. However, men of the four leading legions, who had pressed on to the walls themselves, were driven back with the loss of 700 men, including 46 centurions. Only skilful manoeuvring by Caesar with *legio X*, and *XIII* under the legate Sextius, which had been guarding the small camp, covered the rout, and prevented a greater disaster. Caesar records how, at a subsequent parade, he was sharply critical of the over-confidence of the troops—which his own run of successes had done much to engender. But it may be suspected that Caesar himself was substantially to blame for a gamble that failed to come off. The reverse, however caused, was to dent the impression of Caesar's personal invincibility: the Aedui, oldest of the Roman allies in Gaul, deserted his cause, putting all Caesar's conquests at risk.

THE SIEGE OF ALESIA

Despite this upsurge in his fortunes, Vercingetorix was unable to maintain himself in open warfare, where his Gallic cavalry was routed by German horsemen obtained by Caesar from the far side of the Rhine. He now retired into the hilltop town of Alesia (Alise-Sainte-Reine near Dijon), which Caesar promptly began to encircle with siegeworks, so entrapping his chief adversary and effectively localising the revolt (pl. 8; fig. 28). Learning that a relief force of Gauls was being organised, and conscious that a major trial of strength was now imminent, Caesar used the time to embark on the construction of a much more elaborate sequence of fortifications (pl. 9):

He dug out a 20-foot trench, with perpendicular sides, as broad at the bottom as at the top, and held back the other fortifications some 400 feet behind this trench; with such a vast extent of ground having to be enclosed, it was not going to be easy to keep the whole circuit manned. He was worried that a large party of the enemy could make a sudden attack, either under the cover of night or loosing off a volley of javelins in daytime, on the troops engaged on the construction work. Therefore, leaving a gap of 400 feet, Caesar dug out two trenches of equal depth, each 15 feet wide. The inner one he filled with water, where the ground was low and flat. Behind the two ditches he erected a rampart, strengthened by stakes, 12 feet in overall height. On top was a breastwork and battlement, with large forked branches projecting, where the breastwork and rampart met, to slow up any Gauls who tried to climb over. There were towers put along the fortification, round the entire circuit, 800 feet apart. The necessity of despatching men to gather timber and corn, and at the same time of putting up such massive fortifications, meant that large numbers of men were always some considerable distance away from the encampments. On a number of occasions the Gauls attempted to assault our fortifications, making simultaneous and determined sorties from several of the town gates. Therefore Caesar resolved to strengthen the works even more, so that a smaller number of troops would be able to defend them. Accordingly tree trunks or very stout

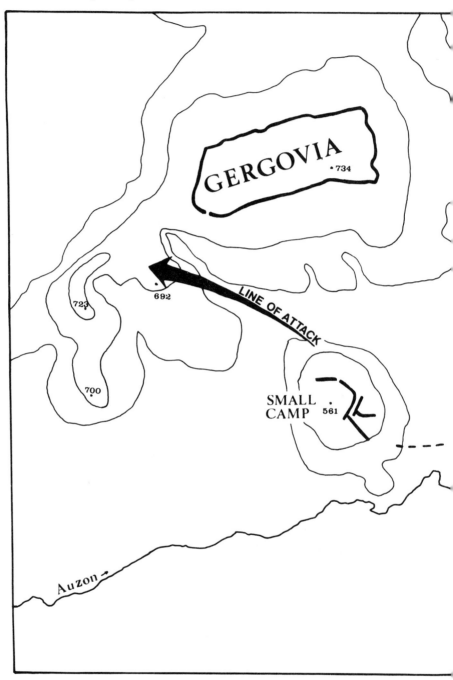

27 Caesar's fortifications at Gergovia, 52 BC (*after Napoléon III and Gorce*)

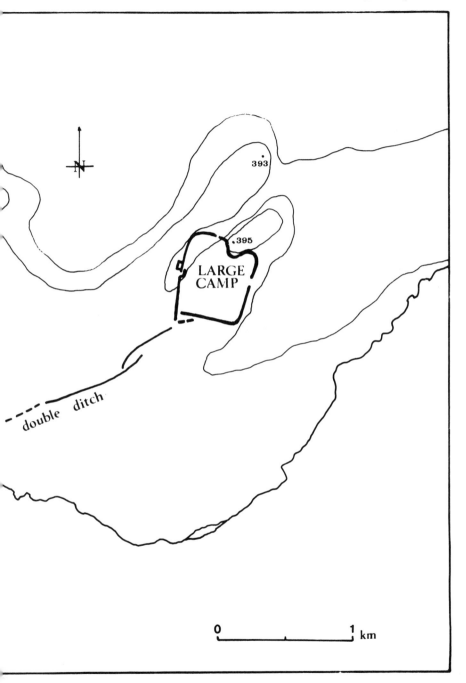

393

.395

LARGE
CAMP

double ditch

0 _____ 1 km

branches were cut, and their tops stripped of bark and sharpened; continuous trenches five feet deep were dug. The tree trunks were set into the ditches with their bottom ends secured to one another to prevent their being pulled up, and with the branches sticking out. In each trench, there were five rows of these tree trunks, linked together and intertwined; anyone who went among them would get impaled on their very sharp points. These were nicknamed 'boundary posts'. In front of them, arranged in diagonal rows in quincunx fashion were pits three feet deep, tapering gradually inwards towards the bottom. In the pits were set smooth logs as thick as a man's thigh, with the tops sharpened to a point and hardened by fire, and projecting only four fingers' breadth out of the ground. To keep these firmly in position, they were supported round about with hardened earth to a depth of one foot, the rest of the holes being filled with twigs and brushwood to keep the trap hidden. There were generally eight rows of these pits, kept three feet apart; they were nicknamed 'lilies' for their resemblance to the flower of that name. In front of these, blocks of wood a foot long with iron hooks fixed in them were set completely into the ground, in great numbers, all over. They were called 'goads'.

When this work was completed, Caesar constructed identical fortifications facing the other way, over a distance of 14 miles, along the flattest ground that could be found, a defence against attacks from outside. The purpose was to prevent the garrisons of the inner ring from being overrun, even if a very large force should attack. To avoid the danger of men having to be sent out to look for food, each man was required to have with him 30 days' rations for himself and food for the horses too.[8]

Such double lines of fortification were familiar Hellenistic practice, but Caesar's have always attracted particular admiration. He was thus able, when the relieving force arrived, to maximise his forces—he had upwards of 45,000 men (more than his account would suggest), against an alleged 250,000 (this figure may be hugely exaggerated). There was some danger now that Caesar himself would be entrapped.

On the first day of battle the two cavalry forces met in combat, with Caesar's Germans finally proving victorious. A surprise attack by the Gauls on Caesar's outer ring of defences proved a costly failure, with all the pits and obstacles proving their worth, and Vercingetorix too slow in assaulting the inner ring in support. In a fresh effort, picked Gallic forces were sent to attack the weakest part of the Roman lines

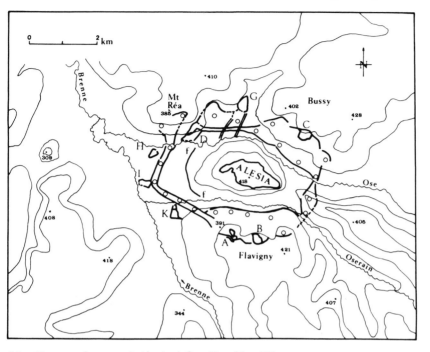

28   Siegeworks round Alesia (*after Napoléon III*)

by day—somewhere north of the town itself—and Vercingetorix mounted a simultaneous attack from within. The Roman lines just held, and Caesar's skilful use of cavalry again proved decisive; the relieving force withdrew, and the besieged surrendered, Vercingetorix becoming a prisoner of Caesar.

The siegeworks at Alesia were the subject of an intensive campaign of excavations conducted in 1861–65 by Colonel Stoffel, on behalf of Napoléon III, who took a keen interest in the work; the results became the centrepiece of a two-volume *Histoire de Jules César* (Paris, 1865–66). The rediscovery of a part of Stoffel's excavation-archive in 1949 prompted a fresh assessment, and further excavation was undertaken. More recently aerial photography has added fresh details. Alesia occupies an isolated hilltop at the western end of a narrow ridge between the rivers Ose and Oserain, both tributaries of the Brenne (fig. 28). It is encircled by hilltops of similar height. Caesar's inner ring of fortifications lay on the intervening low ground, following the water barriers where possible, and the outer ring along the surrounding hills, control of which was essential if Caesar was to ward off relieving forces. Excavation revealed considerable variation in the nature of the fortifications, e.g. in the depth and width of the ditches. In particular the wide ditch which Caesar reports as dug in advance of his inner ring was located only on low ground west of the town (f–f on fig. 28). Caesar may have expected, or hoped, that Vercingetorix' main effort at breaking out would be directed towards the west. Some uncertainty surrounds the purpose of the double ditches which cross the Roman lines in the direction of Camp G; they may have been intended to funnel any sortie from the town towards that camp, but more needs to be known about their relationship to the main lines of fortification. The presence of pits and obstacles was confirmed only on the inner ring. The chief Roman encampments lay on the heights of Flavigny and Bussy, and in the plain to the west, with sizes ranging from 6.3 to 24 acres (2.5 to 9.5 hectares); nothing is known about their interiors. On Flavigny the gaps between the camps were protected by artillery emplacements. Several redoubts were detected along the inner ring, and others inferred, to produce a total of 23. It might be inferred from the Napoleonic plan that Caesar did not include Mt Réa, north of the town, in his defensive circuit, and Caesar's own account appears to confirm this:

> There was a hill on the north side of such large extent that our men were unable to include it within the circuit of the fortifications; they were compelled to place their camp there on gently sloping ground, which left them in a somewhat unfavourable position.[9]

However Harmand has argued, in his definitive modern study of the campaign, that Mt Réa *was* included, and that the hill mentioned by Caesar was Bussy, of which the Roman fortifications included only the south-western extremities. On the other hand, the old excavations produced, in the ditches below Mt Réa, an extraordinary deposit of human bones, horse skeletons, weaponry, military equipment and coins (the latter all datable to 52 BC or earlier) which fit well with Caesar's description of the intense hand-to-hand fighting in this threatened sector of his outer perimeter line. The finds, which include both Gallic and Roman equipment, are necessarily of prime importance in our appreciation of the weaponry in use by the legionaries at this time.[10] In general, modern study has confirmed the details of the siegeworks, though the Gallic fortifications on the slope east of the town were pure hypothesis, and one redoubt is now recognised as a prehistoric barrow.[11]

THE END OF THE WAR

With the fall of Alesia the effective resistance to the Roman invaders was halted, and Caesar evidently hoped that his wearied legions could now enjoy a well-earned respite. But warlike moves by the Bellovaci of the Beauvais region in the winter of 52–51 forced him to campaign against them. Many years ago the site of Caesar's initial encounter with the Bellovaci was confidently pinpointed at Nointel on the River Breche near Beauvais itself, where camps both for legionaries and auxiliaries were identified, together with elaborate defence lines along the river, and two wooden causeways crossing marshy ground between the Roman fortifications and the enemy on the hills beyond. But grave doubts have been expressed. Geographically Nointel does not seem to be well positioned to be the battle-site; moreover the excavated remains seem likely to include elements of Iron Age and even Medieval date. In particular the causeways are permanent structures which would have taken many months to construct. Fresh excavation is much to be desired, and an examination of small finds, if any, before more can be said about what is certainly an intriguing complex. Several other revolts were put down during the year, and the population of Uxellodunum (perhaps the modern Puy d'Issolu in the mid-south) were harshly treated on the capture of the town: all the fighting men had their hands cut off, as an example to deter other potential rebels. By the end of 51 Gaul seemed quiet, and all but reduced to the status of a province, which seems formally to have been established, with the name *Gallia Comata* ('Long-haired Gaul'), at about this time.

THE ARCHAEOLOGY OF CAESAR'S CAMPAIGNS

Some reference has been made to archaeological discoveries. Much more must remain undetected. Nine years of constant marching and counter-marching in areas geographically reasonably well defined by their author, and attacks on cities where detailed accounts of Roman dispositions are preserved, indicate wide potential for future discovery. To be sure, 'camps de César' proliferate on the maps of France. Great impetus was given long ago by Napoléon III, whose project (under the direction of Colonel Stoffel) led to many discoveries, some confirmed by modern excavation. In other cases an excess of imagination led to over-hasty conclusions, and almost always some dating evidence would be welcome. In France aerial photography has been slow in gaining acceptance, except in the Somme valley where decades of outstanding work by Roger Agache have led to the identification of several Roman camps; some could belong to Caesar's time. Here again confirmatory dating evidence from associated small finds is much to be desired. The work of René Goguey in central France, most notably at Alesia, can also be commended. It is to be hoped that further reconnaissance, in areas where Caesar is known to have operated, may help to plot camps on his line of march, perhaps with peculiarities of gate-form or overall shape, which we may come to recognise eventually as Caesarian.

CAESAR'S COMMENTARIES

Our knowledge of Caesar's campaigns—and their chronology— derives almost totally from Caesar himself, who wrote a detailed account shortly afterwards. His *Gallic War*, and the sequel, the *Civil War* (below, p. 101) provide a succinct and factual account. Caesar emerges as the all-conquering general, but his army, especially the soldiers in the ranks and the centurions, are the true heroes. Caesar tells the truth but not the whole truth. Without doubt he had within nine years added all Gaul to the Roman domain; when no active campaigning was in prospect, he maintained the momentum of his success by crossing the Rhine and invading Britain. The former expedition had more political than military value; so too the latter, which was quite unnecessary, but had a huge impact on public opinion at Rome. Britain was an island, of mystery and monsters, on the edge of the known world. Yet while there were some murmurings in the Senate at the necessity of his campaigns, the conquests in general were received with great rejoicings, and as no more than the natural fulfilment of Rome's destiny of eventual world rule. Caesar makes much of his clemency, but this could be interspersed with deliberate acts of terrorism, and he was not averse to 'dirty tricks' when these suited his purpose.

Caesar's account provides the most valuable narrative we could have of the Roman army on campaign, written by its commander. Sulla and other proconsuls had written similar accounts, and Pompey's biography was written by a distinguished Greek scholar, but these have not survived. Caesar was writing for immediate public support, as well as for future historians. Though close to the events he describes, he avoids enveloping the reader with a mass of detail. The account is strictly of the campaigns themselves: we learn almost nothing of the leisure activities of Caesar or his soldiers, or the mundane facts of camp life, or the presence (or otherwise) of women and other camp-followers. Much information we should have liked to know—technicalities of camp-building, the line of battle, the duties of individuals—are assumed as well known. Yet we must be

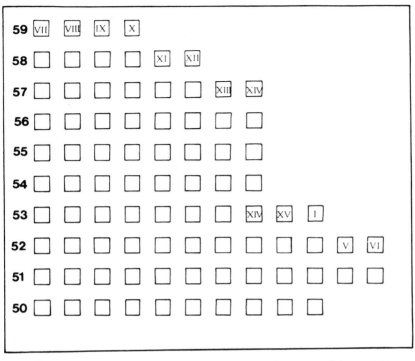

29 Growth of Caesar's army, 59–50 BC. Note: the original *legio XIV*
was destroyed in the winter of 54/53; *legio I* was returned to Pompey in
50, along with *legio XV*

grateful for the picture Caesar provides, of an army of the Late
Republic on active campaign in a hostile countryside, which forms
every schoolboy's picture of the all-conquering Roman forces.

CAESAR'S ARMY

In nine years Caesar had increased his army from four to 12 legions
(fig. 29). Most of the new recruits seem likely to have been
volunteers. The army included many long-serving professionals. The
reader may recall P. Considius, 'reputedly a first class soldier', who
had served in the East with Sulla, and against Spartacus, before
going to Gaul, probably as a *praefectus*.[12] Caesar found that his
performance fell far short of his reputation. The legions each had a
paper strength of about 5000 men, but their manpower could fall
well below that figure, as battle casualties, illness and fatigue took
their toll. All the new formations were raised, during the winter

97

months, from Caesar's own provinces, though some Italians presumably travelled northwards of their own accord, with a view to enlistment. The new legions were raised by virtue, it would seem, of a proconsul's right to call out local forces in defence of his province. Unlike most proconsuls, Caesar had access to reserves of citizens, in Cisalpina. At first he paid and equipped the new legions at his own expense from the profits of the war. At the Luca summit in 56 he was able to get recognition for legions *XI–XIV*, which were henceforth paid by government funds,[13] but the later formations remained dependent for pay on Caesar himself. Caesar enlisted men both south and north of the Po: those living north of the river (the Transpadanes) were not full Roman citizens, but had the status of 'Latins'. Caesar ignored the distinction, and was happy to admit all to his ranks. Late in 52 he formed a militia from the native population of Transalpina to defend its northern border during the crisis of that year; it must be likely that this militia, 22 cohorts in all, formed the basis of the *legio V Alaudae* (the Larks) which we later find among his forces (below, p. 132). Existing legions were supplemented each year by drafts from Cisalpina, so that by the time of his invasion of Italy in 49, Caesar's forces must have possessed a unique coherence and loyalty, which were important factors in his eventual victory.

The cohort was the standard tactical unit in Caesar's army; maniples are mentioned several times, but the word seems a general term for a sub-section of troops, or a small body of men. The centurions (especially those of the First Cohort) are the fighting backbone of the legion, striving for promotion and honour. In the tradition of earlier commanders, Caesar often included them, along with the legates and tribunes, in his war councils. The tribunes, on the other hand, had a less well defined role. They seldom displayed initiative or courage; at worst they were cowardly and unreliable. It is evident that Caesar's army, later to become a supreme instrument devoted to his cause, was initially typical of its time. Caesar himself, much to his later regret, had brought out from Rome a retinue of young nobles and hopeful equestrians 'on the make', chosen for political rather than military potential; doubtless this was common practice. But continuous active campaigning did much to excise dubious elements, to leave a finely honed instrument.

Caesar names many centurions, especially those conspicuous for their bravery, and the epigraphic evidence, which now for the first time begins to illuminate the study of the army, adds several individuals. An epitaph from Capua (pl. 10) records two brothers called Canuleius who served in Gaul with Caesar's *legio VII*. The elder was soon killed in action, but the younger served throughout the campaigns—presumably including Britain—and survived to earn his release.[14] We know also of a Q. Cabilenus who served in *legio VIII*, a Vettidius in *legio XII*, a Vinusius in *legio IX*, and several veterans of *legio VI*.[15]

The artillery which accompanied the legions has always attracted attention: two main types are in evidence—the giant catapults which we normally call *ballistae*, firing heavy stones, and smaller, crossbow-type machines, called 'scorpions', which fired smaller arrows with great accuracy. The fieldcraft and engineering skills displayed have evoked admiration—the siege towers and ramps at Avaricum, the Rhine bridge, the entrenchments around Alesia.[16] These were standard techniques for the well-equipped Hellenistic army, but there seems little doubt Caesar took a particular interest in their organisation, and brought them to a fresh peak of efficiency. An officer of engineers (*praefectus fabrum*) is frequently attested in the armies of the Late Republic, but the post seems in reality an aide-de-camp on a commander's personal staff, and certainly no *praefectus fabrum* appears in any account of battle, or fortification or engineering project in Caesar's writings.

The legates, together with Caesar's *quaestor*, played an important role, and over a decade of warfare we get an excellent picture of the range of their duties and employment. An essential factor in Caesar's command structure, they provided his middle management. The intended purpose of the legate, to act as subordinate commander for a proconsul operating over a wide geographical area with substantial military forces, finds full expression. Caesar had 10 legates, whom he could appoint directly, without reference to the Senate. The legate could command a legion, or two or three legions, together with attendant auxiliary forces. But others had a primarily civil role. In winters the legate commanded a camp, and in general was responsible for maintaining peace and the security of the surrounding region. There was however no particular link between a legate and any individual legion—the post of legionary-legate (*legatus legionis*) was a development of the future. Caesar's legates, as we know from their careers and family backgrounds, were senators of varying junior rank and military experience, and not always of particular intelligence or resolution. Yet most served him for a considerable number of years. Q. Cicero, the orator's brother, hardly seems a natural military commander; he was accepted initially as a favour to his brother, and saw service in Britain and later at Alesia. Some of the early legates fade from sight, but a number of their successors were to play important roles in the ensuing civil conflict. The intelligent Q. Labienus, already of praetorian rank, was the senior *legatus* throughout the Gallic War, and served in positions of increasing responsibility.

In winter the legions were placed in winter-quarters, either singly or in groups. This was normal military practice. If an existing township could be utilised, well and good; otherwise a winter-camp (*castra hiberna*) could be built near a tribal stronghold. During the winter the legions were reconstituted in the time-honoured fashion (above, p. 55). But their numerals were left unchanged. Caesar had inherited *VII–X*, and added others to continue the sequence up to *XV*. Later he also had a *V* and a *VI*, thus bridging the gap between the consular legions (*I–IV*) and his own group. Whether any of these numerals were duplicated in garrisons elsewhere at this time remains unknown.

Caesar's use of auxiliaries is of interest. No Roman cavalry are mentioned (see above, p. 79), though some *equites* served on his staff and assisted the legates. The army on campaign consisted essentially of the legions and cavalry, the latter drawn from the Gauls and later the Germans whom Caesar found his most effective weapon at defeating the Gauls themselves. Gallic infantry are rarely mentioned, and were of dubious military value. The Gallic cavalry was made up of the nobility of each tribe, with the various contingents headed by their chief magistrates or young men of the leading families. A particular tactic of the Germans, of interspersing cavalry and fleet-footed spearmen, was adopted by Caesar, and we may wonder whether such groups are the precursors of the *cohortes equitatae* (part-mounted cohorts) of the Empire (but see below, p. 182). When Caesar arrived in Gaul he found at his disposal a contingent of foreign auxiliaries: Numidian cavalry, Balearic slingers, and Cretan archers; these fade from sight after 57 and were presumably dispensed with and sent home.

THE PROFITS OF THE WAR

The soldiers were motivated by honour and loyalty—but also by financial gain. Caesar himself became extremely wealthy, and it is certain that many, if not most, of the legates were considerably enriched. It was well known at Rome that an appointment to Caesar's staff was a passport to wealth. The ordinary soldiers too stood to gain, from slaves and loot. Such factors were not negligible in their support for Caesar, and he could not afford to ignore them. The baggage train, of which Caesar took the greatest care while the army was on the move, contained the soldiers' accumulated spoils, which he and they were concerned not to endanger. When its overall bulk had to be reduced, as in 54 when the legionaries of Sabinus and Cotta sought to escape from their winter encampment, much heart-searching went on over what was to be left behind. Even so, the quantity taken with the moving column was still large, and when the decision was taken to abandon everything, soldiers broke ranks to save what they could of their own possessions.[17]

CAESAR'S GENERALSHIP

The reasons for Caesar's success are not hard to find: decisiveness and instinct, rapport with the individual soldier and not a little dash of luck. His speed of movement, the legendary *Caesariana celeritas*, astounded Roman and Gaul alike. Yet we must beware of excessive adulation of his achievements. A careful reading of the *Gallic War*— and especially the *Civil War*—reveals Caesar as often rash and impulsive, with little interest in logistics. His swiftness of action could leave the troops ill-supplied with basic foodstuffs. Often, if his brilliance is shown by extracting the army from a difficult situation, it was his rashness which created that situation in the first place.

We hear nothing from Caesar himself about deliberate training programmes, even of newly raised formations. However, his bio-grapher Suetonius tells us that he kept the legions at instant readiness for the march.

> He often did this where there was no need at all, especially when it was raining and on public holidays, and sometimes he would warn them to watch him closely and then quite suddenly steal away from the camp at any hour of the day or night (expecting them to follow). The march was made longer than usual to wear out those who straggled.[18]

This insight, which brings to mind the regular route marches and training programmes of the Empire (and would have delighted Field-Marshal Montgomery!) is unfortunately not dated. The first battle against the Helvetii was nearly a disaster, and other battles brought heavy losses, but these never deflected him from further efforts.

There is little to show that Caesar was particularly interested in changing the army's traditional institutions or organisation. It would be wrong to find in him an important military reformer, as sometimes claimed. He accepted the army as he found it, and tuned the instrument to a fine pitch in his own interest; but there is nothing to suggest that he intended, or introduced, any changes in army service or organisation. It has sometimes been suggested, even stated as a fact, that Caesar discontinued Marius' practice of replacing with a wooden peg one of the iron pins securing the wooden shaft to the iron head of the *pilum*. Instead, the iron immediately below the *pilum*-head was left untempered, so that the missile bent on impact and became unusable.[19] However there is nothing to show that this change, which can be observed in the archaeological record, was made on Caesar's initiative. The use of the wooden pin may have been merely a short-lived experiment. Also ascribed by some scholars to Caesar's time is a change in the shape of the legionary's shield, the *scutum*, from oval to the familiar rectangular form of the Empire. But it is much more likely that this change occurred later, during or even after Augustus' long reign (see pl. 19d and p. 233).

THE APPROACH OF CIVIL WAR

The year 50 passed quietly. Caesar was preoccupied with the rush of political events at Rome, and the need to secure his own future. In 51 he had sent one legion to Cisalpina, to protect its towns from attack from the Balkans, but otherwise, in the late summer of 50, his forces still lay in the far north of Gaul. In September he concentrated them at Trier, and held a special review, perhaps in part to test their temper, for a struggle he must now have suspected as inevitable. Soon after, a force of four or five legions was moved south to Matisco (Mâcon), just within the border of Gallia Comata. In the same year he was compelled to yield up, for a projected Parthian War, a legion (*legio I*) lent to him by Pompey in 53 (above p. 87), and also one of his own. He sent *XV* (incidentally, or deliberately, one of the newest) which was then on hand in Cisalpina, and transferred *XIII* to replace it at Aquileia (fig. 30).

Caesar's immediate aim had always been a second consulship in 48, and protection against prosecution by his enemies until he had entered office. Thereafter he may have planned a further period of active command, most probably in the East; but his opponents in the Senate were determined that its authority should prevail. Caesar continued to profess a willingness to negotiate over his future status, but finally the Senate resolved to act: the consuls were invited, in the traditional wording of the 'Ultimate Decree', to act 'to prevent the State incurring any harm'. At this Caesar himself cast legality aside, and ordered his *legio XIII* across the little Rubicon river, which marked the border between the Cisalpine province and Italy[20]. Under the Roman constitution, the holder of a provincial command automatically forfeited his *imperium* (the right to command citizen troops) when he left his province. The crossing of the Rubicon plunged the Roman world into civil war.

4 Civil War

The reaction of the Senate was sensible and immediate—a state of war was declared, new governors were appointed to Caesar's provinces, and arrangements made for an extensive levy of troops, under Pompey's overall command. But Pompey did not reckon with Caesar's swiftness of action. Pushing forward with *legio XIII* to Ariminum (Rimini, always a vital control point for Italy's invaders and her defenders), and with other legions already on the march to support him, Caesar placed garrisons in a number of coastal towns to control the line of the Via Flaminia (fig. 30). Just as quickly he sent a force to hold Arretium (Arezzo) in the Arno valley, so all but cutting communications between the capital and the north.

This was civil war. Caesar stresses throughout the willingness of his troops to support his cause, in what amounted to a military coup.[1] A great many of his men were of course not from peninsular Italy but from Cisalpina and even southern Gaul, for whom a march into Italy would not provoke the same crisis of conscience. We hear nothing of dissent at fighting other Romans—only occasional rumblings of discontent by the veterans at being kept under arms for such an extended period. Yet it was probably at about this time that Caesar doubled the soldiers' pay (to 225 *denarii* a year), an added factor in their adherence to his cause.[2] We could suppose that his opponents were compelled to match the increase. Of Caesar's officers, only Labienus chose to abandon his cause, and joined Pompey.

CONQUEST OF ITALY AND THE WEST

The speed of Caesar's advance and the apparent welcome being accorded to his forces took Pompey by surprise, and he withdrew from Rome, his preparations for defending it hardly formulated. He retired first to Capua, where the two legions handed over to him in 50 were then billeted, and then, as Caesar continued to sweep forward, into Apulia. His chief problem was difficulty of access to, and of

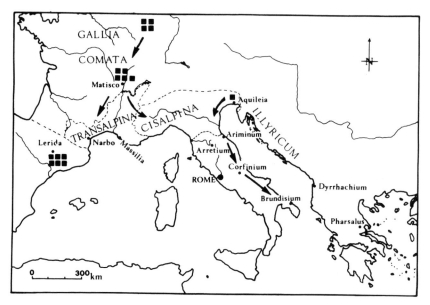

30 Movements of legions, 50–49 BC

obtaining prompt reinforcement from, his own troops in Spain—six legions in all, which legates controlled on his behalf.

The task of delaying Caesar was entrusted to—or assumed by— Cn. Domitius Ahenobarbus, who assembled troops from the Apennine communities and from among his own tenants (with lavish promises of land-ownership in the event of victory), and fortified the important crossroads town of Corfinium (Corfinio) in the central Apennines. When Caesar, now reinforced by legions *XII* and *VIII* and '22 cohorts' allegedly newly levied in Cisalpina (almost certainly this is a euphemism for the *legio V Alaudae*—'the Larks'—and perhaps another legion?), laid siege to the town, Domitius' troops quickly capitulated, handing over their commander to Caesar. A length of ditch located in 1879 outside the town's own defences, and traced over a distance of 130 m, was identified as part of the Caesarian siege-lines.[3]

Pompey had rashly claimed that he could raise an army to oppose Caesar simply by stamping his foot on the soil of Italy,[4] but it was Caesar who quickly gained access to Italy's enormous manpower reserves. Within a few months he had recruited, or pressed into service, about 80,000 men, sometimes taking over units in process of formation in Pompey's interest; by August of 49 he had a legion numbered as high as *XXX*. Some hints of the rapid build-up are visible from the epigraphic evidence: a recruit from Pisa serving in *legio XXVIII*, and a centurion from Mutina in *XXX*—both perhaps enrolled during his advance southwards.[5] Seasoned troops were transferred to form the core of newer legions. We chance to know of a tribune of *legio VI* who later served in *legio XXIX*;[6] perhaps the transfer belongs now. There were quick promotions to be had on both sides as the army was quickly expanded.[7]

Witnessing the irresistible onrush of the Caesarian tide, Pompey decided to leave Italy with the troops he had been able to scrape together. The decision was sensible on strategic grounds: he would keep his forces intact, fall back on the garrisons and resources of the East, and either wait for Caesar to follow, or himself return as the new Sulla. However his retreat cost him the initiative, and the propaganda battle, dented his military reputation, and presented into Caesar's lap the capital, the organs of government, and the state treasury, which effectively financed all his future operations.

Narrowly failing to prevent the embarkation of the Pompeian army at Brundisium (Brindisi)—French excavators revealed the lines of his siegeworks round the town in the late nineteenth century[8]—Caesar left his weary legions to recuperate in Apulia, and travelled to a Rome he had not seen for 10 years. He spent hardly more than a week there before speeding north to deal with Pompey's Spanish army. Already it seems that Caesar had transferred three legions from their winter bases in Gaul southwards to Narbo, to guard against any thrust by the Pompeians towards Italy. Now he ordered them onwards across the Pyrenees, instructed the remaining legions (which lay far away in central Gaul) to follow. Leaving some newly enrolled formations to lay siege to Massilia (Marseilles), which had declared for Pompey, he hastened on into northern Spain, where he found Pompey's legates—Afranius and Petreius (above, p. 77), highly experienced officers—occupying a prepared position near Ilerda (Lerida). Yet they were out-manoeuvred and eventually forced to surrender, with little loss to either side. With all the western provinces now under his control Caesar returned to Italy. By virtue of his office as consul for 48 (he had been elected late in 49), he raised four more legions, with the traditional numbers *I–IV* (above, p. 78), so completing his numerical sequence, which now probably ran uninterrupted from *I* to about *XXXIII* (see Appendix 1).

The prime need was to prepare for a campaign against Pompey himself. Infantry and cavalry from the newly subdued Gallic tribes were added to his forces, and by December of 49 an expeditionary task force of 12 legions had been assembled at Brundisium. Quite clearly all the veteran legions were earmarked, i.e. *VI* to *XIV* (of which six had to march back from northern Spain), together with *V Alaudae* and two of the younger legions—one of the latter we can identify as *legio XXVII*.

Over the winter Pompey had roused his clients, and the kings and princes of the East, in the defence of the legitimate government. In the spring of 48 he returned to the Adriatic, and prepared to oppose a Caesarian landing, or himself launch an invasion of Italy, should circumstances suggest that course. He had nine legions now, having added to his forces one made up from two weak units then in Cilicia, another formed out of retired soldiers resident in the eastern provinces, and two recently levied in Asia Minor. In addition he expected the arrival from Syria of Metellus Scipio with another two. Large numbers of native archers and slingers, and cavalry, had been assembled from Greece, Crete, Asia and Syria.

SIEGEWORKS AT DYRRHACHIUM

The fighting which followed along the Adriatic coastline south of Dyrrhachium (now Durrës in Albania) is among the most fascinating of the Civil War, and demonstrates the confidence of Caesar's men and their high morale (fig. 31). After some difficulties in securing a passage against the strong Pompeian fleet, Caesar succeeded in putting seven legions ashore near Apollonia. Unfortunately the transports were intercepted on the return journey, so delaying the arrival of the remaining legions under Antony, who eventually joined him with another four legions. Two legions were immediately despatched under Domitius Calvinus to prevent Metellus Scipio making contact with Pompey, and if possible to defeat him.

Typically Caesar took the offensive at once. He got between Pompey and his chief supply base at Dyrrhachium (the western roadhead of the Via Egnatia), and, with markedly inferior forces, began the construction of siegeworks to hem in the surprised Pompeians. Some elements of these lines were observed on the ground by Hauptmann Veith.[9] Pompey immediately began the construction of counter-works and numerous exchanges took place between the two sides.

> In all this fighting we lost no more than 20 men; but in the fort itself (marked on fig. 31), every single soldier was wounded, and four centurions in one cohort lost their eyes; and wishing to give proof of their labour and the danger they had been in, they counted out before Caesar around 30,000 arrows which had been aimed into the fort, and when the shield of the centurion Scaeva was brought to him, 120 holes were found in it.[10]

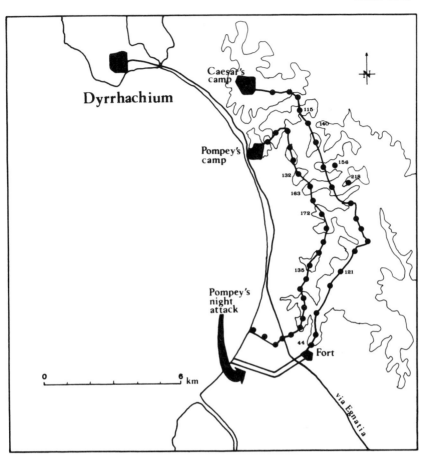

31 Fortifications at Dyrrhachium, 48 BC (*after Kromayer and Veith*).
Note: the general alignment of the fortifications was established by
fieldwork, but the siting of the individual redoubts (marked here by the
dots) is largely hypothetical

Caesar does not say whether Scaeva himself was still fit for active
service! A later author states that he received several serious wounds
and lost an eye.[11] Pompey now launched a surprise night attack by
sea against an unfinished sector at the southern end of the Caesarian
fortifications. Continued skirmishing brought more casualties
among Caesar's men, and at the end of the day Pompey was saluted
imperator (victorious general) by his troops. Caesar broke off the
action as soon as defeat seemed certain, and marched off into the
interior. Inevitably Pompey followed, pleased at this opportunity to
prise Caesar away from his line of communications back to Italy, and

107

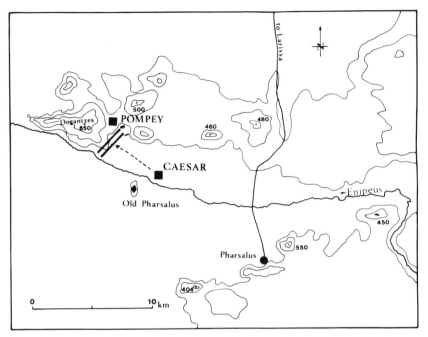

32 The battle of Pharsalus, 48 BC (*after Rice Holmes*)

delighted to have forced him on the defensive. Swiftly crossing the mountains of Epirus by the Metzovo Pass, Caesar reached the plains of northern Greece where he was now joined by Domitius Calvinus, and Pompey by Scipio, so that the two armies were now at full strength, except that both commanders left holding-garrisons in the coastal towns. Caesar restored his troops' morale, and their finances, by the swift capture of the little town of Gomphi (now Palaia Episkopi) which chanced to lie on his line of march.

PHARSALUS

The two armies met in the valley of the Enipeus, west of Pharsalus (modern Farsala). The precise battle-site has been disputed, but it seems most likely that Pompey established his camp on the hill of Dogantzes north of the river (fig. 32), while Caesar arrayed his troops further east.

> Caesar, when he had approached Pompey's camp, saw that his line was drawn up as follows: On the left wing were two legions which had been handed over by Caesar in obedience to the decree of the Senate at the beginning of the civil strife. One was called the

First and the other the Third. That was where Pompey himself was. Scipio was holding the centre of the line with the legions he had brought from Syria. The legion from Cilicia, along with the cohorts from Spain . . . were placed on the right wing. Pompey felt that these were his most reliable troops. He had placed the rest in between the centre and the two wings. The total was 110 cohorts. There were, in all, 45,000 men, and about 2000 recalled veterans who had served with him in earlier wars. He dispersed these throughout the battle line. The other seven cohorts he had posted in the camp and nearby forts. As a stream with steep banks protected his right wing, he had stationed all the cavalry, archers and slingers on the left wing.

Caesar, following his usual practice, had placed the Tenth Legion on the right wing, and the Ninth on the left, though its manpower had been badly reduced in the fighting around Dyrrhachium. He put the Eighth legion next to it, so as almost to make one legion out of two, and ordered them to render each other mutual assistance. He had 80 cohorts stationed in the line, in all 22,000 men. He had left two cohorts as a guard for the camp. He himself took up his position opposite Pompey. At the same time, noticing the Pompeian dispositions described above, and worried that his right wing might be surrounded by a great mass of cavalry, he quickly withdrew one cohort from each legion's third line and made up a fourth line, opposite the cavalry. He explained his plan to them, and stressed that victory that day would depend on their valour. At the same time he instructed the main army in its three lines not to engage the enemy without his express command. He would give the signal with a flag when he wanted them to join battle.[12]

Caesar gives his own forces for the battle as 80 cohorts (equivalent to eight legions), and accords his opponent 110 cohorts (11 legions), but this ignores the fact that Pompey had left up to 22 cohorts on detached garrison duty, so that the two sides were more evenly matched than Caesar suggests. The battle developed as Caesar had expected. The two bodies of legionaries became locked in combat; Pompey's cavalry outflanked Caesar's right, and seemed likely to roll up his line; but at the critical moment Caesar's reserve cohorts caught the Pompeian cavalry in the flank. The third line of the main army now moved up to give added impetus to the attack, and a general rout ensued. Pompey fled and his camp was taken. Caesar's original tactics, and the hard training and calmness of his experienced troops, won the day.

CAME, SAW, CONQUERED

Pompey himself escaped—much to Caesar's annoyance, as he had hoped to secure an agreement for the future—and went by sea to Egypt. In the sorting out of troops which followed the battle, local levies were released, and citizens serving out their normal term in Pompey's forces were marshalled into four legions, probably given the numerals *XXXIV–XXXVII*, and added to Caesar's army. He needed them as a nucleus for the defence of the eastern provinces, the garrisons of which had to be resurrected as soon as possible. The older veteran legions were sent back to Italy, except for *VI*, which Caesar took with him by sea as he set out in pursuit of Pompey; one of the younger legions, *XXVII*, was ordered to follow by land. In fact Pompey was already dead: even before he had set foot on dry land, at Pelusium in the Nile Delta, he was taken unawares in a small boat, in full view of his wife and relations, and murdered. On arrival at Alexandria Caesar and his small force became embroiled in a local struggle between the young pharaoh, Ptolemy XIII, and his sister Cleopatra, and for a time were besieged in the town itself. Reinforcements were brought up and Caesar was eventually able to restore order, with Cleopatra installed as joint ruler along with a younger brother, Ptolemy XIV. Several months were now spent with her, on an 'expedition' up the Nile. Unfortunately this lull in his bellicose activity gave his enemies time to regroup and effectively prolonged the war. By the time Caesar emerged, further trouble loomed: Pharnaces, a son of the great Mithridates, endeavoured to profit by the power vacuum in Asia Minor. After initial successes against Caesar's legates, he was soon swept away by Caesar himself at Zela near Amaseia in north-east Turkey. In a letter to a friend at Rome, reporting the encounter, Caesar dismissed his opponent with almost telegrammatic brevity: *veni, vidi, vici* (Came, Saw, Conquered), one of the great military epigrams.[13]

Serious problems awaited him in Italy and at Rome, where Mark Antony had proved incapable of maintaining order; moreover the veteran legions were impatient of discharge and proper recompense for their services. Some men had already served some 12 years under Caesar alone, well above the norm. However Caesar was soon going to need his veterans: Republican diehards had massed in Africa, and disposed of massive resources; they had a powerful ally in King Juba of Mauretania. Caesar again acted with decision, and landed an expeditionary force consisting of five of the younger legions (*XXVIII, XXX, XXIX, XXVI* and perhaps *XXV*), together with one veteran formation, his *V Alaudae*. But his opponents were ready, and Caesar had to call for help from several of the veteran legions—we can identify *VII, VIII, IX, X, XIII* and *XIV.* A fascinating insight into the conservatism of Roman military institutions is provided by an incident in this campaign: Caesar had to break off his advance for a purification ceremony on 21 March (46 BC), which marked the traditional opening of the campaign season.[14] After a hard struggle the Pompeians were defeated at Thapsus on the Tunisian coastline south of Sousse. In the aftermath most of their leaders met their deaths. A single anecdote serves to indicate the morale of the Caesarians: in response to taunts by Labienus (still serving against Caesar) as to the inexperience of the younger legions, one soldier shouted to him: 'I'm no raw recruit, Labienus, but a veteran of the Tenth legion'. Labienus replied 'I don't recognise the standards of the Tenth'. Then the soldier said 'You'll soon be aware of what sort of man I am'. He threw off his helmet, so that Labienus could see who he was and aimed his javelin in Labienus' direction, and threw it with all his might. He drove it hard into the chest of Labienus' horse and said 'That will show you, Labienus, that it's a man of the Tenth legion who attacks you'.[15] Legion *V Alaudae* gained its permanent elephant-emblem for its exploits in the final battle (below, p. 140). A few of its members, and probably other veterans, were discharged, and began a new life in Africa, in one of a rash of small colonies quickly established by Caesar on the shores of the Cape Bon peninsula.

TRIUMPH AND AFTERMATH

A quadruple triumph (over Gaul, Egypt, Pharnaces and Juba of Mauretania, though not of course over any Roman adversaries) marked Caesar's supreme moment on his return to Rome. Images and painted scenes depicted incidents in the wars, captives were led behind his chariot, the soldiers sang bawdy songs, rich in topical allusion, in the time-honoured manner. One of the prisoners was Vercingetorix, kept imprisoned for this very day, and subsequently strangled, in the old Roman tradition.

All the veteran legions, with the exception probably of *V Alaudae* (the most junior of the group), were now released, and land sought for them in Italy, or in southern France, which some presumably remembered with affection after many years' service. *Legio VI* was established at Arelate, and *X* at Narbo—the provincial capital. Ti. Claudius Nero, father of the future emperor Tiberius, helped to supervise the work. Another legion may have been established in Gaul (making three in all), but its colony has not been identified.

Within Italy, *legio VII* was settled near Capua, in the small town of Calatia, and preparations (not complete by Caesar's death) were made for *VIII* to be established at nearby Casilinum. Many other veterans were settled in smaller groups throughout Italy; few of these settlements can be pinpointed.

But one further round of fighting remained, in Spain, where the last remnants of Pompey's support had rallied round his two sons, Gnaeus and Sextus. Mismanagement of Further Spain after 49 by Caesar's nominee fuelled disaffection among citizens and natives alike. Caesar took the *V Alaudae* and some of the younger legions, including *III* (almost certainly the later *III Gallica*) to Spain, and seems to have diverted the veterans of *VI* and *X*, who must have been en route to their colonies at Arelate and Narbo, if not already settling in. The final battle, at Munda near Osuna in southern Spain, was fierce, but the veterans, few in number but resplendent in honour, again won the day. Excavations at Osuna early this century revealed not only sculptural reliefs of Iberian warriors and weaponry of the period, but many Roman slingbullets and much ironwork, including barbed *pila*, useful in our appreciation of the evolution of the weapon, and large stone balls launched at the defenders of the town by Roman artillery. Gnaeus Pompeius was killed, but his brother Sextus escaped to cause trouble later.[16]

THE IDES OF MARCH

Many important reforms of the constitution, local government, finance and the economy were already in hand at Rome, and Caesar returned to maintain the momentum. But he already had a further campaign in mind—this time in the East, to avenge his former partner Crassus, and to recover the legionary eagles lost in the great defeat at Carrhae (above, p. 87). He may have been more than a little uncomfortable at his own anomalous position within the constitution. Legions from among the garrisons in Macedonia and Syria were earmarked to join the expedition (see fig. 33). We can name several: *II* and *IIII* (from Caesar's consular series in 48), and a legion entitled *Martia* (its numeral is not yet known), and *XXXV* (made up out of former Pompeians) in Macedonia. Among those in Syria and the eastern provinces we can identify *XXVII* (which had been left in Egypt in 47) and two other 'Pompeian' legions, *XXXVI* and *XXXVII*. Doubtless auxiliaries from Gaul and Germany were to accompany him, together with a composite force from the client princes of the East. But the projected campaign never took place. Less than six months after Munda Caesar lay dead at the foot of a statue of

1 Italian hoplites

2   The battle of Pydna, 168 BC, as depicted on the monument of Aemilius Paullus at Delphi

3   Roman soldiers of the later second century BC; detail from the Altar of Domitius Ahenobarbus

4 The army on the coinage:
a military standards, 82 BC
b military standards, 49 BC
c colonisation programme, c.
40 BC d Gallic arms e the
Gauls defeated

a

b

c

d

5 Soldiers of the Late Republic **a** L. Septumius; **b** L. Appuleius; **c** C. Raius Perulla; **d** P. Gessius

6   Bust of Julius Caesar

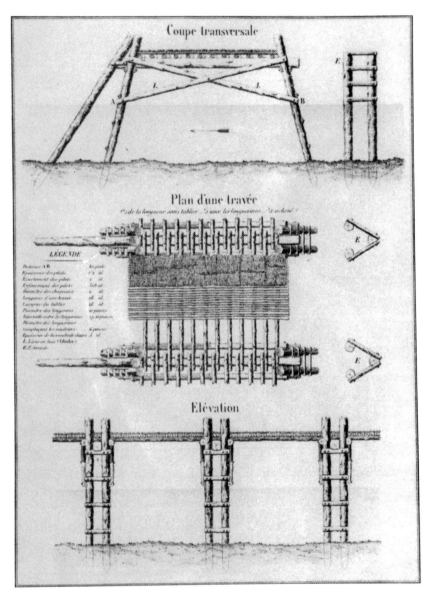

7   Caesar's bridge across the Rhine

Vue prise du camp attaqué sur les pentes du Mont Réa

Vue prise de la position occupée par César (dernière bataille) sur les pentes de la montagne de Flavigny

Vue prise de la pointe du Mont Pennevelle

Vue prise des pentes de la montagne de Bussy

8 Alesia: general views of the site

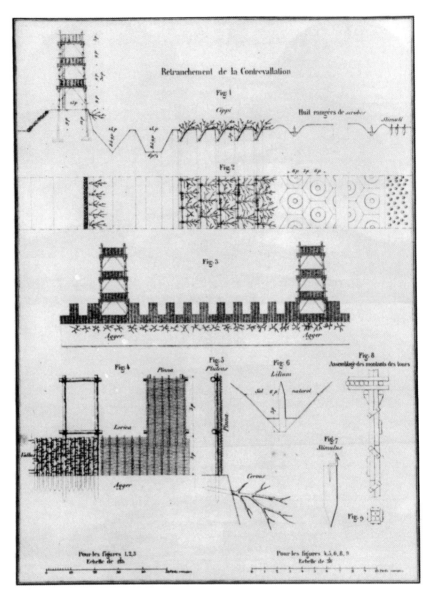

9 Alesia: details of the Roman fortifications

10 Gravestone of the brothers Canuleius, who served under Caesar in Gaul

11 A warship of the Late Republic

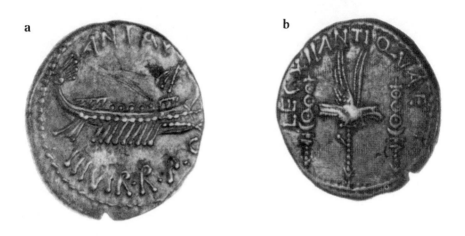

12 Antony's military coinage, 32–31 BC **a** Antony's fleet **b** *legio XII Antiqua* **c** *cohortes praetoriae* **d** *cohors speculatorum*

13 Catapult-shield of the *legio IIII Macedonica*

a

b

14 Emblems and standards: **a** *legio IIII Scythica*; **b** a monument at Venafro

15   Statue of Augustus from Prima Porta, Rome

16 Augustan colonies on the coinage: **a** Emerita **b** Caesarea Augusta **c** Philippi **d** Patrae

17 Imperial propaganda on the coinage: **a** recovery of standards from the Parthians **b** Germanicus recovers an *aquila* lost with Varus **c** Caligula addressing the men of four legions, AD 39 **d** Nero addressing the German Bodyguard, AD 64–66

18   Cenotaph of Marcus Caelius, a centurion who 'fell in the Varian War'

19 The army of the Early Empire: **a** Cn. Musius, *aquilifer*
b C. Romanius, cavalryman of the *ala Noricorum* **c** Monimus,
a Syrian archer **d** P. Flavoleius, a soldier of *legio XIV Gemina*

20 The Praetorian Guard

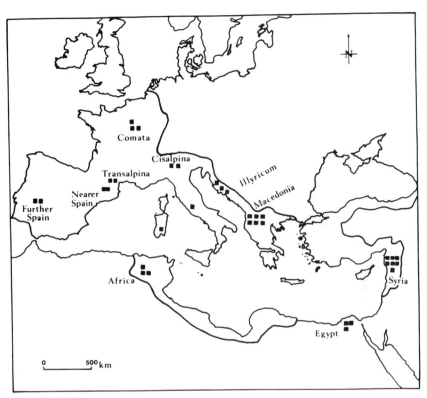

33 The Roman Empire, 44 BC, showing distribution of legions

Pompey—the Senate was meeting in a building he had constructed—attacked by his fellow senators, under the leadership of Brutus and Cassius, and with 23 wounds later counted in his body. In part at least he was a victim of his own success.

The assassination took the city and people, and the army, completely by surprise. But the conspirators, so successful in the planning and execution of the deed itself, had given little thought to the consequences of their success. They had hoped for a return to the normality of political life as they understood it. But it was not long before the temper of the city populace and the veterans was made clear. Caesar's partner as consul, Mark Antony, devised a compromise solution—Caesar's unconstitutional actions as an individual would be quietly forgotten, but his acts and ordinances, so much a basis for all their own positions and the government structures, would be confirmed.

113

ARRIVAL OF OCTAVIAN

But for those who had supposed that Caesar himself could be so easily consigned to oblivion, there was a rude awakening. On the one hand Antony appeared to have neutralised the Liberators (as Brutus and Cassius, and their co-conspirators, styled themselves), but he soon discovered a threat from an unexpected quarter. Among the army at Apollonia 'working up' in Macedonia for the projected Parthian campaign, was Caesar's young great-nephew, Gaius Octavius, his nearest male relative. The news of Caesar's death was received with consternation at Apollonia. It was followed almost at once with the announcement that Caesar in his will had adopted the young Octavius (who now became C. Julius Caesar Octavianus— Octavian). Here was an opportunity indeed. Despite the reasoned pleas of mature relatives and advisers, Octavian resolved to proceed to Rome and claim the inheritance. The hand of fate could not be expected to beckon twice. Landing at Brundisium (Brindisi) he proceeded north by way of the Via Appia to Capua and Rome—to be greeted by ecstatic crowds, among them his adoptive father's veterans, at towns on or near his route.

On arrival at Rome Octavian was treated with some disdain by Antony, who declined to hand over either the Dictator's papers (which he had tampered with) or his family fortune (into which he had dipped his fingers). Octavian now proceeded to stress his links with Caesar, and to put Antony in a bad light for collaborating with the Liberators. Cicero too had hoped that Octavian would prove a temporary phenomenon, hardly likely to last the pace of politics at Rome. In a memorable epigram he denigrated Octavian as a youth to be 'praised, uplifted, and lifted off' (the three Latin words *laudandum, ornandum,* and *tollendum*—the last with a double meaning—defy condensing into English). Octavian was to remember it well.[17]

In June of the year, as part of a reshuffling of provincial commands, to accommodate Brutus and Cassius, now in exile east of the Adriatic on quasi-diplomatic missions, Antony obtained (in place of Macedonia previously assigned to him) Caesar's old province of Cisalpine Gaul, the gateway to Italy from the North, and arranged for the transfer to it of the six legions of the Macedonian garrison. Of these in fact four were eventually transported across the Adriatic— *II, IIII, Martia* and *XXXV*; Antony journeyed to Brundisium to greet them, and to arrange the details of their northwards march to their new posting. While he was so preoccupied, Octavian sensed an opportunity to strengthen his own position: he proceeded to Campania, and persuaded upwards of 3000 of the veterans of

Caesar's legions *VII* and *VIII*, by appealing to his memory and by open bribery, to return with him to Rome. However, he had been less than honest—he was spoiling for a confrontation with Antony; but the veterans were more concerned with avenging Caesar's death, the anomaly of the continued presence of the Liberators in public life, and security of tenure of their own newly acquired steadings.

Octavian was forced to withdraw northwards into Etruria, with the scanty loyal remnants of his forces, still bearing the Caesarian numerals *VII* and *VIII*. Suddenly he received a decisive boost: two of Antony's legions, marching north along the Adriatic seaboard, declared for Octavian, turned westwards along the Via Valeria towards Rome, and took up position in the fortress-colony of Alba Fucens near Avezzano, some 100 kms east of the capital. Both these legions—*IIII* and *Martia*—had been at Apollonia during Octavian's sojourn there; he had perhaps done his homework well, but the gap between success and political elimination had been small.

WAR IN THE NORTH

Antony, after trying without success to persuade them to reverse their decision, resolved to hasten north to Cisalpina with his remaining two legions, and with *V Alaudae* which was still on hand in Italy. The 'sitting' governor of Cisalpina, Decimus Brutus (one of the Liberators) was known to be intending to resist Antony, who felt his military power-base slipping badly. The Senate, in a remarkable about-turn, ordered Octavian, invested with the powers of a praetor, to co-operate with the new consuls of 43, Hirtius and Pansa (both former legates of Caesar in Gaul), and with Decimus Brutus, to eliminate Antony. Brutus himself had retired into the old Roman colony of Mutina (Modena) on the line of the Via Aemilia, 25 miles north-west of Bologna. Hirtius hastened north, with Octavian and his legions nominally under his control, while Pansa raised additional troops in central Italy. Events moved on apace: the two sides clashed at Forum Gallorum (now Castelfranco), a village seven miles south-east of Mutina (fig. 34). Antony launched a diversionary attack on Hirtius' camp, and then bypassed the main senatorial force, in an attempt to catch Pansa and his recruits arriving from the south before they made contact with Hirtius and Octavian. A vivid account of the battle survives in a letter (almost a war correspondent's report from the Front) written to the orator Cicero the following day by his friend Sulpicius Galba, serving as legate to the consul Hirtius.

On 14 April, the day on which Pansa was due to reach Hirtius' camp, I was with him because I had been sent forward a hundred

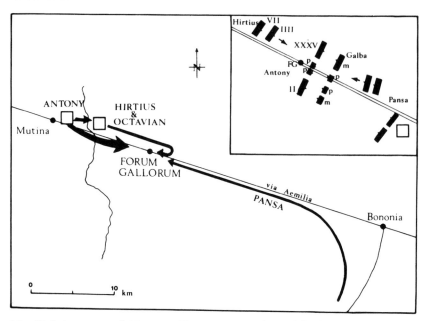

34 Fighting around Mutina, 43 BC Inset: a plan of the battle of Forum Gallorum, Note: **m** = *legio Martia;* **p** = Praetorian Cohort; **fg** = Forum Gallorum

miles to make contact with him and hasten his arrival. That day Antony led out two legions for battle, *II* and *XXXV*, and two Praetorian cohorts, one of which was his own—the other belonged to Silanus[18]—and some part of the recalled veterans. He came out to meet us because he thought we had only the four legions of recruits. But, under cover of night, to make our safe arrival in the camp less chancy, Hirtius had sent the *legio Martia*— over which I usually held the command—and two Praetorian cohorts to us. When Antony's cavalry made their appearance, neither the *legio Martia* nor the Praetorians could be held in check; we were forced to follow after them, being unable to hold them back. Antony was keeping his main force at Forum Gallorum, and wanted to conceal the fact that he had legions present; he only let us see his cavalry and light-armed troops. After Pansa saw that the legion was moving forward without orders, he instructed two legions of recruits to follow him. After we had got across a narrow strip of marsh and woodland, we formed a line that was 12 cohorts long. The two legions (of recruits) had not yet appeared on the scene. Suddenly Antony brought *his* two legions out of the village, into line, and immediately charged. At first the fighting was so intense that neither side could have fought harder; even so, the right wing, where I was stationed with eight cohorts of the *legio Martia*, drove back Antony's *XXXV* at its first onslaught, so that it moved more than 500 paces beyond its original position. Thus when Antony's cavalry looked like outflanking our wing, I began to pull back and to put our light-armed troops into battle against their Moorish horse, to prevent them attacking our rear. Meanwhile I saw that I was in among Antonian troops, and that Antony himself was some way behind me. Immediately, throwing my shield away, I galloped in the direction of a legion of recruits which was coming up from our camp. The Antonians pursued me. Our troops looked as though they would loose their javelins. By some chance I was saved because of quick recognition by our own men.

On the main road itself, where Caesar's (i.e. Octavian's) Praetorian cohort was, the fighting lasted a long time. The left wing, which was weaker, having only two cohorts of the *Martia* and a Praetorian cohort, began to pull back, because they were being surrounded by the cavalry, in which Antony is extremely strong. When all our formations had withdrawn, I began to retreat, the last of all, towards our camp. Antony, thinking he had won the day, believed he could now take the camp, but when he got there he lost quite a number of men without achieving anything at all. Hirtius, learning what had happened, and taking 20 veteran cohorts (i.e. the two legions *IIII* and *VII*) fell upon Antony as he was returning to his camp. He destroyed all Antony's forces and put him to flight on the very spot where the main battle had been, at Forum Gallorum. About 10 p.m. Antony got back to his own camp at Mutina with only his cavalry intact. Hirtius now proceeded to the camp where Pansa's two other legions (not involved in the battle) had endured Antony's onslaught. So Antony lost the larger part of his experienced forces. This however was not possible without some losses in our Praetorian cohorts and the *legio Martia*. Two eagles and 60 standards—all Antony's—were brought back. A fine piece of work! Written from the camp, April 15th.[19]

Galba had served for several years with Caesar in Gaul as a legate, so that he was able to report these events fairly dispassionately, despite the fact that legion was now fighting legion. The historian Appian, writing in the second century AD, but using as his source what may have been another eyewitness account, presents a more chilling picture:

Because they were experienced troops they raised no battlecry, since they could not expect to terrify each other, nor while the fighting was in progress did they utter a single sound, either as victors or vanquished. As there could be neither outflanking movements nor charges in the marshes and ditches, they stood close together, and since neither could push the other back, they locked together with their swords, as in a wrestling match. No blow failed to find a mark. There were wounds and slaughter, but no cries—just groans; men who fell were immediately borne away and others took their place. They had no need either of admonition or encouragement, since each by virtue of his experience acted as his own general. And when they grew weary they drew apart from each other for a brief space to get their breath back, just as in gymnastic contests, and then rushed again at each other. Amazement took hold of the newly enrolled troops who had come up, as they beheld such deeds done with such precision and in such silence.[20]

Antony was driven back towards Mutina, but Pansa had been mortally wounded, and died soon after. A few days later a second encounter took place, outside Mutina itself. Antony was again worsted, but Hirtius was killed, so allowing Octavian to assume informal command of the whole senatorial army. Decimus Brutus was freed from siege, but, snubbed by Octavian soon after, he endeavoured to make his way to the East through Dalmatia, and was trapped and killed there.

Antony meanwhile, still with his favourite *legio V Alaudae* intact, and remnants of *II* and *XXXV*, retired westwards to make contact with Aemilius Lepidus, proconsul of Transalpina and Nearer Spain, and Munatius Plancus, proconsul of *Gallia Comata* (the wide areas newly added to the Roman domain by Caesar). Both governors, and Asinius Pollio in Further Spain, had been raising fresh troops and recalling veterans in the expectation of fresh fighting. In particular, Lepidus was able to re-form Caesar's old *VI* from its colony at Arelate, and *X* from Narbo.

THE SECOND TRIUMVIRATE

Despite an expectation in Rome that the proconsuls, especially Plancus, would declare for the Senate and resist Antony, in fact (much to Cicero's disappointment) they quickly joined him, yielding up their troops to his overall command. Octavian countered by marching on Rome and securing election as consul. This achieved, he returned north, to a conference with Antony held on an island in a river near Bologna, with Lepidus acting as convenient arbitrator, in October of 43. This 'summit' resulted in a formal pact—known to history as the Second Triumvirate, by which the three men formed a commission, with the vague but alarming remit 'to regulate the state', effectively superseding the normal organs of government. The three disposed of their enemies—including Cicero—without delay and turned to the chief task of eliminating Brutus and Cassius, who now controlled all Roman territory East of the Adriatic.

An army of 22 legions was made ready, under the joint leadership of Antony and Octavian, and including all the re-formed Caesarian formations. Over the summer of 42 these were ferried across the Adriatic to Dalmatia, and the two leaders advanced along the Via Egnatia towards the old city of Philippi. Meanwhile Brutus and Cassius, moving westwards from the Dardanelles along the same road, pushed back some legions sent ahead of the main Triumviral army, and took up a position below Philippi, on low hills to either side of the Via Egnatia itself. Here they could keep contact with their fleet at Neapolis (Kavalla) and await reinforcement from the client kings of the East. Among the two armies only one legion on the Triumviral side (*legio IIII*) is named by the literary sources as participating, but many others can be assumed as present: *VI, VII, VIII, X Equestris*, perhaps *XII*, and (among the younger legions) *III* (now or later given the title *Gallica*), and probably *XXVI, XXVIII, XXIX* and *XXX* (all of which participated in the land settlement schemes that followed the battle). Among the 17 or so legions fighting with the Liberators we must assume most of the former garrisons of the East—legions which by accident of being stationed by Caesar in these parts after Pharsalus now found themselves on the opposite side from his avengers; here we can definitely name *XXVII, XXXVI* and *XXXVII* and probably assume others such as *XXXI* and *XXXIII*. Their ever-thinning ranks had been filled out by recruiting among many non-Romans, and to find suitable officers Brutus had appealed to young Romans spending a term or two at the 'university' in Athens—including Cicero's son, and the future poet Horace, who was to fight—and run away—in the ensuing battle.

PHILIPPI

The two armies thus confronted each other along the Via Egnatia (fig. 35). The Triumvirs' camp lay astride the road itself, with a rampart and ditch extending southwards into the edge of the marshes which flanked both battle-lines to the South, to prevent any encircling movement. Like earlier battles—such as Pharsalus and

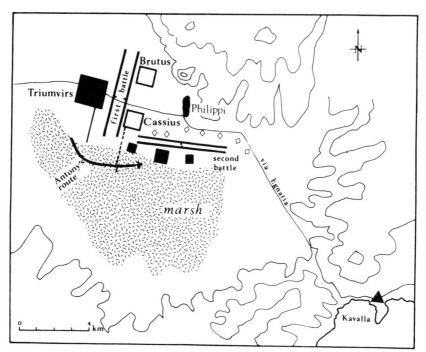

35   The battle of Philippi, 42 BC (*after Kromayer and Veith*).

Forum Gallorum—this was an encounter between trained forces, with all the expertise that generations of experience in Mediterranean warfare could teach. There could be no expectation of easy victory, or of favours from the other side. But the extra experience and *élan* of Caesar's veterans could be expected to be crucial. Antony, who assumed direction of the Triumviral forces—Octavian was in any case unwell—repeatedly drew up his forces and offered battle, but Brutus and Cassius refused. In a manoeuvre of typically Caesarian boldness, Antony attempted to outflank the Liberators' position by cutting a path south and east through the marshes, and laying pontoons.[21] But Caesar's luck did not hold for Antony, and the infiltrators were intercepted by a counterwork when their mission was all but achieved. These encounters brought on a general battle, in which Brutus (on the Liberators' right wing) was victorious over Octavian and captured the main camp. But Antony (on the Triumvirs' right) had succeeded in driving back Cassius and took his camp in turn. Cassius' somewhat premature suicide brought to a close what had in effect been a draw. There now followed a lull of nearly three weeks, during which Antony succeeded in gradually surrounding Brutus, by leap-frogging his forces along his adversary's south flank, and changing the direction of threat by 90°. Brutus extended his own lines to avoid encirclement, and was finally goaded into offering battle. But he was driven back on his own fortifications and his legions disintegrated. Brutus too took his own life.

When the Liberators' army was rounded up, some 14,000 men were incorporated into the victorious army, which was itself reconstituted. The old Caesarian veterans were segregated and despatched to Italy, along with newly-released time-served members of the younger legions raised in 49–48, which had fought with them on the Triumvirs' side. Sufficient men remained to fill out 11 legions, and these were organised round cadres formed by some of the most senior and loyal Triumviral legions (below, p. 133). Of the time-served men, destined for Italy, some 8000 volunteered to continue in service, and were formed into Praetorian cohorts, to be divided equally between the two Triumvirs present. The town of Philippi became a Roman colony as *Iulia Victrix Philippi*. An inscription reports a veteran of *legio XXVIII* settled there, and coins indicate the presence of members of the old Praetorian cohorts (pl. 16c), now released.[22]

At a meeting to decide fresh tasks, Antony claimed the more prestigious duty of reorganising the East, and of putting into effect Caesar's planned Parthian campaign. To this end Antony retained eight of the reconstituted legions. Among them we can identify *VI* (now *Ferrata*), *X Equestris, III Gallica, V Alaudae*, perhaps *XII* (later *Fulminata*) and others we shall meet with again. Octavian returned to Italy with just three legions: *VII* and *VIII*, the old Caesarian units which he had drawn to his side in Campania in 44, and *IIII* (probably now with its title *Macedonica*), one of the two legions which had defected to him from Antony in the previous year. Antony for his part was probably glad to be rid of them: *IIII* in particular, even if reconstituted, would be anathema to him. The other defecting legion—the *Martia*—would doubtless also have been retained by Octavian, but by cruellest fate it had been intercepted during the crossing of the Adriatic, allegedly on the very day of the first battle at Philippi, and its personnel almost wholly destroyed, along with Octavian's own Praetorian cohorts.[23]

On returning to Italy, Octavian's urgent task was to arrange for the settlement of the time-served veterans; generous promises made before the campaign now required fulfilment. The rewards had already been made known before the task force set off for Greece, causing a wave of revulsion: 18 cities 'renowned for their prosperity, the excellence of their land and their properties' were earmarked to provide the necessary allotments, and their country-based populations turned out.[24] The veterans, some 40,000 in all (including recalled Caesarian veterans, many of whom now received a fresh plot of land) benefited, each man obtaining up to 40 *iugera* (25 acres), sufficient for himself and his family. The ill-will of the people fell on Octavian, but he persisted, pushing through the whole programme within six months, securing for the future the loyalty of the veterans and of his own army who could look to similar rewards in due course.

Most of the new colonies can be identified: the historian Appian names five (Capua, Beneventum, Nuceria, Venusia and Ariminum). Other literary references allow us to add Bologna and Ancona. The sufferings of the poet Vergil whose family lost its property at Mantua allow us to add nearby Cremona, and the family of the poet Propertius lost land at Assisi as veterans flooded into the colony at Hispellum. The evidence of inscriptions adds Luca, where veterans of *XXVI* were settled alongside the old Caesarian *VII*, and Octavian's reconstituted *VIII* was established at Teanum where one of its veterans is known—the man had served in *legio VIII Mutinensis*; the epithet (which is found only here[25]) must derive from the legion's participation in the battle at Mutina (Modena) in 43. Other colonies of the time seem likely to have been at Asculum, Tergeste, Hadria (where a soldier or tribune of *legio XXIX* has been pinpointed), and Aquinum which has a settler from *legio III* (perhaps the later *III Gallica*).

THE PERUSINE WAR

While Octavian was grappling with the problem of settling the impatient veterans without totally alienating the remainder of the population, fresh thorns appeared in the form of Antony's wife, Fulvia, and his younger brother Lucius Antony, now consul for 41 with a newly raised army of six legions at his disposal. Both proceeded to champion the cause of the dispossessed, and lay obstacles in Octavian's path. A war of words soon developed into minor skirmishes, and then into open conflict. First, Lucius occupied Rome, but was forced to withdraw in the face of Octavian's approach. Eventually he took refuge in the old city of Perusia (Perugia), on a ridge at the north-west end of the great Umbrian plain. Here he planned to appeal to the local population, some evicted from their farms by the colonists at nearby Hispellum, and to wait for very substantial Antonian forces—under Asinius Pollio and Ventidius Bassus—to march from Gaul and Cisalpina to his relief. His calculations went astray. Octavian hemmed him in with siegeworks, and closed the roads to the North against the relieving forces.

Appian gives a detailed account. Octavian's first action was to construct a palisade and dig a ditch round the town, for a distance of 56 stades (seven miles/11 kms), and to extend these works to reach the Tiber itself, to prevent river-borne food supplies or reinforcements getting through. Next

> he speedily increased the strength of the fortifications and doubled the depth and width of his ditch so that it was 30 feet wide and 30 feet deep. He increased the height of his rampart and built 1500 wooden towers along it at intervals of 60 feet. There were also frequent forts and every other kind of entrenchment. The lines faced both inwards and outwards, to hem in the besieged and to ward off attacks from outside.[26]

The total length of the works accords well with the most likely circuit which takes in the circle of ridges and hillocks which all but surround the hilltop fortress itself. On the clear winter days (there is regularly a haze in summer) Octavian's ramparts and his troops would have been in full view from the city across the intervening low ground. No traces of these fortifications have been detected (information from Professor Filippo Coarelli of Perugia University), but it must be supposed that a programme of fieldwork would help to locate them. The area needing to be searched is not over-large.

In fact the support of Pollio and Ventidius—and Munatius Plancus who had joined them from the South with two legions (probably from the colony at Beneventum which he was then engaged on founding)—was lukewarm, in the absence of a specific directive from Antony himself, and they declined to force a passage, leaving Lucius at Octavian's mercy. After fierce fighting (vividly related by Appian)[27] and unsuccessful attempts to break out, and with hunger sapping the morale and strength of his army, Lucius sensibly surrendered. He was released and his army dispersed, but Octavian's wrath fell (rather unfairly, we could suppose) on the magistrates and city-councillors of Perusia, who were executed. The city was then set ablaze, but whether by accident or design was never established.

An unexpected and almost unique insight into the fighting round Perusia, and the propaganda war being waged by both sides, is provided by the survival of substantial numbers of lead slingbullets, some inscribed with the names of the legions, their officers and commanders (fig. 36).[28] The collection of bullets in the archaeological museum at Perugia, some 80 examples, does not seem to have been added to for some considerable time. The bullets, which are on

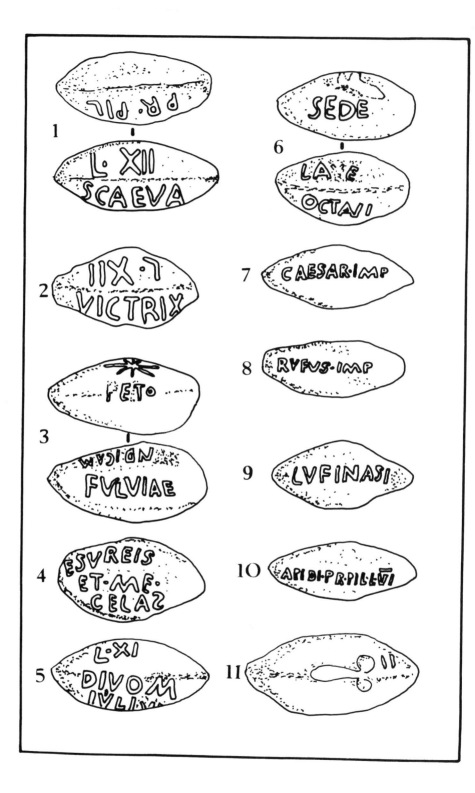

1. PR·PIL / L·XII SCAEVA

2. ꟿ·XII / VICTRIX

3. FETO / VSION FVLVIAE

4. ESVREIS / ET·ME· / CELAS

5. ꟿ·XI / DIVOM IVLI

6. SEDE / LA·E OCTAI

7. CAESAR·IMP

8. RVFVS·IMP

9. ·LVFINASI·

10. AP·DI·P·R·PIL·LVI

11.

average 40mm in length and 10–15mm in diameter, tapering to a point at both ends, must have been made by the million, and were a normal adjunct to the military armoury of the time. Many, perhaps all, of the bullets found at Perugia were manufactured during the siege, as their brief messages, impressed into the moulds from which the lead bullets were made, make clear. Both sides in the siege made use of such projectiles; they cannot always be distinguished. Several mention the legions whose members presumably launched them; many can, from the presence of a thunderbolt emblem, favoured by Octavian's legate Salvidienus who directed the siege, be placed in the army of Octavian, and thus provide a useful digest of his forces. Legions with the numerals *IIII, VI, XI* and *XII* (one bullet giving it the epithet *Victrix*) are definitely attested; much less certainly there may be records of legions *VIII* and *XIX*. A few give the names of centurions or tribunes, perhaps given responsibility for the production of the missiles. We learn of Scaeva, chief centurion of *legio XII*—whom it is tempting, and perhaps right, to identify with Caesar's valiant centurion (above, p. 107). In addition some bullets exhibit an abbreviated coarseness, denigrating the leaders of the opposing factions, emphasising physical defects (e.g. Lucius' baldness), doubting their virility, and envisaged as being aimed directly at the protagonists—Octavian, Lucius and Fulvia—to strike them in particularly embarrassing or tender parts of the male or female anatomy. Bullets deriving from the Caesarian side emphasise their links with Caesar and give Octavian his formal title as *Caesar imperator*. On the other hand bullets fired outwards by the besieged dismiss him as Octavius, denying the legitimacy of the Caesarian connection. A number are indecipherable, but some of these are almost certainly obscene. In general the tone recalls the ribald ditties bawled by Caesar's troops at his Triumph, and reflects soldiers' language in all ages.

FROM THE PERUSINE WAR TO ACTIUM

With the conclusion of hostilities Octavian turned to the repair of Italy's prosperity and the restoration of morale among its population. Antony's lieutenant Ventidius conducted a successful campaign against the Parthians and returned home to celebrate a Triumph in

---

36 Slingbullets from Perusia. Note reference to the centurion Scaeva
1, Fulvia 3, the deified Julius Caesar 5, Octavian 6,7, and his legate
Salvidienus Rufus 8. Scale 1/1 OPPOSITE

38, but Antony himself was driven back from Armenia with great loss, only alleviated by the brilliance of his strategic retreat. His repeated appeals to Octavian for access to the Italian recruiting grounds were diverted or ignored. Octavian himself, after an uncertain start, began to get the upper hand against Sextus Pompeius, still at large in the Mediterranean; his lieutenant Agrippa defeated Sextus' naval forces in two battles off the north-east coast of Sicily in 36. Some of Sextus' legionaries were incorporated into Octavian's army, and many time-served men were released, after a near mutiny at Messana. Lepidus, who had been in virtual exile as proconsul in North Africa, and who had helped Octavian by landing forces on the west coast of Sicily, was forced into retirement.

Relations between the two remaining Triumvirs continued to deteriorate, and Antony found himself increasingly isolated, denigrated and misrepresented. His liaison with Cleopatra became common knowledge, and the story was easily exploited to his discredit. Octavian meanwhile continued to win plaudits by successful if minor campaigns in Illyricum, always emphasising the regularity and legitimacy of his rule, to the detriment of Antony. Finally Antony was pushed into an intolerable diplomatic position, and unwillingly found himself at war, disowned by Octavian and a compliant portion of the Senate. Yet he did not lack friends, who saw in him a more worthy successor to Caesar than the calculating Octavian, and risked all to follow him.

About the detailed activities of the armies of Octavian and Antony in the decade between the Perusine War and the outbreak of war between them we are not well informed. Appian names a *legio XIII* among Octavian's forces in southern Italy in 36, and also reports *legio I* as forming a temporary garrison at Puteoli (Pozzuoli on the Bay of Naples).[29] Otherwise we can see, in the epithet *Fretensis* borne under the Empire by a *legio X*, an allusion to the *Fretum* or *Fretum Siculum*, the Roman 'Channel' between Italy and Sicily, and the scene of several encounters between Octavian's ships and those of Sextus Pompeius in 38–36. Perhaps this *legio X* was then serving on shipboard, as a *legio classica* (below, p. 127). Rather unexpectedly we know rather more about Antony's legions. Tacitus, in a description of a battle in AD 69, refers by chance to the participation by the legion *III Gallica* in Antony's Parthian War. A commemorative coin, issued during the Parthian War of the Emperor Lucius Verus in AD 166, names *VI Ferrata*, apparently alluding to the bicentenary of its participation in Antony's similar campaign.[30] More important, in the later 30s Antony issued to his army coins which named its component legions. The coins, mostly *denarii* in silver, though a few gold *aurei* are known, shared a common obverse showing a galley (pl. 12a), and a reverse showing a legionary *aquila* between two standards. The legend on the obverse names Antony as ANT(*onius*) AVG(*ur*)—emphasising his one legitimate public appointment as a state priest; the legend on the reverse gives the numeral of one of the legions. Coins commemorating legions numbered *I* to *XXX* are known, but scholars have seriously doubted the genuineness of those with numerals above *XXIII*, which have to be dismissed as modern forgeries extending a popular series.[31] In addition, *denarii* are known which record *cohortes praetoriae* (pl. 12c), and a *cohors speculatorum* (pl. 12d), evidently an inner élite force and personal bodyguard. A separate coin issue gave details of the titles borne by some legions: we learn of *XII Antiqua* (pl. 12b), *XVII Classica* and *XVIII Libyca*. The epithet *Antiqua* should indicate a legion claiming a Caesarian pedigree, *Libyca* some service in North Africa or off its coast, and *Classica*, a period of service at sea with the fleet—in fact we know that four legions were embarked during the final battle on Antony's warships, and *XVIII* may have been among them. Many others of his legions doubtless had titles which we chance not to know.

The occasion for the issue of this distinctive coinage is not clear, though numismatists tend to place it in the period 33–31. No literary source makes reference to it. However it must be very likely that the issue was struck to honour and pay the troops present on the west coast of Greece for the final battle in September 31. The use of the galley as an emblem on the obverse of the series is particularly appropriate. Antony's forces at that time (see below) probably amounted to 23 legions.

The coins have survived to modern times in very substantial numbers. This was due in part to the poorness of the silver content, which meant that the coins remained longer in circulation, well into the second century AD. The issue itself must have been extremely large—if indeed it was distributed to all the members of 23 legions (which would have a paper strength of 115,000 men). The issue could represent one pay-instalment (the soldiers received their pay on a four-monthly basis). In that case each man would have received 75 of the *denarii*, making some eight million in all. On the other hand, if the issue is in fact a donative paid to the troops on the eve of the battle, it could have been much larger.

THE BATTLE OF ACTIUM

In response to the Senate's declaration of war—nominally against Cleopatra—Antony marshalled his forces over the winter of 32–31, and prepared vigorously to defend his most westerly provinces, Macedonia and Greece. His land army contained 19 legions, with four more on shipboard. Octavian promptly transferred his army —about 24 legions—to Epirus, and when Agrippa succeeded in entrapping part of Antony's fleet in the Gulf of Ambracia (access to which was controlled by the promontory of Actium), Octavian quickly brought his full army up in support, and encamped on the north side of the Gulf (fig. 37). Antony in turn was forced to move his legions and main fleet northwards to rescue the entrapped contingent; he established his camp on the south side of the Gulf. As soon as the main body of his troops had arrived, Antony, in a typically Caesarian move, crossed the narrow mouth of the Gulf on a bridge of boats, established a second camp on lower, but unhealthy, ground, and sent a cavalry force round the Gulf to the north-east, intending to blockade Octavian and starve out his army. But the outflanking group was defeated, and Antony in turn found himself short of supplies, as Agrippa pounced on and eliminated his various supply bases and staging posts along the coast.

Finally, on 2 September 31, Antony made a move to attack Agrippa's fleet, and broke through to safety with a small force together with Cleopatra's own squadron. But the majority of ships were sunk or surrendered. The land army, which had watched helplessly from the shore, attempted to retreat towards the north-east, making for the Dardanelles and the safety of Asia, but, increasingly disillusioned, and deserted by the senatorial officers, its representatives began a protracted negotiation for surrender: the older soldiers thought principally of discharge and retirement, and the younger men of their future service. After a week of talking it was agreed that Antony's troops should receive identical treatment on their release to Octavian's time-served men (i.e. land and money); the citizens among the younger men could remain under arms, if they wished, though the non-citizens were dismissed to their homes; and several legions were transferred intact into Octavian's army, carrying forward their numerals, their distinctive titles and battle-honours (below, p. 134). Meanwhile Antony and Cleopatra, reaching Egypt safely, attempted to regroup and rearm, but the tide had turned too far, and, on the approach of Octavian, their remaining troops (including a force under the legate Scarpus in Cyrenaica; see p. 134) deserted, and both committed suicide. Octavian was now master of the Roman world.

The conclusion of hostilities ushered in a further spate of veteran settlement. Octavian's own men were accommodated in some 28 colonies in Italy itself, while Antony's men received land in the

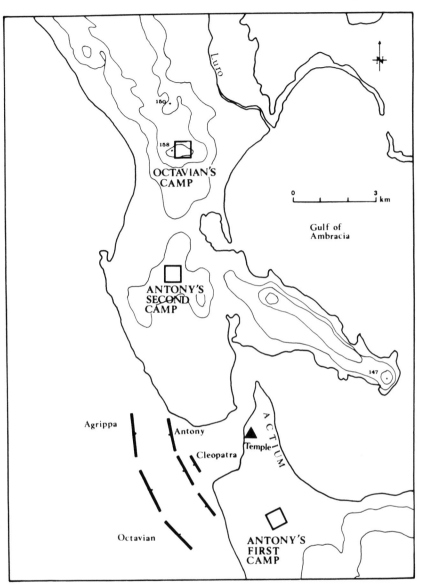

37 The battle of Actium, 31 BC (*after Kromayer and Veith*)

provinces. In Italy the civilian population was ejected from the designated towns—which included Brixia, Venafrum, Sora and Ateste, and many others in Campania, Cisalpina and Etruria—with promises of compensation, probably fulfilled out of the spoils of Egypt. Evidence for colonies in the provinces is rather scanty, but we can

129

38 Tombstone of Marcus Billienus, who fought at Actium in *legio XI*, and adopted the surname *Actiacus*. After the naval battle (*proelio navali facto*) he was settled in the colony of Ateste (Este) and became a town-councillor. (*ILS* 2443; Museo Civico, Vicenza). Drawn by John Callan

perhaps identify Patrae (where veterans of *X Equestris* and *XII Fulminata* are known), Beirut (which has veterans of *V* and of *VIII Gallica*) and perhaps Troy (a veteran of a *legio XVI* is attested there) (pl. 16d). Now, or perhaps a little later, a *legio VII* and a Praetorian cohort provided the manpower for four small colonies in Mauretania. Carthage was refounded in 29, perhaps for Antonian veterans.[32] In commemoration of Actium, some of the veterans settled by Octavian at Ateste in north-east Italy assumed the title *Actiacus*, 'Actium-fighter', in permanent commemoration of their part in the victory (fig. 38).[33]

Very quickly Octavian turned the energies of the legions from civil strife to new projects and foreign wars, with a view to repairing the neglect of nearly two decades, and to the pacification of half-won provinces, securing their borders against attack, and extending the Empire even further.

5 The Emergence of the Imperial Legions

It is often credited to Octavian—or *Augustus* ('the revered one') as he became in 27 (see below, p. 145)—that after Actium he substantially recast the army of the Civil Wars, disbanding old formations and creating new legions loyal to himself. As an example, it is common to adduce the three imperial legions *II, III* and *VIII*, all entitled *Augusta* ('Augustan'), an epithet which, it is alleged, specifically identifies them as fresh creations of his Principate. The aim of the present chapter is to argue that the army of the Roman Empire had substantial and evident roots in the civil wars of the Late Republic and that many, perhaps the great majority, of the legions found in service from Augustus' reign onwards were already in being before Actium, some indeed before the death of Caesar. The surviving evidence does not permit every stage on the process of transition to be perfectly understood, but some quite distinct phases can be discerned.[1]

In fact, for a study of the origins of the familiar legions of the Empire, it is necessary to begin with those units which Caesar found as the garrison of the Gallic provinces and Illyricum on his arrival in the north in 58, and the formations which he raised during his tenure of office, i.e. legions *VI* to *XIV*, together with *V Alaudae*, that special creation deriving from provincial militia raised in or about 52. Many of these legions continued to exist in recognisable form into the Empire (see Appendix 2). It might seem from this last statement that Caesar effectively established the self-perpetuating, standing legions of the Empire, with their fixed numerals and distinctive titles. But it was not his plan to do so. In 47–44 Caesar released from service legions *VI–XIV* (their repeated pleas for discharge will be recalled), and only *V Alaudae* remained in service down to 44 when it is found brigaded somewhere in southern Italy, perhaps awaiting formal discharge, unless it was intended as the core of the army for the projected Parthian campaign. Caesar proposed to conduct this war against Parthia with the aid of the younger legions of the 49–48 levies. Caesar thus followed normal practice: with the end of a major war, the legions of time-served men were released into civilian life.

Caesar's death, and more importantly the arrival on the political scene of Octavian, were vital stages towards the creation of the imperial army as we know it. The events of the Ides of March aroused the anger of the veterans, and both Antony and Octavian re-constituted several old Caesarian formations to bolster their forces and support their policies. Octavian, as we have seen, re-formed *VII* and *VIII* in Campania; Antony regrouped *V Alaudae*, and Lepidus in Transalpina took advantage of his proximity to Caesarian colonies there to re-establish *VI* and *X* (and perhaps another). Ventidius Bassus made attempts in Italy at reconstituting legions numbered *VII, VIII* and *IX*, but it is not clear that any of these survived even to the time of Philippi. A *legio XII Antiqua*, found later with Antony, has an epithet, 'Ancient', which suggests that it was claimed as the descendant of Caesar's *XII*. There is no certain evidence for the re-forming of legions *XI, XIII*, and *XIV*, but this may be due simply to the incompleteness of the literary and the epigraphic record.

The old Caesarian legions were in the forefront of the fighting at Philippi. After that battle Antony and Octavian released substantial numbers of time-served men, and regrouped those remaining into 11 legions (above, p. 121). The soldiers released now will have been the old Caesarians recalled in 44, and most of the founder members of the younger legions of 49–48, whose six-year service norm was now complete.

REORGANISATION AFTER PHILIPPI

It would have been normal practice now for the legions to be renumbered, in a fresh numerical sequence, perhaps beginning with a legion *I*. However, this did not happen. We are in the position of being able to identify almost all the legions which emerged from the post-Philippi reorganisation (see Appendix 1, p. 199). Octavian took back to Italy his *VII* and *VIII*, together with *IIII Macedonica*, which had defected to him in the summer of 44. Of the eight legions that remained with Antony, we can identify the old Caesarian *V Alaudae, VI Ferrata, X Equestris*, and almost certainly *XII* (the later *Fulminata*), together with *III Gallica*, probably one of Caesar's consular series of 48 (Appendix 1). The other three cannot be identified, but all must surely have been continuators of existing legions.

It was presumably militarily convenient to use existing legions as the nuclei for the reconstituted army. More important perhaps was the political dimension—both Octavian and Antony wished to be seen (and to continue to be seen) as Caesar's natural successors, to whom the Dictator's old legions were necessary as a visible testimony of support. Thus what can be seen in the long-term as a vital stage in the transition to the army of the Empire was taken primarily in the interests of the political survival of the chief protagonists in the struggle for power.

In the following decade Octavian filled out his own numerical sequence of legions. Already available he had the three ferried back to Italy after Philippi, and a quite substantial number of legions recruited in 45–42, which had been left behind as garrisons for the western provinces at the time of the battle. Particular attention may be directed at those legions, apparently five in number, raised by Pansa in 43 in preparation for the war against Antony in northern Italy (above, p. 115); several survived till Actium and probably into the Empire. Octavian did not hesitate to duplicate legionary numerals already in use by Antony. The latter had serving with him *V Alaudae, VI Ferrata* and *X Equestris*. Soon we find Octavian's army boasting of a *V* (the later *Macedonica*), *VI* (the later *Victrix*) and *X* (soon to be *Fretensis*). Of these, *V* and *X*, and less certainly *VI*, bore under the Empire a bull-emblem which would normally indicate a foundation by Caesar (below, p. 139); but the true Caesarian legions with these numerals (*Alaudae, Ferrata* and *Equestris*) were with Antony.

ACTIUM AND AFTER

That the army of the Empire had in part at least reached its final form in the decade after Philippi seems clear from the events following Actium itself, when some of the Antonian legions were incorporated into a previously existing numerical sequence, so producing the duplication in numbering which was to last throughout the Empire. Legions added now from Antony's army were *III Gallica, V Alaudae, VI Ferrata*, and *X Equestris*. Less certainly we could add to this list *IIII* (soon to be *Scythica*)—which matches Octavian's *IIII Macedonica* (see below, p. 206). Antony's army had boasted a *XII Antiqua*, (above, p. 133); that epithet by itself suggests a claim to Caesarian antecedents. The legion ought to be identifiable as the later *XII Fulminata*. Certainly veterans from *XII Fulminata* and *X Equestris* may have been settled together at Patrae in 30, a collocation which could suggest an Antonian origin for both (pl. 16d). Another legion to be ascribed to Antony before Actium is the imperial *III Cyrenaica*, which from its title could be identified as part of Pinarius Scarpus' force in Cyrenaica at the time of Actium (above, p. 128), unless raised initially by Lepidus before 36.

It is significant that the Antonians should set such store by the survival of their legions. The attitude probably indicates an appreciation that the legions were now semi-permanent institutions in an army of which they were concerned to form part. Many legions had remained in existence throughout the Civil Wars, and had kept the same numerals, which were now firmly established. From Octavian's point of view, it was surely politically advantageous to be seen as reunifying the old Caesarian army under his single leadership, as the Dictator's rightful heir. Other hints of reorganisation at this time seem implied in the title *Gemina*, 'Twin', which identifies a legion formed by the amalgamation of two existing formations. The history of X *Gemina* can be reconstructed with some plausibility: it is the successor to Caesar's Tenth legion, his favourite in Gaul. This legion, it will be remembered, had acquired the title *Equestris* in 58. A growing number of inscriptions report the title: a tribune at Pompeii, two veteran colonists settled at Patrae after Actium, and most interestingly a dedication in the Forum of Augustus at Rome, erected by centurions and soldiers of the *legio X Gemina Equestris* (see below, p. 209): hence a valuable link and explanation of its pedigree. The *legio X Equestris* went East with Antony after Philippi; it must have been a prime candidate for incorporation into Octavian's army. But why did the distinctive and glorious title *Equestris* give way to the rather colourless *Gemina?* A solution is to hand: Suetonius reports that, apparently after Actium, Octavian had to put down a mutiny by a Tenth Legion, which was demanding excessive rewards.[2] It may be that he subsequently diluted the remaining Antonian legionaries with new recruits, or some legionaries from other formations loyal to him, so producing the new title 'Twin'. Dio specifically informs us that Octavian's reorganisation after Actium produced legions with the title *Gemina*.[3] The old title *Equestris* evidently survived in use for a while, but was eventually discarded. For legions *XIII* and *XIV*, also *Gemina* under the Empire, we have no direct evidence. Perhaps these too were former Antonian legions, but we know nothing about the circumstances of the amalgamations which produced their titles. The *legio XV* of the early Empire was one of Octavian's legions before Actium—that is if we accept the view that it acquired its distinctive epithet *Apollinaris* for services in that battle; the temple on the promontory at Actium was dedicated to Apollo, to whom Octavian was particularly attached. Nothing is known about the early history of legions *XVI–XIX*; because *XVII–XIX* were destroyed in AD 9 (below, p. 168), few inscriptions attest their members, and no titles or emblems are known which might assist an appreciation of their formative years, though Octavian's army before Actium was certainly large enough to have contained legions with all these numerals. Legions *XX* (later *Valeria Victrix*) and *XXI* (*Rapax*) are first heard of during Augustus' reign; their origins are unknown to us. The final, highest-numbered legion of the Augustan sequence is *XXII Deiotariana*. Quite clearly this title derives from the name of the Galatian king Deiotarus, who sent troops to aid Pompey and later Caesar (below, p. 141), and who died in 40. It is not unreasonable to suppose that Antony utilised this force in the campaign against Octavian. The latter may have taken over this Deiotaran legion at once after Actium, or better in 25 when the Galatian kingdom was finally added to the Empire. The numeral, placed at the end of the numerical sequence, suggests a freshly given number, and indicates that the full Augustan complement of legions (28 in all) was already in being by 25.

Older theories that the sequence of legions was built up gradually in the course of Augustus' long reign can no longer be entertained. Mommsen believed that Augustus retained 18 legions after Actium and added eight more in AD 6, and a further two in AD 9 (for the significance of these dates, below, pp. 163, 168). Hardy supposed that all the legions numbered above *XVI* were the product of recruitment from AD 6 onwards.[4] These older views seemed to derive some support from the fact that all the higher numbered legions are found on the northern frontiers; in particular the reader will note a neat collocation of legions *XVII–XIX* together on the Lower Rhine in AD 9 (below, p. 168). There could at any rate be some suspicion that Augustus did attempt some clockwise numeration of legions (as in the Republic?), with low numbered legions in Spain, and higher numerals along the Rhine and Danube. But warfare throughout the reign must have disrupted any system; if *XVII–XIX* were together in AD 9, it had not always been so (below, p. 159).[5]

TITLES AND EPITHETS

Useful evidence for the legions in the Civil War years derives from their titles, many of which disappear later. The use of distinguishing epithets for military units is a familiar practice in all ages. In modern times we are familiar with such formations as the *82nd Airborne*, the *Royal Green Jackets*, the *Argyll & Sutherland Highlanders*, the *Leibstandarte*, the French *Légion étrangère* and many others. The distinctive titles and nicknames describe origins, a special function or capability, but end as honorific epithets, instantly descriptive of high quality and distinction.

Roman legions began to employ such titles in the Civil War period.

It is surprising that they had not done so before, e.g. during the Second Punic War, when legions were retained in service over many years, and had time to develop *esprit de corps* and battle traditions. Certainly no record survives. At the time of the Social War we have some hints of titulature, but unsubstantiated.[6] The practice of reconstituting legions each winter (above, p. 78) must have militated against any continuity of tradition. It is only in the later first century BC that titles emerge and become important.

We may think that Caesar's legions in Gaul would have developed and adopted titles, to reflect particular victories, e.g. against the Nervii, or after the sieges of Avaricum or Alesia, or after landing in Britain. Caesar, as the master propagandist, can hardly have been unaware of their potential morale-boosting value, but his writings give no hint that any titles were awarded or adopted. Almost certainly, however, the famous *legio X* obtained as its epithet the title *Equestris* ('Mounted' or better, 'Knightly') from an incident in 58 (above, p. 84). The *legio V*, the *Alaudae* (French: Alouettes) seems to have acquired the nickname 'Larks' while a semi-regular unit of provincial militia in Transalpina, before a numeral had been given (above, p. 98). The *Alaudae* is the only legion of the Empire to have as its title a noun, plural and normally indeclinable, rather than an adjective. The title derives from a bird-crest evidently worn on the helmets by founder members, a familiar Celtic practice.[7] During the civil war against Pompey there were plenty of suitable occasions for the coining, award or adoption of splendid titles. But for the period before Caesar's death we happen to know of only one title, *Martia*, which came to be attached to one of the legions stationed in Macedonia; it may have been acquired during service in Africa in 46 BC.[8] In 44–43 Cicero took pains to extol the merits of the *legio Martia*, then under Octavian's command, as a counterweight to the *Alaudae*, currently the mainstay of Antony's army. Such was the preoccupation of Cicero with the title itself that we do not know the legion's numeral.[9]

After Caesar's death many more titles are recorded in our sources; the existence in rival armies of legions with the same numerals surely encouraged their coining and use. Equally it seems that titles could change with some frequency: some were probably nicknames that not every soldier wished to perpetuate. Sometimes two or more titles appear to be in use, if not contemporaneously, at least in rapid succession, by what from other evidence might seem to be the same legion. If our epigraphic records had been fuller, we should probably have found the profusion even more disconcerting. Titles are found now which fade from sight after the Civil Wars (see Appendix 1).

The Emergence of the Imperial Legions

Sometimes, however, epithets acquired during these years continued in use later. *Legio X* acquired its permanent title *Fretensis* from exploits in the *Fretum Siculum* or 'Channel' between Italy and Sicily during the war between Octavian and Sextus Pompeius. Its naval emblems under the Empire—dolphin and galley (below, p. 140)—help to confirm its early history. The *legio VI Ferrata* ('Ironclad') surely acquired its distinctive title in the Civil War, perhaps already under Caesar. Graham Webster kindly suggests that some peculiarity of equipment, for example iron chest-protectors worn with the normal mail shirt, could have occasioned the epithet. The earliest evidence for the use of the title belongs soon after 40.[10] The *legio IIII Macedonica* clearly derived its title from its sojourn in Macedonia before 44.[11] Equally early is the title *Gallica* (reflecting service in Gaul) used by *legio III*; it can only have been acquired before the battle of Philippi, after which the legion was stationed permanently in the East.

We must not suppose that, because a legion with a distinctive title attested during the Civil Wars is not found under the Empire, the legion itself, rather than simply its title, has been suppressed. Thus, in my view, *II, III* and *VIII*, all called *Augusta* under the Empire, were directly descended from legions in Octavian's army before Actium. *Legio VIII Augusta*, with its bull-emblem, is surely the old legion of that numeral, which served with Caesar in Gaul; *legio II Augusta* may be identifiable with the *II Sabina* reported on an inscription of a Civil War veteran at Venafrum (Venafro) and with the *II Gallica*, the veterans of which received land at Arausio (Orange) in 36–35 and are commemorated on the Augustan Arch there. The antecedents of *III Augusta* cannot yet be established. The new titles presumably reflect some degree of reconstitution, or some particular success in the wars of Augustus' reign, which he wished specially to commemorate. Any earlier titles borne by the three legions inevitably disappeared from view in the face of such resplendent epithets. Dio notes that a legion was deprived of its title *Augusta* after a reverse in Spain in 19.[12] It may well have been *legio I* (below, p. 157). If so, the legion did not disappear, but is recognisable as the later *I Germanica* of the Rhine garrison. One of the familiar legions of the garrison of Roman Britain, *legio XX*, had under the Empire the titles *Valeria Victrix*; both titles, or at least the former, have long been supposed to have been adopted during Augustus' reign, as a result of sterling service during the Pannonian revolt of AD 6–9, when the legion was commanded by the legate Valerius Messallinus.[13] The two titles were thus translated as 'Valerian and Victorious'. But it must be doubted whether Augustus, at that late stage in his reign, would have allowed the fresh coining of a title from the family name of a leading senator. Even more improbable is the theory that one of the legion's permanent epithets could have derived from the name of Valeria Messallina, Claudius' consort until her demise in AD 48. A recent study has suggested, almost certainly correctly, that the titles are best translated, 'Valiant and Victorious', with the former deriving from the Latin verb *valere* ('to be valiant or strong'), and that both were acquired by the legion in the aftermath of Boudica's revolt in Britain in AD 60–61, to match the epithets *Martia Victrix* granted to the *legio XIV Gemina* which also contributed to the victory.[14]

Interestingly many epithets—even those of which common use was made in the Civil War years—fade from use under Augustus and the Julio-Claudian Emperors, only to become common again under Nero, or more certainly at the time of the civil war of AD 68–69, which rent the Roman world apart after his suicide. It may well be that the stressing of battle honours and old titles became more pertinent when legion was again fighting legion. From the Flavian period of the later first century AD, legionary titles are found in use on inscriptions as a matter of course.

LEGIONARY EMBLEMS

Towards establishing the background and early history of the imperial legions, a study of their emblems is of particular assistance. It will be remembered that the Roman legion before Marius had five standards—an eagle, wild boar, minotaur, horse and wolf. Marius gave pre-eminence to the eagle, which henceforth became the principal standard of all legions. But other distinctive symbols were also in use. Zodiacal signs are found as emblems of individual legions under the Empire; their appearance on relief sculpture, building records and the so-called legionary coinages issued by third century AD emperors and usurpers, provides a useful, though incomplete, digest.

Legions with a bull as their emblem are asserting a Caesarian origin: the bull was the zodiacal sign associated with Venus, legendary founder of the Julian family. The bull is found with legions *VII, VIII Augusta* and *X Gemina*, all of which had served with Caesar in Gaul, and with *III Gallica* and *IIII Macedonica*, which were probably formed by him in 48.

Legions with a capricorn emblem attest a foundation (or reconstitution) under Augustus. For Augustus the capricorn was an important emblem symbolising good luck. It was the zodiacal sign under which he was conceived. Legions with the capricorn are *II Augusta, XIV Gemina, XXI Rapax,* and, it may be, *IIII Scythica* (pl. 14a and below, p. 229). As *IIII Scythica* is normally thought of as serving with Antony in the decade before Actium, some reconstitution later may be implied. Alternatively we may have to rethink its early history. *Legio IIII Macedonica* has both the capricorn and the bull (pl. 13): the capricorn could have been added to an existing bull-emblem when the legion was brought back to Italy by Octavian after Philippi and became part of his new army.

But not every Caesarian legion had (or retained) a bull-emblem under the Empire: *V Alaudae* had an elephant, the result of an incident in 46 at the battle of Thapsus.[15] Caesar himself, though he records acts of heroism in the battle by members of *V Alaudae* against charging elephants, makes no mention of the resulting emblem.[16] Clearly reminiscent of its participation in the sea-battles of the Civil War are the naval emblems of the *legio X Fretensis*: in addition to the bull (alleging a Caesarian origin), the legion used a dolphin and a galley. One legion, *XI*, has Neptune, presumably a reminiscence of service at Actium, in which we know it took part.[17] Other emblems are less easy to explain: *VI Ferrata* with the wolf and twins (i.e. Romulus and Remus), and *XIII* and (less certainly) *XVI* with the lion; the latter is another zodiacal sign, especially linked to Jupiter. *Legio II Augusta* has the pegasus, the winged horse of Greek mythology (as well as its capricorn), and a pegasus may appear also with *III Augusta*, but the precise significance is not clear. Not all the emblems we know need originate in the Augustan age. The boar, a familiar battle-emblem of the Celts, was used by *XX Valeria Victrix* and sometimes by *X Fretensis*. For some legions no emblem seems to be attested; but the picture would doubtless become more complex, if we knew more.

NON-ROMANS IN THE LEGIONS

The rapid build-up of the army during the Civil War, and the urgent need of the various protagonists to enlarge their forces with all speed in provinces far from Italy, brought into the legions many men who would normally have been excluded—they lacked citizenship, the essential qualification. Already in Gaul Caesar had been augmenting his forces from Transpadanes who had only Latin status, and (as already referred to) in 52 he raised 22 cohorts of provincial militia in Transalpina. 'One legion he even recruited from the Transalpini and trained and equipped it in the Roman style and gave it a Gallic name—it was called *Alauda*. Later on he gave citizenship to all its members.'[18] It is interesting that in his *Gallic War* Caesar himself never mentions the *Alaudae* by name preferring vague references to 'cohorts', which suggests that he was sufficiently conscious of the legion's unorthodox origins, to wish to conceal them. Doubtless after his arrival in Rome in 49, or after Pharsalus at the latest, there was no further need for deception, and the legion was formally assigned its numeral, *V*.[19]

To match Caesar's surreptitious build-up of his forces, Pompey's legates in Spain raised a *legio vernacula*, a 'homebred' legion, from young men born in Spain itself. Later Cn. Pompeius in 45 had two such *legiones vernaculae*, and another 'made up out of Roman settlers'.[20] This is a useful distinction: the vernacular legions drew upon the local native population, and the other upon Romans living in Spain. In Asia Minor, Domitius Calvinus in 47 had a legion 'made up out of militia-men called out in the emergency';[21] it bore the title *legio Pontica* (indicating its origin in the kingdom of Pontus), and fought against Pharnaces, after whose defeat at Zela it is not heard of again. Almost certainly the numerous legions hurriedly raised by Pompey in Asia and Macedonia, by Plancus, Pollio and Lepidus in the West, by the Pompeians and (later) Lepidus in Africa, and by Brutus and Cassius and (later) Antony in the East, contained many non-Romans, in addition to residents and colonists. By the later stages of the Civil War we could suppose that commanders would be happy to accept any recruits of suitable bearing and physique, whatever their cultural background or civic status.

In the East a number of dynasts and client kings had begun to organise their troops in the Roman manner. The army of king Deiotarus of Galatia contained by 47 at least two such 'legions' 'which had been established on our disciplinary system and using our types of weaponry'. They were defeated in an early battle against Pharnaces; Deiotarus then regrouped the survivors into one legion which fought at Zela (above, p. 110).[22] The legion is likely to have continued in some form till Actium, and it achieved the accolade of formal incorporation and amalgamation as a legion into the Roman army in 25 at the latest, as *XXII Deiotariana*, after which it was stationed in Egypt. The kings of Mauretania and Numidia had 'legions' which intervened in the Civil War from time to time.[23] Less certainly some of the troops of Herod the Great were organised as legions, and attention might be directed, if the evidence allowed, at the forces of Egypt under Achillas, which Caesar encountered in 48–47; some input from Roman 'advisers' and soldiers of fortune can be presumed, among them some of these soldiers left behind by the proconsul Gabinius to protect the King of Egypt in 55.[24] It is easy to imagine that other kingdoms on the fringes of the Roman world were influenced by the example of her continuing military success. By the

THE LEGIONS OF THE EARLY EMPIRE
(to be read in conjunction with Appendix 2)

Legion	Originator and date of formation	Meaning of title and implications	Emblem
I Germanica	Caesar, 48 or Pansa, 43?	served in Germany	?
II Augusta	Pansa, 43?	reconstituted by Augustus	capricorn, pegasus
III Augusta	Caesar, 48 or Pansa, 43?	reconstituted by Augustus	pegasus?
III Cyrenaica	Lepidus in Africa, 40–36 or Antony, 40–31	served in Cyrenaica (under Antony?)	?
III Gallica	Caesar, 48	served in Gaul	bull
IIII Macedonica	Caesar, 48	served in Macedonia	bull, capricorn
IIII Scythica	Antony, 40–31	campaigned against Scythians on lower Danube, 29–27	capricorn (see p. 229)
V Alaudae	Caesar, 52	'The Larks'; formed from native Gauls	elephant
V Macedonica	Pansa, 43 or Octavian, 41–40	served in Macedonia	bull
VI Ferrata	Caesar in Gaul, 52	'Ironclad' (see p. 138)	bull
VI Victrix	Octavian, 41–40	Victorious in Spain	? bull
VII Claudia	Before 58	after loyalty to Claudius, AD 42	bull
VIII Augusta	Before 58	reconstituted by Augustus	bull
IX Hispana	Before 57 or Octavian	after service in Spain	?

Legion	Raised	Note	Emblem
X Fretensis	Octavian, 41–40	after naval victory in *Fretum Siculum* (Straits of Messina), 36	bull, dolphin, galley, boar
X Gemina	Before 58	'Twin', after amalgamation following Actium	bull
XI Claudia	Caesar, 58	after loyalty to Claudius, AD 42	Neptune
XII Fulminata	Caesar, 58?	'Equipped with Thunderbolt'	thunderbolt
XIII Gemina	Caesar, 57 or Octavian, 41–40?	'Twin', after amalgamation	lion
XIV Gemina	Caesar, 54 or Octavian, 41–40?	'Twin', after amalgamation	capricorn
XV Apollinaris	Octavian, 41–40?	'Sacred to Apollo', in commemoration of Actium battle (p. 135)?	?
XVI Gallica	Octavian, 41–40?	after service in Gaul	? lion
XVII	Octavian, 41–40 or later?	—	?
XVIII	Octavian, 41–40 or later?	—	?
XIX	Octavian, 41–40 or later?	—	?
XX Valeria Victrix	Octavian, before 27?	'Valiant and Victorious' (see p. 138)	boar
XXI Rapax	Octavian, before 27?	'Grasping' (in predatory sense)	capricorn
XXII Deiotariana	on annexation of Galatia, 25	after Deiotarus, king of Galatia	?

close of the Civil Wars there must have been many men under arms who were not citizens by birth, or if Italian by descent had not lived in Italy for many years. Local natives were doubtless attracted by the promise or prospect of full citizenship, and financial rewards in the event of victory, but few achieved them.

Before the last generation of the Republic, legionaries by definition had been Roman citizens acting in defence of, or to further the interests of, their homeland. The revelation that other sources of manpower could be tapped was a legacy of the Civil Wars, to become increasingly important later.

6 The Age of Augustus

The victory at Actium ushered in a long period of prosperity and internal peace. In 27 there took place a radical reform of the constitution. Octavian ceased to rely on powers irregularly acquired during the Civil War. Instead he agreed to accept, at the hands of the Senate, a large 'province' consisting of Gaul, Spain and Syria. It was not his intention necessarily to go out as *proconsul*, but following the precedent set by Pompey in Spain, he would rule through legates responsible and loyal to himself. As Gaul, Spain and Syria contained the bulk of the Empire's military forces, he effectively retained control over the army. At the same time he took a fresh title *Augustus*, 'the revered one', by which he was subsequently known; it was a new name for a new era. Augustus was to remain in control at Rome for a further 40 years.

The list of legions (see Chapter 5) was substantially complete by Actium, but otherwise the army was much as before. Certainly the long drawn out conflict had heightened the general efficiency of Roman forces, and produced a large body of near professionals. The size of the army had expanded dramatically in 49, when Caesar advanced southwards into Italy, and remained at a high level until Actium when some 60 legions were in commission. Rival commanders recruiting in the name of the Roman state had brought to arms many whose interest in fighting was low. The historians exaggerate the rapacity of the soldiery in these years, and give prominence to outbreaks of unrest and mutiny. Yet the latter were generally not the result of greed, but reflected more a desire for discharge by men who merely wished to go home. The vast numbers drawn into his service by Caesar in 49–48 were reconciled to the traditional requirement of six years, but when that was completed and the Liberators defeated at Philippi, they were anxious for a prompt release. Indeed of the 36,000 men entitled to discharge after the battle, only 8000 were keen to stay on in the army—this gives a useful insight into the professional core of legionaries at this time.[1] Thus the citizen army of the Civil Wars contained two types of soldier: 1 the professional who was anxious for long protracted service, and liked the life (or knew no other), and 2 the short-stay recruit who was concerned to return to civilian life as soon as possible. Many of those who enlisted in 49–48 were presumably conscripted, in the traditional manner, by a *dilectus*. The two groups have to be carefully distinguished: the later Roman historians, familiar only with the long-service army of the Empire, found the unrest incomprehensible, and attributed base motives to account for it.

THE NEW ROMAN ARMY

The army of the Roman Empire differed from that of the Republic in many ways. The individual legions (and auxiliary regiments) remained permanently in commission with the same names, numerals and titles, and were renewed by constant supplementation. The soldier served for an extended period, and looked on the army as a lifetime's occupation and career. A proper financial structure ensured the payment of wages. At the end of service there was a fixed reward, on the implementation of which the soldier could rely. It is to Augustus that the credit belongs for effecting these changes.

We have already seen that many of the legions of the Empire were already in being during the Civil Wars and were retained thereafter. But the decision to maintain them on a permanent basis, in peacetime, was by no means a foregone conclusion at the start of Augustus' reign. Augustus might, after 31, have disbanded the existing legions, and reverted to the old system, raising fresh levies as required. In the past a large army had been maintained for many years, e.g. against Hannibal, but at the end of hostilities the legions were released all the same. But in the later first century Augustus had to face the reality that Rome now controlled, and felt obliged to defend, an enormous territory, extending round the Mediterranean basin, northwards into central Europe, and eastwards into Asia. The very distance between Rome and the provincial borders she had to defend was now a significant factor. A substantial standing army— well above the 10–14 legions in service before the Civil Wars—was required. Of course many of the soldiers were already long-serving professionals, and permanent garrisons had been maintained in Rome's provinces for many generations. But the legal and administrative framework had not kept pace. It was time for some rationalisation.

The historian Cassius Dio, writing of events in 29, reports two speeches made before Augustus by his advisers Agrippa and Maecenas, in which the best way of securing the continuation of the Roman state and defence of its empire was discussed.[2] Agrippa (whose speech survives only in part) apparently advocated the retention of the traditional system (by which men would be conscripted to serve short periods, and then released into civilian life). Maecenas, on the other hand, argued for a long-service army of volunteers, and despite Agrippa's contention that the latter could form a threat to the security of the Empire—and the Emperor— carried the day.

The speeches need not be judged the true record of a real debate between the two. In part at least they reflect the political situation of Dio's own time (early third century AD) and were aimed at a contemporary emperor, perhaps Caracalla[3]. Nevertheless there could easily have been some discussion on the future make-up of the army, in the immediate aftermath of Augustus' return from Egypt and the completion of the great colonisation programmes. However, we know of no changes introduced at this time. But in 13, after Augustus' return from Gaul, he ordained that army service in the legions should in future be fixed at 16 years, to be followed by a four year period 'in reserve', to be rewarded by a fixed cash gratuity.[4] The announcement followed closely upon another land-settlement scheme in 14, about which we have only sketchy information; numerous colonies seem likely to have been founded or reinforced, especially in the provinces. The impact on Italy seems less easy to assess and may have been relatively minor. Perhaps public outcry against the settlements, or the difficulty in obtaining suitable land, prompted the emperor to substitute simple cash payments.

CHANGING CONDITIONS OF SERVICE

The jump from six years (the likely norm in the Late Republic) to 16 seems surprising, but service had been lengthening out during the Civil Wars. The gap of just 16 years between the settlement programmes of 30 and 14 BC surely suggests that many who joined up as replacements for the Actium veterans had served for about 16 years. Augustus could claim merely to be implementing a Republican practice: 16 years was the legal upper limit to the period that a man could be called upon to serve during his adult lifetime. Polybius mentions that, in times of special crisis, a total of 20 years might be demanded;[5] so that Augustus' decision to require an extra four years in reserve may have seemed thereby less outrageous.

By itself this longer service-requirement in the legions all but forced intending recruits to think of the army as a lifetime's occupation. It seems fairly clear that Augustus expected the ranks to be filled by volunteers. In AD 5 some alterations were made to the conditions of army service. The number of years which the new recruit had to serve under arms was raised to 20 years, with a further period (not specified, but probably at least five years) in reserve.[6] The cash gratuity was now fixed at 12,000 sesterces for the ordinary soldier, a lump sum equivalent to about 14 years' pay; centurions doubtless received much more. Seemingly as part of this same package, but recorded separately by Dio under the following year (AD 6), Augustus established a military treasury, the *aerarium militare*.[7] Its function was to arrange the payment of gratuities. Augustus 'primed the pump' with a large gift of money, but in the longer term the *aerarium*'s revenues were to come from two new taxes imposed from this time onwards on Roman citizens: a five per cent tax on inheritances (i.e. a sort of death duty) and a one per cent tax on auction sales. The introduction of these taxes caused an uproar, but, as Augustus knew well, taxation was preferable to the dislocation, bad feeling and financial ruin, which had been the consequences of land settlement programmes of the preceding generation. Augustus thus shifted a part of the cost of the nation's defence from his own purse to the citizenry at large. But the wages of serving troops continued to be paid by the imperial treasury; Augustus could brook no interference, or divided loyalties, there.

At some point, undefined within his long reign, Augustus ordained that soldiers must not marry during service, and frowned even on the custom of senior officers taking their wives to provincial postings. Such a ban, familiar to students of the imperial army, did not apply under the Republic, when short terms of service were the norm. Its advantages, at least as seen from Rome, were obvious: the troops had to be mobile, and a marching column is best unencumbered by a long tail of families. Later, when the legions came to occupy permanent fortresses, the ban remained in force; but soldiers took local women, and raised families, and considered their marriages to be quite regular. Eventually the ban was lifted by Severus at the close of the second century AD.

AUGUSTUS AND HIS SOLDIERS

A grave danger in the Late Republic had always been for troops, under a skilful or unprincipled leader, to identify their interests with the commander himself (Sulla and Caesar are obvious examples), and be drawn into the political arena. One of Augustus' aims, and certainly one of his achievements, was to separate troops and commanders, to occupy the army in ambitious foreign conquests and keep it loyal to him alone. Both the troops and the commanders were to look to him for rewards and advancement.

Throughout his reign Augustus was concerned to maintain a bond between the soldiers and himself: he was their patron, they his clients. Their loyalty, and the closeness of the bond, were continually emphasised, especially on the coinage, which the soldiers received from Augustus as their pay. Victories were his, and to be publicised. The Emperor, and his family, took the credit and held Triumphs in Rome, and gave donatives. Frequently in his early years, Augustus personally took the field to show himself to the army, and to be directly involved in its chief campaigns and successes. He needed also to satisfy the aspirations of the senatorial aristocracy, now deprived in large part of their traditional rewards and honours. But he still took care to set their commands in the context of a civilian career structure, within which military responsibilities were to be seen as a necessary element, not a chief end. Active commands in the field were not to be held over-long, lest too close a bond develop with the troops or provincial interests.

OFFICERS AND GENTLEMEN

Thus Augustus himself, as proconsul, governed a substantial part of the Empire through his legates, the *legati Augusti*—a phrase which encompassed both the senior commanders, who governed the Emperor's provinces (with powers equivalent to a propraetor under the Republic) and the commanders of the legions which formed their garrisons. We have already seen how legates were employed by Caesar, and the system (though less well documented) continued throughout the Civil Wars, and into Augustus' reign. The more junior legates continued to command one or more legions, or a composite body of troops, especially when encamped together, as the occasion demanded. It is only towards the very end of Augustus' long reign that we begin to find the designation legionary legate (*legatus Augusti legionis*)—indicating that men were being appointed to command individual named legions, and remained with them for a number of years.[8] These legionary legates would be young men in their late twenties or early thirties, men who had held at least one magistracy at Rome, as Quaestor, Aedile or Plebeian Tribune; some holders would already have been former Praetors. But by the end of the Julio-Claudian age the status of the legate was becoming fixed in the promotion ladder of the senatorial career. Command of a legion went to a man who had already served as Praetor—a reversion to the practice of the middle Republic.

For equestrian officers the expansion of the army and the Empire, and the growth in the number of the provinces, brought a wide variety of appointments. Former legionary tribunes were employed as military governors of tracts of newly won territory, or as commanders of fleets, or as prefects of regiments of auxiliary infantry or cavalry. As the reign progresses, and inscriptions, our chief source-material, become more abundant, we can observe how the tribunate was becoming an intermediate step in a career structure, not an end in itself. Greater opportunity opened up also for centurions, who could now rise into the Equestrian Order, and become tribunes and prefects: talent had mattered more than birth in a Civil War context, and doors hitherto closed were for a time opened up.

The structure of the legion itself was left untouched, except that mention should be made again here of the category of reservists created by the Augustan military reforms of 13. Men who had completed the basic 16 years of service were retained for a final four years 'under a special standard' (*sub vexillo*). After the changes introduced in AD 5, the group consisted of men who had already passed their twentieth year of service. These reservists remained with the legion, but were excused the normal round of camp duties. Theoretically they were to be called upon only in emergencies, but the distinction was soon eroded, to be a cause for discontent later (below, p. 170). The group seems likely to have numbered about 500 men in any one legion.

AUXILIARIES

It is time to say something about the place of the auxiliaries in the new Augustan scheme. During the later Republic it had become customary for a Roman army on campaign outside Italy to be assisted by native infantry requested from local allied tribes and client kings. Caesar in Gaul made extensive use of Gallic and later Germanic cavalry, which proved extremely effective during the Civil Wars. Meanwhile Pompey, Brutus and Cassius, and later Antony, drew heavily on the armies of the kings and dynasts of Asia Minor, Syria and Egypt.

Large numbers of such troops served during the Civil Wars, for

39 Roman helmets of the early empire from **1** Nijmegen and **2** Cremona (*after Connolly*); drawn by John Callan

extended periods, often far from their homelands. By the time that peace returned, their potential role and function were fully perceived, as a necessary and valuable complement to the legions themselves. *Cohortes* of infantry and *alae* (wings) of cavalry fought alongside the legions in the Augustan wars of conquest and expansion. Units of combined infantry and cavalry are also found (cf. above, p. 100). An inscription of Tiberian date mentions a *praefectus cohortis Ubiorum peditum et equitum* ('prefect of a cohort of Ubii, foot soldiers and horsemen'),[9] which is an early example of this type of unit, of which we shall hear more later (below, p. 182). At the end of the Civil Wars many of the auxiliaries were presumably sent home, but some regiments certainly remained in being, like the legions themselves. Some of these early units, many of them cavalry squadrons of Gauls and Germans raised by Caesar or his successors from the Gallic provinces, retained distinguishing epithets deriving from their first (or an early) commander—for example, the *ala Scaevae*, presumably named after Caesar's old centurion (above, p. 106)—or a senior Roman officer—for example the *ala Agrippiana*, or *ala Siliana* (perhaps after Agrippa, and a member of the consular family of Silii). These, and others, became permanent units of the standing army. But many others, probably still a majority, were raised according to the needs of the moment, under treaty obligations, for a short- or long-term engagement, and served close to, if not in, their homelands. An interesting phenomenon is a small number of citizen-cohorts; we know of a *cohors Apula* (i.e. 'raised in Apulia') and a *cohors Campanorum* ('raised in Campania'). The circumstances of their formation are unknown. Less certainly belonging with this group are two *cohortes Italicae*, which must have been raised in Italy, but the civic status of their members is unclear; they need not have been citizens by birth.

Frequently those units raised in the provinces by treaty obligations were commanded by their own chiefs or nobility; citizenship was a common and appropriate reward for such officers' loyal service, but we have no evidence that the common soldier received any material reward when he went home. Some units were presumably paid for and kept supplied by their own communities. But for those units which had become a formal part of the army's structure, we can presume an extended period of service, probably matching the legionary's. Such regiments were generally commanded by ex-centurions, or ex-legionary tribunes, but the set hierarchy of appointments found later had not yet been established. Augustus even designated young men of senatorial family to command *alae* of cavalry in pairs.[10] This was not an early experiment in job-sharing, but designed to increase the number of military posts available to young men of senatorial background.

SEA-POWER AND THE NAVY

The importance of sea-power, and the control of trade-routes in the Mediterranean, had become pre-eminent in the Civil Wars from 49 onwards. Armies had repeatedly to be transported to theatres of operations far from Italy, in the face of hostile naval squadrons. Pompey, the Liberators, and most obviously Sextus Pompeius, maintained large fleets, a threat to Italy and the city's food supply. The ships could be heavily manned with soldiers. Several legions bore in the Civil War period the title *Classica* (see Appendix 1). Sea-power was a cornerstone of Antony's control over the eastern Mediterranean: one of the common types on his coinage was a galley. Those who controlled the eastern Mediterranean could draw on the fleets of Rhodes, the cities of Syria and the Levant, Asia Minor and of course Egypt, and the expertise of professional admirals in the Hellenistic mould. Caesar and later Octavian were forced to build almost from scratch. During his preparations for war against Sextus Pompeius, Octavian established secure port-facilities at Forum Julii (Fréjus in Provence); some structures have been located by excavation. More important, under the direction of the naval-minded

Agrippa, major installations were developed on the Bay of Naples at the Lucrine Lake, which was opened to the sea, and itself linked by a channel to Lake Avernus further inland, which offered a safe, inner harbour; tunnels from Cumae and Puteoli facilitated the transfer of men and stores. Many of the associated warehouses and dockside facilities of this great complex, named the *Portus Julius* (after Octavian), have been detected and planned, by underwater archaeology in the Bay, and by aerial photography over its waters.[11] After Actium, Antony's warships and crews were sent to Forum Julii, but it was soon resolved that the chief bases of a permanent Roman fleet should be in Italy itself. Facilities were built at Misenum, at the western tip of the Bay of Naples, and at Ravenna close to the head of the Adriatic. At Ravenna an inland lagoon south of the town was adapted to form a safe anchorage, and linked directly to the river Po by a canal, the *Fossa Augustea*.[12] The *Portus Julius* at the Lucrine Lake was soon abandoned, despite the energies expended on its construction, perhaps because of subsidence or—less convincingly—a powerful business lobby of merchants exploiting the oyster beds for which the Lucrine had long been famous. Each of the two principal fleets was placed under a *praefectus classis*, often an ex-tribune who could already have held a command with the auxiliary forces.

TROOPS IN THE CITY

Augustus established, for the first time, what was in effect a military garrison at Rome itself. Most important were the Praetorian Cohorts. Under the Republic a magistrate on campaign could have a small escort and bodyguard, called a *cohors praetoria* (cf. above, p. 84). After Caesar's death both Octavian and Antony formed large bodyguards from among Caesar's veterans. After Philippi those veterans who declined the offer of land-settlement remained to form a plurality of *cohortes praetoriae*, at the disposal of the two Triumvirs (see also above, p. 116). After Actium Octavian retained his *cohortes* to form a peacetime bodyguard. We know it better as the Praetorian Guard. There were nine cohorts in all, each probably 500 men strong, with small mounted contingents. How the total number of cohorts was decided upon is not known. Augustus may have been intending to avoid the figure of 10 cohorts, as too reminiscent of a legion in the public mind; on the other hand the total of nine could have reflected some fusion of his own and Antony's former cohorts after Actium.[13] Conscious of a breach in Republican tradition in maintaining a military force at the capital, at first Augustus stationed only three cohorts in Rome, at any one time, and the men were distributed in small groups in lodging houses. The remainder were billeted in neighbouring towns, none of which has been identified.[14] Initially the Praetorians lacked any overall commander, but in 2 Augustus chose two *equestrian praefecti praetorio* to exercise command jointly. During the Civil Wars the *cohortes praetoriae* had been drawn from the ranks of the legions—after Philippi new cohorts were made up entirely from time-served legionaries disinclined to accept the profferred discharge and land settlement.[15] They were thus a *corps d'élite*; but under Augustus (and thereafter) their members were recruited directly from civilian life. In 13 service in the Guard was fixed at 12 years (increased in AD 5 to 16 years)—this was surely a total length of service, not to be computed in addition to any previous legionary service, and marks an important transition. Their pay was set at one and a half times the legionary's rate, and later increased to three times, a source of discontent and envy among the legions on the wilder frontiers.[16] Augustus also maintained from the Civil Wars a small 'personal protection' squad, the *Germani corporis custodes* (German bodyguards), drawn from tribes of the Rhineland (pl. 17d).

In addition he established a police force for the city, three *cohortes urbanae*. These were entrusted to the senatorial *praefectus Urbi*. The number of *cohortes* was perhaps intended to match the three *cohortes praetoriae* which Augustus retained within the city itself. Finally, Augustus in AD 6 established a permanent fire-brigade, replacing the various *ad hoc* groups which had existed up to that time. Seven cohorts of *Vigiles* were formed, mainly from freedmen, each cohort responsible for tackling fires in two of the 14 *regiones* into which the city was now divided. Effectively the city now had a garrison some 6000 men strong (excluding the *Vigiles*), which maintained order, and the status quo, in what had become the Mediterranean's largest city, with a population of nearly one million.

FOREIGN POLICY

If the Augustan Age was marked in Italy by a return of peace and stability, it saw also a great burst of activity in the provinces, as new areas were overrun and existing provinces consolidated, after a long period of neglect and abuse during the Civil Wars. Augustus himself, his chief confidant Agrippa, and later his step-sons Tiberius and Drusus, took a major role, and the army was kept at full stretch throughout most of the reign. A sequence of successes, some none too easily won, produced a succession of splendid Triumphs in the city for the Emperor, his family and a number of his legates, advertising the continuing success of his policies and the work of the armies now campaigning far from home.

The literary record of this work is often paltry, and the epigraphic and archaeological sources distressingly thin by comparison with later periods, so that we cannot trace in every detail the movement of troops or identify their encampments. Most years saw a cycle of the concentration of a province's army into a summer camp (*castra aestiva*) in readiness for active campaigning, or to meet a potential threat; in the autumn the legions were distributed to a number of winter bases (*castra hiberna*), much as during Caesar's Gallic conquests. The winter bases might be used repeatedly, so that some wooden hutments or even stone structures were put up and remained standing over the years, but it is probably too soon to speak of these *hiberna* as 'fortresses'. Such developments lay in the future.

It is only with the fuller record provided by Tacitus' *Annals*, which provide an account of the Empire's history starting at Augustus' death in AD 14, that we can begin to identify and locate garrisons with something approaching certainty; while some dispositions can be retrojected into the later years of Augustus himself, much remains obscure. Often legions are attested under Augustus in provinces far removed from their later haunts: the distribution of legions in the Empire's frontier provinces was by no means settled at this time.[17] Augustus was anxious to occupy the army's energies, and to define and secure the borders of Roman possessions, but he was cautious about extending the Roman domain too far from its Mediterranean heartland, except where insecurity of the frontiers demanded action. Thus he resisted demands for the incorporation of Britain, southern Arabia and Parthia from a public which felt that nothing was now beyond the power of Rome's invincible legions.

GAUL AND SPAIN

By virtue of his newly acquired responsibilities, Augustus directed his attentions first to Gaul, and travelled there in the summer of 27. We know little of the disposition of troops in Gaul at this time, but presumably the bulk of the legions lay in *Gallia Comata* on or near the Rhine itself. It seems likely that some posts had already been established on the Rhine, at Strasbourg and Vindonissa, garrisoned by regular auxiliary units, or by native levies acting in the Roman interest. Other troops seem likely to have been in Aquitania, to control the south-west corner of Gaul.[18] We can assume five or six legions as the garrison of Gaul, among which were probably *XVII–XIX*, and *XXI*. A small winter-camp located by aerial photo-

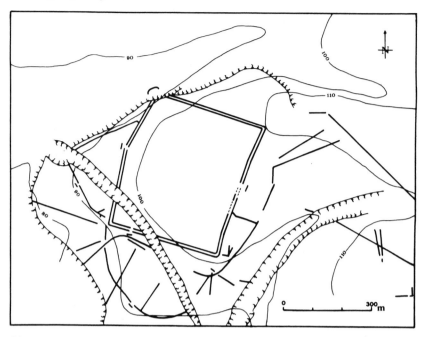

40 Winter-camp near Folleville in the Somme Valley, revealed by aerial photography (*after Agache*); 39 acres (15.9 hectares). The extent of the surrounding earthworks suggests that the camp had more than a temporary occupation. An Augustan date seems likely

graphy near Folleville in the Somme valley may belong now (fig. 40). Communication with Italy was improved by the final subjugation of the Alpine Salassi who straddled the St. Bernard Passes, and a colony for veterans of the *cohortes praetoriae* was established in their territory at Aosta (*colonia Augusta Praetoria*) in 25. A length of ditch found during an early excavation just outside the town and initially interpreted as part of the defences of the Roman camp on the site of which the colony itself was planted, is now seen as a natural water-course.[19] Soon after, defensive posts established on the Walensee protected Helvetia from Raetian attacks from the East, and forts were placed on the Rhine itself at Basel, Oberwinterthur, and at Zurich on the line of communications south-west towards the heartland of Gaul.

From Gaul Augustus moved on to Spain, and inaugurated a long series of campaigns against the Cantabrians, Asturians and other tribes of the north and west of the Iberian peninsula. Up to seven legions took part, some perhaps brought by Augustus from Gaul; we have records of *I, II Augusta, IIII Macedonica, V Alaudae, VI, VIIII,* and *X Gemina.*[20] Two of these were former Antonian legions (*V* and *X*), now transferred to the west. Fighting continued until 19. In that year a legion, perhaps *I,* which had already acquired the distinctive epithet *Augusta* for some unspecified achievement (witnessed by Augustus himself in Gaul or Spain?) was stripped of the title (above, p. 138).[21] Soon after the legion was transferred to the Rhine frontier. *Legio VIIII* aquired its permanent title *Hispaniensis* (later the form *Hispana* was preferred) from its participation in these wars—the title is attested already by the middle of Augustus' reign.[22] *Legio VI* also became *Hispaniensis* from its service in Spain but the date of the award is not known. After the tribes had been subdued, the strength of the resident garrison could be reduced to three legions by the later years of Augustus.[23] Boundary markers, testifying to the extent of the *prata legionis* ('legion's pastureland') of one of the garrison units, *legio IIII Macedonica,* place it at or near Aguilar de Campóo on the Pisuerga River (the name Aguilar derives from *aquila*).[24] The bases of the other two legions of the late Augustan garrison—*VI Hispaniensis* and *X Gemina*—are not certainly known (but see below, p. 193). Colonies for time-served veterans of the Spanish campaigns were established at Merida in Lusitania (*colonia Augusta Emerita*)—men from legions *V* and *X* received land there in 25 (pl. 16a)—and at Zaragoza (*colonia Caesarea Augusta*) probably in 19. Veterans from three legions (*IIII, VI* and *X*) of the now reduced garrison received land there (pl. 16b).

PARTHIA AND THE EAST

Attention had for some time been turning towards the eastern frontier. In 25 Galatia was added to the Empire on the death of its King Amyntas, and during the same decade other client states were remodelled or regrouped in the wake of Antony's defeat. Some of Antony's legions remained as permanent garrisons in the eastern provinces: *VI Ferrata* and *III Gallica* in Syria, *III Cyrenaica* and (less certainly) *XII Fulminata* in Egypt. They were joined by Octavian's legion *X Fretensis* (which seems to have been for a time in Macedonia before moving east).[25] At Amyntas' death, his troops, already trained in the Roman manner (above, p. 141), were reconstituted to form a legion numbered *XXII,* entitled *Deiotariana* from Amyntas' predecessor, Deiotarus; it was sent to Egypt. Other legions—*V Macedonica, VII,* and *VIII Augusta*—almost certainly served in Asia Minor early in Augustus' reign, perhaps under a legate in Galatia.

The chief enemy in the east was Parthia, and Roman reverses

under Crassus and later Antony, combined with a failure of a Parthian attempt to annex Syria in 40–39, had shown both powers the value of a common desert frontier. The chief bulwark of Roman power was the legionary garrison in northern Syria, placed to guard against possible incursions by the Parthians. In 6 we know that the garrison of Syria was three legions,[26] and by the end of Augustus' reign it had increased to four. The bases of the legions at this time are not reported.[27]

In 20 Rome achieved a new understanding with Parthia, which was presented as a diplomatic triumph: the eagles and standards, and even some prisoners, lost with Crassus in 53, and other commanders, were restored. The Roman propaganda machine was quick to trumpet this success throughout the Empire (pl. 17a). The famous statue of Augustus from Livia's villa at Prima Porta just outside Rome seems to depict on the breastplate a youthful Tiberius receiving back, on Augustus' behalf, an *aquila* from a Parthian representative (pl. 15).

In Egypt, exploitation of the country's resources and native population continued under the Roman mastery. Three legions were based there after Actium, under the overall charge of an equestrian *praefectus Aegypti*: one at Nicopolis on the eastern outskirts of Alexandria (a modern name for the site is Kasr Kayasira i.e. *castra Caesaris*), where Octavian had established his camp in 30 and defeated Antony in a last encounter. Another legion was at Babylon, near modern Cairo, and the third somewhere in Upper Egypt—most probably at Thebes.[28] One member of the garrison, *legio III*, perhaps obtained its title *Cyrenaica*—if it was not already in use (above, p. 134)—from a successful police action on the province's western border; for a while *legio XXII* may also have borne the title *Cyrenaica*.[29] The name of the third legion of the garrison, later transferred, it would seem, to Syria, is not certainly known, but may have been *XII Fulminata* (above). An expedition in 25 to capture the flourishing port of Eudaemon (Aden) at the mouth of the Red Sea, in which detachments of one or more of the legions took part, was a complete failure.[30]

The rich corn lands of Africa were protected by a garrison of one legion, *III Augusta*, based at Ammaedara (Haïdra), which by AD 14 had been linked to the east coast of Tunisia by a new arterial road, built by the legion *ex cast(ris) hibernis* ('from its winter camp') to Tacape, the modern Gabes.[31] The title *Augusta* could be linked to a successful campaign against desert tribes in 19, which earned a Triumph for the *proconsul* Cornelius Balbus. It would not be surprising if other legions served in Africa under Augustus; we have a little evidence for *legio VIII Augusta*, of which two serving members died in the province at an early date.[32]

THE NORTHERN FRONTIER

In the last two decades of the first century BC, the emphasis shifts dramatically to the northern borders of the Empire, which consisted of a great arc from the Rhine delta, through the Alps and the northern fringes of Macedonia and Thrace to the Black Sea. Achieving a rational and defensible limit to Roman possessions in the north was to occupy Augustus for the remainder of his reign. In 29–27 M. Licinius Crassus, grandson of the Triumvir, had successfully overrun the whole area between Macedonia and the lower reaches of the Danube, earning a Triumph over the two chief tribes, the Getae and Bastarnae (sometimes known collectively as Scythians).[33] His army probably contained *V Macedonica* and perhaps *VII* and *XI*; it must be likely that *IIII* aquired its title *Scythica* at this time. *Legio XX* too was on the lower Danube at some stage during Augustus' early years.

Augustus himself went to Gaul in 16, in response to an incursion by the Germanic Sugambri, who defeated the army of the legate, M. Lollius; one of the legions, the *V Alaudae* recently transferred from Spain, even lost its eagle-standard, the ultimate disgrace.[34] The whole Alpine mass was finally subdued by Tiberius and his younger brother Drusus, who in 16–14 carried Roman arms northwards to the line of the upper Danube, and created new provinces of Raetia and Noricum. Two legions, *XVI* and *XXI*, seem likely to have formed the initial garrison of Raetia, perhaps in a joint base at Augsburg-Oberhausen, and a detachment of *VIII Augusta* is reported during Augustus' reign at the Magdalensberg hillfort in Noricum.[35] A major base of about this time was at Dangstetten north of Basel, which was held for a while by *legio XIX*.[36]

With the Rhine and Danube barriers reached for some considerable part of their combined lengths, it might have seemed that the Romans had reached natural barriers in the north. But from 13 Drusus carried Roman arms to the Weser and even to the Elbe, and after his death in 9, Tiberius consolidated these gains, and a whole new province, *Germania*, seemed about to be added to the Empire. As a literary source for the northern wars we are fortunate to have an account written by the historian Velleius Paterculus, who served in Germany and Illyricum as a *praefectus equitum*, then as legate. Velleius has been little regarded as a historian, because of excessive adulation of Tiberius, yet his is a valuable and contemporary

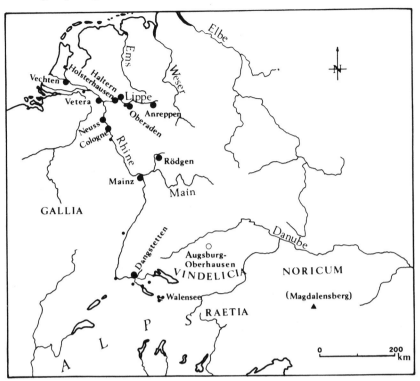

41 Roman sites on and beyond the Rhine before AD 9 (*after Wells*).
Note: small dots indicate forts occupied by auxiliary regiments

viewpoint, from the pen of an officer who actually took part in many of the campaigns. During Tiberius' virtual exile on Rhodes (6 BC–AD 2), there was something of a lull, but with his return Roman armies again campaigned beyond the Rhine; Tiberius' winter camp in AD 4–5 was close to the head-waters of the River Lippe.[37] In AD 5 the Romans again stood on the bank of the Elbe.[38] A fleet sailed up the river from the North Sea and joined forces with the legions.

A great deal has been learnt in recent years, by archaeological excavation and fieldwork, about the progress of the armies of Drusus and Tiberius (fig. 41). For example, the base for amphibious operations along the coast of Friesland was at Vechten on the Old Rhine, from which the *fossa Drusiana*, on the line of the River Vecht, led to the Zuider Zee and the northern Ocean. Less certainly, a large base at Nijmegen, of some 103 acres (42 hectares) may belong in this early period. Vetera near Xanten, at the junction of the Rhine and the Lippe, was the jumping off point for all Drusus' operations

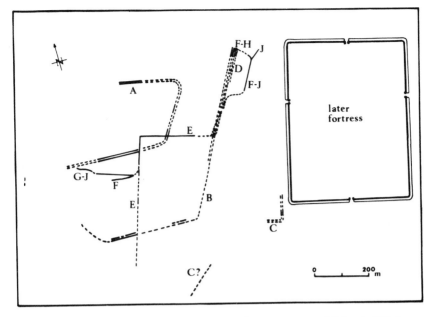

42 Augustan period camps at Neuss (*after Bogaers and Rüger*). Ditch-systems belonging to nine different camps have been located west of the later (Claudian) fortress

into the North German plain. A winter-base for two legions, rebuilt several times on different alignments during the Augustan period, has been located there. Further south, the encampment at Neuss was likewise rebuilt many times under Augustus, to house forces of varying sizes, up to four legions (fig. 42); the earliest occupation of the site cannot belong much after 20. One of the early camps has produced a record of *V Alaudae*. At nearby Cologne a base was also in use before AD 9: it served for a while as the camp of *legio XIX*, which was destroyed in the Varus disaster (below, p. 168).[39] On the upper reaches of the Rhine, the most important base was at Mainz (Mogontiacum), at the junction of the Rhine and the Main, from which access could be gained to all of southern Germany. The general picture gained from the archaeological evidence is of fluidity of movement: not all the bases can have been occupied at the same time; differences of emphasis and objectives from year to year will account for periods of abandonment. Doubtless more bases will be found in due course.

Some estimate can also be gained of Roman movements east of the Rhine along the main communication and invasion routes into

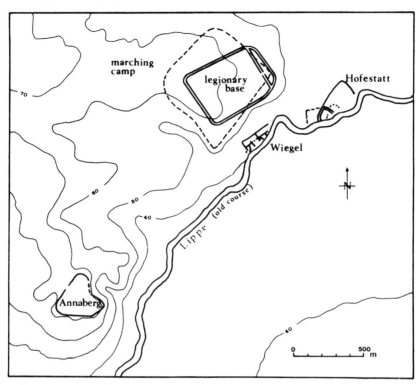

43 Haltern: general plan of Roman sites (*after Wells*), comprising a winter camp for one legion (Fig. 44) which overlies a marching camp for two legions; a fort on the Annaberg hill, and depots at Wiegel and Hofestatt, partly eroded by the river

Germany itself. Along the valley of the Lippe the progress of Drusus and later Tiberius is marked by a very large marching camp at Holsterhausen, and another (for two legions) at Haltern (fig. 43). The latter was subsequently overlaid by a winter-base for one legion (fig. 44), from which a lead-pig with the name of *legio XIX* has been recovered.[40] Further east a two-legion winter base and a small fort have been located at Oberaden (from which much military equipment, including *pila*, has been recovered), and traces of a Roman camp have been detected at Anreppen, fully 80 miles east of the Rhine. These are clearly links in a chain leading towards the Elbe. The literary sources name one of these winter-bases as Aliso, which Cassius Dio tells us was first built in 11, and was still being used in AD 9;[41] perhaps Aliso should be identified with Haltern. The ground-plan of Haltern is a valuable guide to the layout of a Roman timber-built legionary encampment, preceding the stone-built fortress at Vetera (fig. 52) by 50 years and Inchtuthil (fig. 47) by almost a century.

Further south, Drusus' route had been along the Main, into the Wetterau. A small supply base has been found at Rödgen, 35 miles east of the Rhine, and other sites are suspected. Rödgen, whose interior is dominated by granary and store buildings (fig. 45), can be seen as an intermediate point along the chief Roman campaign route to the east. It is surely clear now that the Romans maintained semi-permanent bases east of the Rhine itself, and spent the winters there (as Dio himself makes clear)—they did not retire behind the Rhine at the end of each campaigning season.[42]

REVOLT AND DISASTER

In AD 6 Augustus resolved to put the finishing touches to this magnificent extension to the Empire by extinguishing the power of King Maroboduus, who had built up a powerful kingdom in modern Bohemia, the suppression of which would allow the new frontier of Roman power to run directly from the Elbe to the Danube. Tiberius was to advance north and west from the Danube at Carnuntum. His army included legions *XX, XVI, XXI, XIII. VIII, XIV* and *XV; VII* and *XI* lay in the new province of Moesia just to the east. The army on the Rhine under Sentius Saturninus, marching eastwards from Mainz, comprised legions *XVII, XVIII* and *XIX* (veterans of many years' campaigning in Germany), *I,* and *V Alaudae.* But Augustus confidence proved delusive: the lands already overrun in the middle years of his reign were thinly held, incompletely pacified and inexpertly ruled. In AD 6 all Pannonia and Dalmatia rose in revolt. Tiberius, already on the march, was forced to turn back. There was hard fighting; legions were summoned from Galatia and the East, veterans recalled, and volunteers enlisted; some of them were taken north without delay by Velleius Paterculus.[43] Tiberius devised a pincer movement, which caught the rebels between his own legions and reinforcements arriving from Moesia. Acts of heroism abounded

---

44 Haltern: the winter base (*after von Schnurbein*); 44.5 acres (18 hectares), later increased to 49.5 acres (20 hectares). Only the excavated remains are shown. The headquarters building **a** was centrally placed, with the legate's house next to it **b**. Notice also a hospital **c**. Several major buildings have defied precise identification of their purpose OVERLEAF

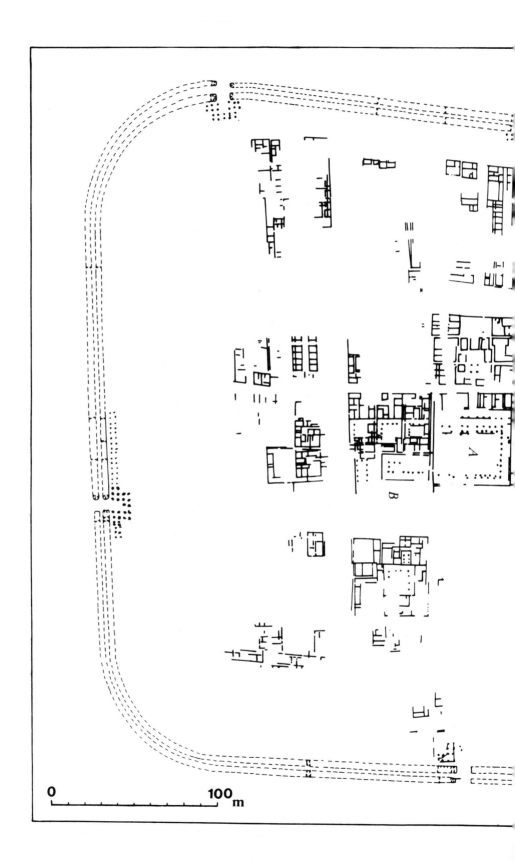

0   100 m

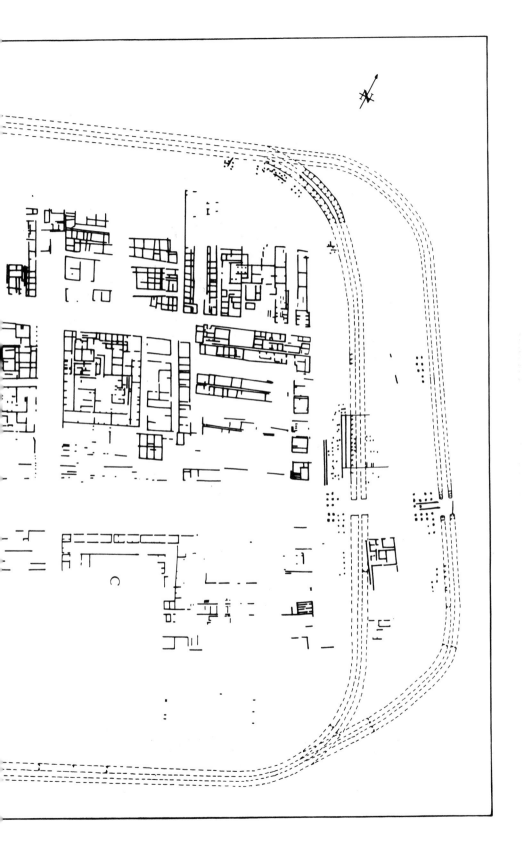

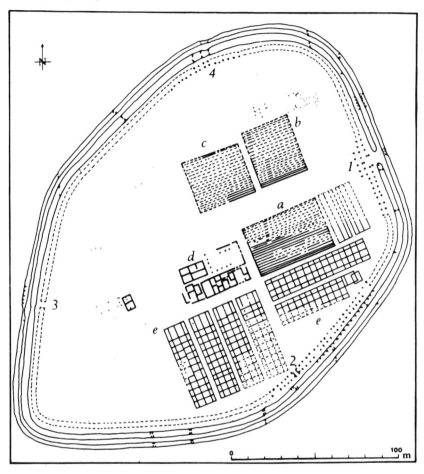

45 Supply base at Rödgen (*after Schönberger and Simon*); 8 acres (3.3 hectares) Note: three large granaries **a–c**, a headquarters building/commanding officer's house **d**, and barracks **e**. There were four gates (1–4); the chief entrance lay on the east side

in the old Roman tradition: *legio XX* under its commander Valerius Massallinus, though operating at, or reduced to, half its normal strength, cut through encircling forces and reached safety (see fig. 46).[44] The army was stretched to the limit. Velleius marvels that in AD 7, a total of 10 legions, over 70 auxiliary cohorts and 16 *alae* of cavalry, 10,000 veterans and a large force of volunteers, together with allied cavalry supplied by the king of Thrace, were concentrated at Siscia on the Save River. Such powerful masses had not been seen together since the Civil Wars.[45]

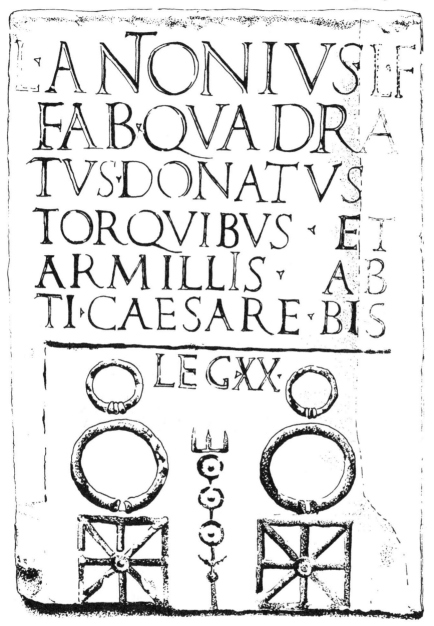

46 Gravestone of L. Antonius Quadratus, at Brixia (Brescia), veteran of *legio XX*. Quadratus fought in Augustus' northern wars and was 'twice decorated by Tiberius Caesar'. His decorations (bangles, torcs and medals, on a leather harness) are shown below, to either side of a military standard. (Drawn by John Callan)

167

Slowly but surely Roman control was re-established over the Balkan lands; but just as news of victory was announced in Rome, a further, much more serious disaster rocked the capital. The legate of the army on the Rhine, whose area of responsibility encompassed all Germany to the Elbe, was P. Quinctilius Varus, an eminent lawyer and husband of Augustus' great-niece. He had five legions with which to control this vast area: three (*XVII, XVIII* and *XIX*) with him in northern Germany, and two more (*I* and *V Alaudae*) under a legate, his nephew L. Asprenas, in the south. Varus and his three legions were drawn away from their winter bases (probably on the Lippe), and into an ambush, by renegade German auxiliaries under Arminius. His entire force of some 12,000–15,000 legionaries, together with six cohorts of auxiliary infantry and three *alae* of cavalry, was surrounded and killed in the Teutoburg Forest, somewhere beyond the Ems. Those who surrendered were mutilated, sacrificed at altars to deities of the Celtic world or butchered in cold blood. Six years later, an expeditionary force under Drusus' son, Germanicus, penetrated again to the site of the battle. The historian Tacitus reports the soldiers' reaction to the scene:

> Across the open ground were whitening bones, scattered where men had fled, or heaped up where they had made a stand. Splintered weapons and horses' limbs lay there, and human heads, fastened to tree-trunks. In nearby groves were the barbaric altars at which they had sacrificed the tribunes and centurions in cold blood. Men who had survived the battle or escaped from captivity, told how here the legates had fallen, and there the eagles were captured, where Varus had suffered his first wound, and where he took his own life. And they told of the platform from which Arminius had delivered a harangue, and of his arrogant insults to the standards and eagles; the gibbets and the pits for the prisoners. So, the Roman army, which had come to the spot six years after the disaster, in a mixture of mourning and mounting hatred against the enemy, laid to rest the bones of three legions. No one knew if he was burying a stranger or a member of his own family; they thought of them all as friends and kin.[46]

All Roman fears of the Celtic and Germanic warrior hordes, stilled since Caesar's day, returned afresh; there was panic in the city and fears of an imminent invasion. Levies were conducted, even in Rome itself. An inscription mentions a *dilectus ingenuorum* (i.e. a levy of free-born citizens)[47] in the city, which stiffened the legions and also produced a series of *cohortes ingenuorum*. Now, if not also in AD 6, slaves and freedmen were enrolled and formed into *cohortes volun-*

tariorum. At least 32 such cohorts were formed, and some despatched at once to guard the Rhine frontier.[48]

Varus' nephew Asprenas, whose force of two legions had lain on or near the Upper Rhine, moved quickly northwards, rescued the holding garrison which Varus had left at Aliso, and took up station on the Rhine itself, before the Gauls had time to waver in their allegiance.[49] A vivid testimony to the Varus disaster comes from Vetera, in the form of a memorial to the centurion Marcus Caelius from the north Italian town of Bononia (Bologna), and who had belonged to the First Cohort of *legio XVIII*. Poignantly the inscription grants permission for Caelius' bones, should they ever be recovered, to be placed within the monument (pl. 18). Doubtless Caelius' remains were among those buried on the battlefield by Germanicus' soldiers in AD 15.

The three legions lost with Varus, *XVII, XVIII* and *XIX*, were never reconstituted, and the total number in service fell to 25. The loss of the entire garrison on the lower reaches of the Rhine necessitated a reshuffling of the legionary forces of the Empire to plug the gaps at the northern end of the defence line, and to prepare for the permanent defence of the river barrier. Legions *I* and *V Alaudae* had moved with Asprenas to the Lower Rhine; they were now joined by *XVI* and *XXI* from Raetia (which now lost its legionary garrison), one legion (*II Augusta*) perhaps from Spain (but its whereabouts in the middle of Augustus' reign are poorly documented), and three from Illyricum (*XIII Gemina, XIV Gemina* and *XX*). Roman forces on the Rhine now stood at eight legions.

THE STRAIN OF EMPIRE

The reverses of AD 6–9 had imposed a severe strain on the machinery of the new professional army. A vivid commentary is provided by Tacitus' account of the mutinies which broke out among the legions on the Rhine and in Pannonia in AD 14, when the news of Augustus' death was reported to the frontier armies.[50] Few can have doubted that Tiberius would succeed to his power, but the change of ruler provided an opportunity for the soldiers to voice their grievances, and to put pressure on Tiberius at a critical moment. Trouble began in Pannonia where the garrison of three legions, under the legate Junius Blaesus, lay in a summer camp near Emona (Ljubljana). Recent recruits from among the city populace in Rome took the lead: some centurions, including '*cedo alteram*' Lucilius (his nickname 'Gimme another' derived from his predilection for using and often breaking his vine-stick cane over the backs of the soldiers in his company), were murdered or beaten up.[51] Older soldiers with special grievances, who were surely at the centre of the mutiny, complained of their protracted service (up to 30, even 40 years), the inadequacy of their eventual reward (often a plot on a barren hillside), the harshness of discipline imposed by corrupt centurions, and the low level of pay—especially when compared with the Praetorians who enjoyed a life of ease in Rome. They wanted a strict limit to the length of service: the 16 years of the Republic maximum, and prompt payment of gratuities, in cash, just as Augustus had promised in 13 (above, p. 147). We need not believe every word and allegation, but there is evidence here of dissatisfaction with the conditions of service in the army. The Varus disaster, and the dearth of new recruits willing to come forward, had delayed the release of those who had already completed their due time. Men conscripted at the height of the emergency jibbed at the prospect of a further 20 years or more on the wild northern frontier. In the Late Republic men conscripted during the Civil Wars could look to a release after about six years, but the new system allowed for no such short-term engagement. We may conclude that the transition from the short-service to the long-service army was not easily accomplished, and far from popular among the traditional sources of the legions' manpower.

Tiberius despatched his son Drusus and two Praetorian Cohorts northwards to confront the mutineers. Aided by a sudden eclipse of the moon, Drusus worked on the soldiers' superstitions, and dampened their ardour. The ringleaders were identified and hunted down, and the legions distributed to their winter bases. Similar unrest affected the much more powerful army on the Rhine. The four legions forming the garrison on the lower reaches of the river lay together in a summer camp, perhaps at Neuss, or at any rate not far from Cologne. Here again conscripts levied in AD 9 were in the forefront. Discipline broke down, and many centurions were beaten to death; the soldiers took to running the camp. Germanicus, who held a special command over Gaul and the Rhine armies, arrived to confront them, but made little impact and had to concede the chief demand: discharge after 16 years, and immediate payments of the cash gratuities. However the interception, by bands of soldiers, of Germanicus' wife and two year old son Caligula—'Little Boot' (from the miniature legionary's uniform the soldiers had given him, with noisy hobnailed boots)—who were being sent away by night to the protection of a Gallic tribe, brought remorse.[52] The whole incident may have been engineered by Germanicus himself; at any rate he knew how to take advantage of it. Discipline was restored in a ferocious spasm of blood-letting, with the legionaries disposing of the ringleaders and unpopular comrades. Tiberius was far from impressed at Germanicus' handling of the mutiny and soon revoked the concession on shorter service. The soldiers' energies were used up in a sequence of ambitious raids into Germany, which did much to restore public confidence at home. But it was to be the end of Roman ambitions to reach the Elbe.

7 The Army of the Early Roman Empire

In a memorandum written shortly before his death in July AD 14 Augustus indicated his view that no attempt should be made by his successor to extend the Empire, but that his energies should be directed towards the consolidation of provinces and territory already held.[1] Rome already controlled directly—or through client kingdoms closely identified with her cause—most of the lands round the Mediterranean basin upon which her security depended. Yet the impetus for expansion remained, and new provinces were added throughout the following century. In some cases, this represented merely the absorption of client kingdoms as suitable opportunities came to hand—Cappadocia (AD 17), Mauretania (AD 40), Thrace (AD 46), eastern Pontus (AD 64), Commagene (AD 72) and Arabia (AD 106). The frontier on the Rhine was pushed forward in stages from the upper reaches of the river, as the Romans strove to find a workable dividing line with the barbarian tribes. At other times the lure of further conquest proved too strong, and the emperors intervened further afield, often without real justification, as in Britain, the attempted conquest of which pulled the Romans further from their Mediterranean focus; Trajan's conquest of Dacia (modern Romania) in AD 101–6 removed a long-standing menace and eased pressure on the Danube defence line, but involved the Romans more than ever in the tribal movements of central Europe. In the East the age-old rivalry with Parthia required a periodic demonstration of Roman strength and resolution, involving the kingdom of Armenia to which both powers laid claim. The reader may recall the outburst of Domitius Corbulo, legate of the Lower German army, when instructed by Claudius in AD 47 to stop aggressive forward movements against the Chauci of the north German plain—*beati quondam duces Romani* (the Roman generals of old were the lucky ones).[2] The event shows not only Claudius' good sense, but the consciousness among Roman commanders of a heroic past which they felt drawn to emulate.

The Roman army of the Empire was a professional force of legionaries, auxiliaries and fleet personnel who enlisted for extended periods and who regarded the army as a lifetime's occupation. Enlistment was not 'for the duration' of a particular war, but for 25 years (26 in the navy), and men were sometimes retained even longer.

LEGIONS

The legion of the Empire was a force of between 5000 and 6000 men (surprisingly the precise total is nowhere reliably attested), organised into 10 cohorts, and armed, dressed and equipped in uniform fashion, with bronze helmets (fig. 39), mail shirts (later replaced by 'segmented' iron cuirasses), a curving rectangular shield, the short Spanish sword, a dagger, and two javelins, of differing weight. By the mid-first century AD, if not before, the array of equipment had reached a more or less permanent form. The rectangular *scutum* was introduced in place of the traditional oval shape, perhaps under Augustus, although the oval shield was retained by the Praetorians (see pl. 20) as part of their parade-equipment, and for a time by other legionaries (pl. 19d). There may have been a longer changeover period than we might at first suppose.

A favourite battle line-up was the *triplex acies* (the 'triple line' of cohorts), but a double line is also attested, and the very flexibility of the cohort structure allowed almost any variation. The cohort was and remained the chief tactical unit and contained six centuries; the century of 80 men was the basic administrative unit. Each century was divided into 10 squads, each of eight men, who would share a tent on campaign (hence the Latin word *contubernium* used to describe a squad) and a barrack room in a permanent fortress. Attached to each legion was a small group of cavalry, the *equites legionis*, about 120 men in all. The cavalry of the imperial legions were recruited from among the legionaries themselves, with no requirement to own property (as in the Republic), and their chief function seems to have been as escorts and messengers. No independent role was envisaged. These *equites* seem to have been billeted along with the centuries of legionaries, which may help in part to account for the extra length of many legionary barrack-blocks, which can have a dozen or more individual rooms instead of the 10 required for their component *contubernia*.

It might seem therefore that maniples were a thing of the past. In the epigraphic record, which begins to assume importance under Augustus, and provides a flood of evidence about the imperial army, the maniple is nowhere mentioned. For example, construction work carried out by a legion is attributed to the legion as a whole, or to a particular cohort or century. Men are described in army records or on their gravestones as serving in a particular century or cohort, but never in a maniple. Yet some remnants of the Republican system can be detected. The centurions in each cohort retained under the Empire the old titles of the Republic: each cohort had centurions entitled *pilus prior* and *pilus posterior*, *princeps prior* and *princeps posterior*, and *hastatus prior* and *hastatus posterior*. These titles reflected the three-fold division of the old Republic legion into lines of *pilani* (*triarii*), *principes* and *hastati*. Within each cohort the order of seniority among the centurions reflected their former positions in the old battle-lines of the Republic. The senior centurion of each cohort was the *pilus prior*, followed by the *princeps prior* and the *hastatus prior*; then by the three *posterior* centurions in the same order. We could suppose that each *prior* centurion in fact continued (as in the Republic) to command the pair of centuries which made up the maniple, but no source, literary or epigraphic, gives any hint that he did. The lack of epigraphic references to maniples indicates that the term lacked any practical significance, though Roman historians of the Early Empire continued to use the word *manipulus* to denote a 'company' or 'group' of soldiers, and *manipularis* for an ordinary soldier in the ranks; there are no implications for current organisational structure.[3] Ground-plans of fortresses and forts often show pairs of barracks facing each other, as at Numantia under the Republic.

THE FIRST COHORT

A growing body of evidence seems to show that the First Cohort of the legion (the *cohors prima*) was for a time organised differently from the others. The ground plan of the Inchtuthil fortress in Perthshire (Scotland), which dates to c. AD 84–86 (fig. 47), shows clearly that the First Cohort of the occupying legion (probably *XX Valeria Victrix*) had only five centuries, not the usual six, and that these five centuries were of double size, i.e. they contained some 160 men instead of eighty. Epigraphic evidence from this time and later attests only five centurions in the cohort, their titles being *primus pilus*, *princeps*, *hastatus*, *princeps posterior* and *hastatus posterior*. There was no post of *primus pilus posterior*. At Inchtuthil the barracks of the centuries of the First Cohort face inwards in pairs, and are fronted by five small courtyard houses; the most elaborate of these houses, equipped with a hypocaust to provide underfloor central heating, lay

INCHTUTHIL : GENERAL PLAN OF THE LEGIONARY FORTRESS

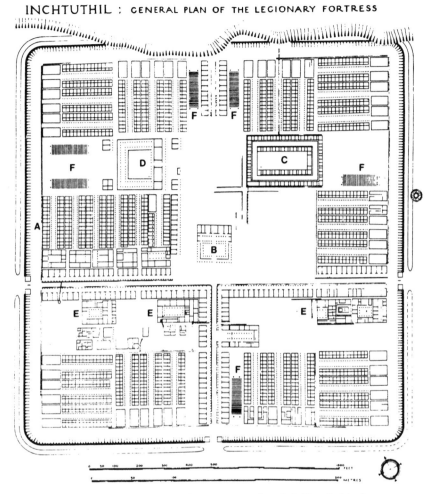

47 Legionary fortress for one legion at Inchtuthil (Perthshire), Scotland (*after Richmond*); 53 acres (21.5 hectares). Most of the ground-area was taken up with barracks of individual centuries, arranged in groups of six (i.e. in cohorts), except for those of the First Cohort **a** which lay next to the headquarters building **b**; see p. 174 for discussion. Notice also the hospital **c**, workshop **d**, tribunes' houses **e** and granaries **f**. This is the most complete plan, preserved in the Richmond papers at the Ashmolean library, Oxford. (Reproduced by permission of the Librarian)

nearest to the headquarters. It was surely the house of the *primus pilus*. In effect each centurion of the First Cohort commanded a double century, of maniple size. The vivid picture of legionary organisation provided by Inchtuthil has perhaps been too readily accepted as standard for legionary bases of all periods throughout the Empire. The extra size and unusual organisation of the First Cohort may be a Flavian innovation, the extra manpower for the cohort being provided by the grafting on to it of the body of reservist *veterani* (above, p. 150) which had continued to exist as a separate group until this time. Yet we might still wonder whether the unusual organis-ation of the First Cohort goes back to the Republic.[4] At any rate we must await a more comprehensive (or comprehensible) ground-plan of a legionary fortress of the Julio-Claudian age to become available before much more can be said on the matter.

HIERARCHY OF COMMAND

The legion was commanded under the Empire by a *legatus legionis*. We have already seen that by the end of Augustus' reign legates were being appointed to a specific legion. Legates under the Republic could be of almost any age and seniority, but in the Early Empire most had already been praetors, and from the Flavian period this became the rule; legateship of a legion now had a definite place in the hierarchy of office and promotion. The post was held for about three years, and a successful or at least non-controversial tenure would lead without much delay to the prefecture of a Treasury at Rome or the governorship of a small province.

Below the legate there came as ever the military tribunes. It seems that one post was usually reserved for a senator (*tribunus laticlavius*, whose toga had the senatorial 'broad stripe'), and five were assigned to equestrians (*tribuni angusticlavii*, 'narrow-stripe' tribunes). So far as we can tell, the role of the tribunes was to act as administrative assistants or advisers to the legate, and they held no definite military command, (say) over individual cohorts. The senatorial tribune would be in his late teens or early twenties, enjoying (or enduring) his first taste of the military life, under the close supervision of the legate. In the hierarchy of command the senatorial tribune always ranked next to the legate, by virtue of his 'noble' birth. Next in order of seniority came not the remaining five tribunes, but the *praefectus castrorum*, the prefect of the camp. This post is not heard of under the Republic, when the tribunes had general charge of laying out and maintaining order in the camp. The earliest record of a *praefectus castrorum* belongs in 11.[5] Under Augustus and his immediate successors we find ex-tribunes and former chief centurions (*primi pili*) being designated as camp prefect, but by the later Julio-Claudians it had become customary for the post to be held by a man who had just demitted office as *primus pilus*; it would be his last post before retirement. Obviously the job required considerable and detailed knowledge of the legion, its personnel and the daily round of duties. When the tribunes declined in experience in the Late Republic, it was natural that the post should be transferred to a centurion. Though it has been argued that the prefect was appointed to a camp rather than to a legion (so that when two or more legions were encamped together, there could be only one *praefectus castrorum*), it is much more likely that from the first each legion had its *praefectus*; certainly Varus' army of three legions in Germany in AD 9 had three *praefecti*— one was left at Aliso, and the other two were with the army on the march.[6] The *praefectus castrorum* had, as his name would imply, general charge of the encampment or base—its cleanliness and sanitation. In addition he saw to the maintenance of the artillery, the medical services and hospital, and supervised weapons training. In general, as the reader will have observed, the *praefectus castrorum* provided a degree of professionalism and continuity, which the two senatorial officers might seem to lack. In Egypt the *praefectus* was the commander of each legion, in the absence of the legate and senatorial tribune (Egypt was barred to senators). After the two legions had been combined in one camp at Nicopolis, a single specially-selected *praefectus* appears to have exercised command over both.

Next in order of seniority within the legion came the five equestrian tribunes. Under Augustus these tribunes had sometimes come from among the centurionate, so that they already possessed some military experience, and went on to a command with the auxiliary cavalry or in the Guard. Claudius, in an attempt to regulate the sequence of military appointments held by equestrians, ordained that the regular sequence should be *praefectus cohortis* (i.e. of a cohort of auxiliary infantry), then *praefectus equitum*, and finally *tribunus militum legionis*.[7] Obviously he felt that a command over citizen troops ought to be the senior position. But this did not become the regular sequence. From the reign of Nero, or at least from the Flavian period, it was normal to serve first as *praefectus cohortis*, then as *tribunus militum*, and finally *praefectus equitum* (or, as it was more normally entitled by that time, *praefectus alae*). The legionary tribune under the Empire held, as we have seen, no independent command, so that his downgrading vis-à-vis the auxiliary prefects should not be surprising. Thus from the Flavian period an equestrian tribune would already have seen service in the auxiliaries, and so be able (if asked) to bring to the legate some practical advice on the handling and disposition of the auxiliary forces in his command area. Equally the equestrian officer would have the chance to see a legion in action from within, a help towards his own decision-making when (or if) he went on to further commands, in the auxiliary cavalry. Most equestrian tribunes would be in their late 20s or early 30s on appointment, and the most successful were destined for posts as procurators in later life.

In the pre-Marian army the tribunes of the first four legions to be levied each year (this was the normal size of a consular army) were elected in the popular assembly from suitably qualified candidates (above, p. 40). We have no record of this procedure in the last generation of the Republic when consular legions were only rarely raised. However in the Augustan age a number of inscriptions report equestrians who served as *tribunus militum a populo* (military tribune 'by the people's vote' or 'elected by the people'). We might think to see here a relic of the old system continuing or newly revived. Rather it seems that such posts were entirely honorary, and were conferred on local worthies throughout Italy. The intention may have been to recall the old Republican tradition, but successful candidates were not expected or intended to officer a legion in the field. The *praefectus fabrum*, who in the Late Republic had served as aide-de-camp to a general in the field, continued to have this role down to Claudius; thereafter, though the post continued to exist, it seems to have become an honorary position, held by young equestrians, often with no military aspirations, either on the staff of a senatorial proconsul or a senior magistrate at Rome.

THE CENTURIONS

Below the tribunes was the chief centurion, the *primus pilus*, who commanded the first century of the first cohort and had charge of the legionary eagle. The close link between the *primus pilus* and the eagle is confirmed by relief sculpture. The eagle-standard is a common motif on the tombs of *primipilaris* centurions (pl. 14a).[8] The centurions of the legion, including the *primus pilus*, numbered 59 in all. Within the centurionate itself there was a fixed order of seniority, only partly understood today. In general it seems that the centurions of the tenth cohort were junior to those of the ninth, and so on, so that promotion could consist of a movement towards a lower numbered cohort, i.e. towards the right in the old Republican battle-lines. At the same time, a centurion who commanded any *prior* century (of the pair making up a maniple) seems to have been senior to any commander of a *posterior* century, with the exception of the First Cohort.

The centurions of the First Cohort were collectively known, at least from the time of Caesar, as the *primi ordines* ('the first ranks'). Some have supposed that under the Empire this phrase also encompassed the senior centurions of each of the other cohorts, but (*inter alia*) the ground-plan of the Inchtuthil fortress shows (at least for the Flavian period) that the *primi ordines* were just five in number: five little courtyard houses (not much smaller than those of the tribunes) lay in front of the centuries of the First Cohort; all the centurions of the other nine cohorts, including the *pilus prior* in each, occupied the normal small apartments at the end of their century's barrack block. The ambition of every centurion was to reach the First Cohort, i.e. the *primi ordines*, and within it to rise to be *primus pilus*. This was the pinnacle of success for the ordinary soldier, his equivalent of the senator's consulship. The post of *primus pilus* under the Republic, and almost certainly under the Empire too, was a one-year appointment. Initially of course the legion itself had only a life of one year, and even in Caesar's time, when legions were retained over a number of years, a man who had been *primus pilus* could, after his year of office, and if he was remaining in the army, revert to a centurion's position. The post automatically elevated the holder under the Empire into the Equestrian Order, and the way was now open for a *primus pilus* to move on to the post of *praefectus castrorum* or (for especially able candidates) to a tribunate in the Rome garrisons, and finally a procuratorship.[9]

On average a man of reasonable literacy and good conduct could reach the centurionate in 15–20 years. Most centurions were enlisted men promoted after long service; others were transferred to be legionary centurions from the Guard after completing the standard 16 years of service in Rome. A minority were directly commissioned *ex equite Romano* (i.e. from among men of the equestrian property status). It would be attractive to see here some continuation of the Republican tradition of service by the *ordo equester*. Rather it seems that these equestrians could be intended as a fast-stream of entrants, intended for quick promotion. The fact that they considered the centurionate at all, as opposed to service as a prefect or tribune, is a useful indicator of the centurion's status. The centurions should not be thought of as sergeants, but as middle ranking officers, company commanders. They provided continuity of standards and traditions. Equally however they must have been bastions of conservatism, averse to innovation and change.

Below the centurionate there was a host of junior posts, positions and titles, either in the administration of the legion as a whole, or the individual century (which was the basic administrative unit). Many grades of craftsmen and technicians are also reported. Only a few such posts are attested epigraphically before the close of the first century AD, but it is difficult to suppose that this hierarchy had not come into being much earlier.

RECRUITMENT

Legionaries under the Empire were mostly volunteers, drawn initially from Italy (especially the north), but increasingly from the provinces. Statistics based on nomenclature and the origins of individuals show that of *all* legionaries serving in the period from Augustus to Caligula, some 65 per cent were Italians; for the period of Claudius and Nero the percentage was 48 per cent, and in the Flavian period and up to Trajan (i.e. to AD 117) the figure was 21 per cent. Thereafter the contribution of Italians to the manpower of the legions was negligible. The figures presented above refer to *all* legionaries; however it can be easily seen that there quickly opened up a dichotomy in recruitment patterns between the western and eastern provinces, with legions in the West drawing upon Gaul, Spain, and Northern Italy, while those stationed in eastern provinces very quickly harnessed the local sources of manpower. An inscription from Coptos near Thebes in southern Egypt, which appears to belong within the reign of Augustus, names 36 soldiers serving in two legions of the garrison there.[10] All but three of the men came from the eastern provinces: Asia, Galatia and Syria in particular. Most were non-citizens by birth, given the citizenship and Roman names on enlistment. It will be remembered that even in the Civil War generals based east of the Adriatic had made increasing use of local material, whatever the civic status or cultural background of the individual. At least one Galatian legion was accepted wholesale by Augustus into the permanent army (above, p. 141).

It seems clear that Augustus whenever possible avoided the forcible conscription of Italians, except at the time of the Varus emergency. His complaint at that time of a *penuria iuventutis* (a dearth of young men) does not imply that the population had fallen dramatically, rather that Italy's youth were unwilling to come forward of their own accord as volunteers; he severely punished an *eques* who deliberately cut off the thumbs of his two sons to disqualify them from military service.[11] In AD 23 Tiberius formally discontinued attempts to persuade Italians to enlist; only the vagabond and the destitute had been coming forward.[12] Instead he turned to the provinces as the chief source of willing recruits, both the descendants of Roman colonists and residents, and the increasingly Romanised native populations. The decision by Augustus to prefer a long service professional army initiated a gradual change in its racial composition. Instead of being a Roman army in the strict sense—made up of Romans or even of Italians—it now became an army defending Rome. The impact on the army of long service far from the Mediterranean homeland is graphically shown in Tacitus' account of the civil wars of AD 68–69. Legionaries of Vitellius' Rhine army, marching through northern Italy in the spring of AD 69, seemed to the local residents an uncouth and foreign band.[13] At the second battle of Cremona, in October of the same year, members of the Syria-based *legio III Gallica* turned at dawn to greet the rising sun in oriental fashion.[14] Legionaries of the Rhine army shared common bonds with the civilians at Cologne.[15] The same legionaries found the Italian summer unbearably hot (like Celtic invaders of earlier centuries); many succumbed to disease, especially those who were encamped at Rome in the Trastevere district, and others who attempted to quench their thirst by drinking from the Tiber.[16]

TRANSFORMATION OF THE LEGIONS

Many of the men had served half a lifetime on the frontier, which now seemed more of a normal environment than the homelands they had now all but forgotten. Fresh dispositions and postings for the legions after AD 70 helped to break up local ties for a time, but the trend towards localised recruitment continued to gather pace, so that the area from which the legion drew its recruits was shrinking, firstly to the province where it was stationed, then to the immediate vicinity of the fortress. Many recruits were the illegitimate sons of serving soldiers or veterans. This transformation is one which has been experienced by many developed societies, by which the burdens of military service are shifted from the well-off to the disadvantaged; 'a rich man's war and a poor man's fight' is an adage which can be applied to the Roman as well as to more modern worlds. Yet while existing legions drew most of their recruits from the adjacent provinces, new legions were always raised in Italy itself, perhaps in deference to tradition or to avoid disrupting normal recruiting patterns (Appendix 3). Italians continued to supply the bulk of recruits for the Praetorians and Urban cohorts.

The average age of recruits on enlistment (as established by information culled from gravestones which give a legionary's length of service as well as age of death) was between 18 and 23. The lower legal limit was 17, though we do find a number of even younger men, perhaps recruited in a time of crisis, or deceiving the recruiting officers as to their true age, or forgetting (or hiding) their real age in middle life. About half the recruits survived their 25 or more years of service to earn discharge. This is not so much an index of the high casualty rates of ancient warfare as of the low life-expectancy of the times. One survey has suggested that soldiers were more likely to reach their early 40s than civilians; soldiers were well and regularly fed, and cared for by an efficient medical service.

Those soldiers who did survive mostly preferred to remain after discharge in the province they knew, where they had made friends and acquired 'wives', and where they may have established business interests, and even bought some land in anticipation of retirement. Sometimes the emperors established veteran-colonies in the provinces, in which each man received a plot of land in lieu of his gratuity. But it seems that most did receive their reward in cash, and stayed either in the settlements which grew up alongside long established fortresses, or in a larger town not too far away.

THE AUXILIARIES

Under the Empire the *auxilia* were drawn from a wide range of peoples throughout the provinces, especially on the fringes of the Empire. Those units raised in the western provinces generally took their names from a tribe or region, those in the east from a city; this dichotomy reflects the origin of the latter in the local defence forces of particular principalities, and of course the greater urbanisation of the eastern provinces. They acted as the army's light infantry and cavalry (pl. 19b, 19c). As we have seen, the infantry were organised into cohorts and the cavalry into wings (*alae*)—this term had been applied under the Republic to the Allied contingents, both infantry and cavalry, which operated on the flanks of the legions; under the Empire it was restricted to cavalry. In the Civil Wars contingents of auxiliaries varied in size; there was no set total. But by the early Empire, and perhaps already under Augustus, the numbers in each regiment were standardised. Most cohorts and *alae* contained about 480–500 men (and were consequently entitled *quingenaria* i.e. 'five hundred strong'). But from the time of Nero, or more certainly from the Flavian period, larger-sized units, called *cohortes milliariae* and *alae milliariae* ('thousand strong') were formed and contained between 800 and 1000 soldiers (fig. 49). In addition there were mixed units of infantry and cavalry, the so-called *cohortes equitatae*. Already in Gaul Caesar had employed mixed units of Germans, which usually

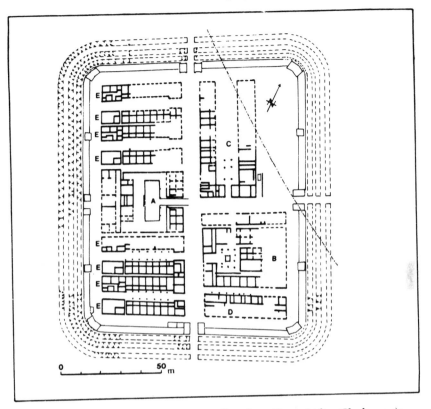

48 Auxiliary fort at Valkenburg, Holland, c. 40 AD (*After Glasbergen*); 3.7 acres (1.5 hectares), probably built for a *cohors quingenaria equitata*. Notice headquarters **a**, prefect's house **b**, 'long barracks' **c**, hospital **d** and barracks **e**

had cavalry and infantry in equal numbers (above, p. 101), but it is probably wrong to envisage a direct line of descent: the proportion of infantry to cavalry in a *cohors equitata* was probably 4:1, and we have no evidence that in battle they were supposed to fight as a composite group. The cohorts were organised into centuries and *contubernia* on the legionary model; thus a normal *cohors quingenaria* contained six centuries of 80 men. The milliary cohorts had 10 centuries of 80 men. The *ala quingenaria* was divided into 16 troops (*turmae*) of horsemen, each of 32 men, making 512 in total. An *ala milliaria* had 24 troops of 32 men (768 total). Cohorts which were *equitata* counted some cavalry in addition, four and eight *turmae* according to whether the cohort was *quingenaria* or *milliaria*, making totals of 608 and 1056.

Initially, as we have seen, many auxiliary regiments were

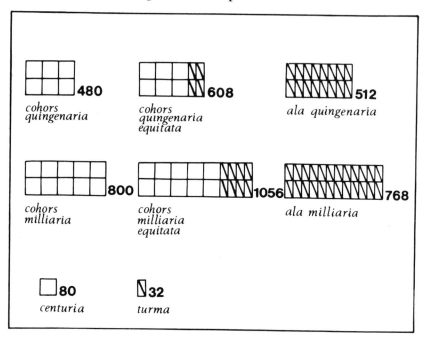

49 Regiments of the *auxilia*: Comparative sizes. However, the centuries in *cohortes equitatae* may have contained about 60 men rather than 80, so reducing the overall totals

commanded by their own chieftains; others had from the beginning ex-centurions or ex-legionary tribunes in command. But by the beginning of the Flavian period, with the rationalisation of command-sequences and the lessons of the civil war and native revolts of AD 69–70 very much in mind (many auxiliary units under their own tribal aristocracies had deserted), the prefectures of *cohortes* and *alae* of auxiliaries were the preserve of equestrians. The regular sequence was *praefectus cohortis—tribunus legionis—praefectus alae* (above, p. 177). The picture was complicated by the creation of the 'milliary' units, whose commanders had to be properly graded within the system. Thus we find that the commander of a *cohors milliaria* with the title *tribunus* was equated in seniority with the tribunate of a legion (so that it could be held as an alternative to the tribunate); the command of an *ala milliaria* was judged to be the most senior post of all, and held after the prefecture of an ordinary *ala*. Centurions ceased from the Flavian period to be offered commands in the *auxilia*; thereafter all those senior centurions thought capable of higher command went to Rome to be tribunes in the cohorts of the garrison there.

It would seem that at first no rewards were offered to auxiliaries on completion of service. Tiberius made some individual grants of citizenship to long-serving individuals, but from Claudius' time citizenship and *conubium* (that is, regularisation of existing or future marriages, so that any children would be citizens also) were established as the due rewards for a man who had completed his 25 years under arms. This was an important landmark in the integration of the auxiliaries into, and their acceptance as part of, the regular military structure. It seems likely that most of the auxiliaries of the Early Empire were conscripted, though some must always have been volunteers. Many regiments served at first in or close to their own tribal zone. The reader may recall unrest in AD 26 among Thracian auxiliaries at the likelihood that they would be posted to other areas;[17] Thrace at this time was a client kingdom, and not yet formally a province. A great many of the auxiliary units on the Rhine in AD 69 were from local tribes, and so the more easily persuaded to defect to the nationalist Civilis. But after the suppression of this revolt, most were disbanded or transferred to distant provinces. For a while, recruitment was kept up from the tribe of origin, but by the later first century the regiments of auxiliaries, like the legions, were undergoing a shrinkage in the area of recruitment, and ceased to maintain an ethnic composition, though traditions of weaponry, religion and dress might continue for a while. This loss of ethnic homogeneity by itself removed the *raison d'être* for the employment of native chieftains in command, and they fade from sight. Only in the case of some eastern regiments, especially archers from Syria and the Levant, can we detect a continuing flow of recruits from their native districts (pl. 17c). The citizen cohorts (above, p. 152) which had been formed under Augustus likewise continued for a time to preserve their separateness, and to draw recruits from free-born citizens, but they too were eventually assimilated to the remainder of the auxiliaries, and took in non-citizens of any origin. Sometimes, but probably not before the Flavian period, a non-citizen auxiliary regiment could be given citizenship en masse, in the field, in return for sterling service; the unit itself henceforth employed the designation *C(ivium) R(omanorum)*, but all future recruits remained non-citizens until discharge—citizenship went only to those serving at the moment of award.

Initially there had been a sharp distinction between citizens who served in the legions and non-citizens who went into the auxiliaries. But gradually the distinction became blurred. We have already seen that non-citizens were being accepted into the legions even under Augustus. So too citizens are found in the auxiliaries; perhaps these were men who had failed to meet the physical requirements for legionary service, or who saw in the auxiliaries a less arduous regimen with better hopes of advancement. By the close of the Julio-Claudian period, a man's physical and mental attributes could be more important than his family background and status in determining which branch of the armed services he was likely to enter.

THE NAVY

Mention should also be made of the imperial navy. After Actium, as we have seen, Augustus concentrated his ships at two bases, Misenum and Ravenna, to watch the western and eastern Mediterranean. These two ports continued to be the chief bases of the Roman fleets for three centuries or more. Under the Empire, the fleets had, we may think, not much to do. Little is heard about piracy or other seaborne hazards. The ships served to transport troops to new postings, and protect the grain supply to the city. Detachments from both Misenum and Ravenna were based in Rome, to handle the awnings at theatres and amphitheatres there. The overall manpower of both fleets remained at a high level, with about 10,000 sailors at each base. Under Augustus and his immediate successors the fleets were commanded by equestrian officers, often ex-legionary tribunes, and later by freedmen of the Emperor's household. But after AD 70 the commands were integrated into the equestrian civil service, and became two of the most senior posts; the Elder Pliny, encyclopaedist, naturalist and a senior procurator in the government service, was prefect of the fleet at Misenum when he lost his life in the eruption of Vesuvius in AD 79.[18] Professional admirals in the Hellenistic mould, briefly renascent in the Civil Wars of the Late Republic, are not heard of again, nor (with very few exceptions) are the squadrons of the eastern dynasts; these were incorporated along with the kingdoms and principalities into the Roman system. Control of a fleet no longer required any professional skills in seafaring, or a particular interest in naval warfare; administrative competence was the only expertise demanded. Detached squadrons on the Rhine, Danube and the English Channel played a more serious role in the maintenance of security in the frontier context. Here again their commanders were equestrians in the course of a procuratorial career.

The fleets' manpower was drawn from free-born provincials, like the auxiliaries; slaves were not used, as in popular modern tradition.

The Ravenna fleet drew a substantial number of men from the Balkan provinces and Pannonia, the Misenum fleet from Sardinia, Corsica, Africa and Egypt. No experience of sailing, or a home on the coast, were deemed of special importance in the selection of men, any more than in modern navies. The men served 26 years (one year more than the legionaries and auxiliaries), receiving—like the latter —citizenship and regularisation of marriage on discharge. From the time of Vespasian sailors began to use Latin names, and this general improvement in status is marked also by the award, probably made under Domitian, of the title *praetoria* to both main fleets, indicating an acceptance of their role in the central defence of the Emperor's position. The title matches the *cohortes praetoriae* of the imperial bodyguard. The civil war of AD 68–69 saw the creation of *legio I Adiutrix* from the fleet at Misenum, and *legio II Adiutrix* from Ravenna; the latter saw service under Agricola in Britain. The title *Adiutrix* indicates that they were envisaged at first as offering 'Support' or 'Assistance' to the regular forces. It seems that founder members of both legions remained non-citizens until discharge, but fresh drafts were drawn from the normal sources thereafter so that they were quickly assimilated. After Actium we hear no more of legions serving on shipboard, presumably because the military presence of such heavily armed infantry was deemed no longer necessary.

THE PRAETORIAN GUARD

In Rome itself the chief military force was the Praetorian Guard, which Augustus had set at nine cohorts, each of 500 men. Its duties were the protection of the Emperor—one cohort at a time stood guard at the Palace, carrying weapons but in civilian dress. The Guard was commanded by equestrian prefects, sometimes two in number (as under Augustus), or more often one. The post could be extremely influential, and Aelius Sejanus (sole prefect from AD 14) was quick to recognise the potential, in controlling access to, and the flow of information to, Tiberius, especially after the emperor's retirement to Capri in AD 26. Sejanus in AD 23 had persuaded Tiberius to authorise the concentration of the cohorts in a new camp on the eastern suburbs of the city, the *castra praetoria*. Substantial remains of its walls are standing today, and the camp still houses the barracks of Rome's resident military garrison. It may also have been Sejanus who secured an increase in the size of the Guard, probably to 12 cohorts.[19] On parade the highly paid Praetorians wore ornate helmets and breastplates, and retained the oval *scutum* of the

Republic which the legionaries had discarded in favour of the familiar rectangular shield (pl. 20). On campaign, as depicted on Trajan's Column, their equipment is indistinguishable from that of the legionaries themselves. Each cohort was commanded by a tribune, usually an ex chief-centurion of a legion who had held similar commands in the *Vigiles* and the Urban Cohorts.

Under Vitellius (AD 69) the number of cohorts was raised to 16, partly by infusions from legionaries of the Rhine army; the strength of each cohort was increased to 1000.[20] The legionaries on the frontiers had always been jealous of the high pay and easy life of the Praetorians (above, p. 170). By transferring selected legionaries to the Guard Vitellius satisfied their craving, and also restored the Guard for a while to the position it had held in the Civil War of the Late Republic—that of a *corps d'élite* within the Roman army. Vespasian seems to have reduced the number of cohorts to nine (the original total), though the strength of each cohort probably remained at 1000; somewhat later in the first century Domitian brought the number of cohorts up to ten. From his time therefore the Guard resembled a legion in its organisation, but it was much more powerful—equivalent to two legions in manpower. The Guard continued in the Early Empire to be recruited by direct intake from Italians, with a sprinkling of men from the more civilised provinces. Evidently Italians were happy to join the Guard, with its high pay, short service-term (16 years in the Early Empire), and residence in the capital. There was of course far less chance of injury or death. From the Flavian period, when the cohorts were regularly required to go on campaign when the Emperor himself took the field, an élite cavalry unit—the *equites singulares Augusti*—was formed from men selected from the *alae* of the provincial garrisons, to act as the Guard's cavalry arm.

URBAN COHORTS

Other bodies of troops were to be found in the capital: the Urban Cohorts, three in number, under tribunes, which formed the day-to-day police force of the capital. Their members served for 20 years, under the control of the *praefectus Urbi*. The Urban Cohorts bore the numerals *X–XII* in continuation of the original Praetorian sequence. Already under the Julio-Claudians other Urban Cohorts were brought into being, and outstationed at Pozzuoli (*cohors XV*) and Ostia (*cohors XVII*), to protect the warehouses full of newly-arrived corn, at Carthage (the collection point for African corn before its shipment to Italy), and at Lyons (*cohors XIII*), presumably to protect the mint there. Like the Praetorians the Urban Cohorts were drawn from Italians. Initially each cohort was 500 men strong, but they seem to have been doubled in size by Vitellius—who added legionaries to their number (probably these were men for whom no place had been found in the Guard). From the Flavian period we find *X, XI, XII* and *XIV* stationed in Rome, with *XIII* at Carthage and a reconstituted unit, *cohors I Flavia Urbana*, at Lyons; it is not known whether others were still at Ostia or Pozzuoli.

THE *VIGILES*

Finally, the *cohortes Vigilum*, the city's fire-brigade, recruited from freedmen who served for six years. Each of the seven cohorts had a permanent base (*castra*) and two *excubitoria* (i.e. fire-stations where those on duty awaited the call to action), one of which was in each of the two regions under its control. Like many modern fire-brigades the *Vigiles* were under military command—their tribunes had seen service as *primi pili* in the legions (and would go on to similar commands as tribunes in the Urban Cohorts and the Guard); their centurions were former Praetorians. Their commander, the *praefectus Vigilum*, a senior procurator, had jurisdiction over crimes committed in the city by night, when of course many of his men would be actively on patrol. But the military role of the *Vigiles* should not be overestimated; they carried no weapons. The range of equipment which inscriptions attest (buckets, axes, pumps, blankets and ladders) is entirely consistent with their primary role in the fighting and dousing of fires. They also had catapults for the demolition of dangerous or threatened buildings. Yet the *Vigiles* could influence events: they played a significant part in the fall of Sejanus in AD 31. While Sejanus himself sat in the Senate House listening to a deliberately long-winded communiqué from Tiberius on Capri, Sutorius Macro, a former *praefectus Vigilum*, acting on the Emperor's instructions, dismissed the detachment of Sejanus' Praetorians who had been guarding the building, and put in their places some *Vigiles* who remembered him and were prepared to accept his authority. This sealed Sejanus' fate.

HIGHER COMMAND STRUCTURE

In the organisation of higher command, the line of development from the Late Republic is clearly seen. In each province controlled by the Emperor, supreme civil and military command was combined under a *legatus Augusti pro praetore*; in a province with more than a single legion (and in the Early Empire there could be up to four in one province), the legate was an ex-consul. Small provinces with a single legion were ruled by a legate who was an ex-praetor; in such cases the legate also commanded the legion itself. He had both the military and civil control over a specific area, like the legates of the Late Republic (above, p. 40). All the legates were appointed by the Emperor—he had 'delegated' to them some portion of his office as proconsul. Within a consular province each legion was commanded by a *legatus Augusti legionis* who was likewise appointed directly by the Emperor. It seems likely that each legionary legate had command over the auxiliary regiments brigaded with or attached to the legion. In Britain it has been suggested that in the second century AD the legate of *II Augusta* (based at Caerleon from the Flavian period onwards) had general supervision over the auxiliary regiments based in South Wales; the legate of *XX Valeria* at Chester had control over those in North Wales and the West Midlands; and the legate of *VI Victrix* at York had control over the garrisons northwards to Hadrian's Wall and beyond.

This fragmentation of command was in part a deliberate political decision to restrict the power of an individual legate, in the interests of the Emperor's continued tenure of his office. The system worked well enough for two centuries. Noticeable also is a conscious effort to secure a balance of force throughout the Empire. For example, in AD 73 (a suitable terminal point for our study, when forces had been reorganised in the wake of the civil war of AD 68–70 and the Jewish War of AD 66–73), there were four legions in Lower Germany and three in Upper Germany (fig. 51). In the Danube area two legions could be found in Pannonia, four in Moesia and one in Dalmatia. In the East there were three in Syria, one in Judaea and two in Cappadocia, together with two in Egypt. The total of 28 is made up by the four now in Britain, one in Africa and one in Spain. It will be noticed that the Rhine group totalled eight, the Danube group seven, and the eastern legions eight. The presence in an adjacent province of a group of legions of roughly similar size was an obvious deterrent to an ambitious legate. For example, when Camillus Scribonianus persuaded the then garrison of Dalmatia (*VII* and *XI*) to declare against Claudius in AD 42, the legionaries, when they perceived that they could get no support from the garrisons of Pannonia and Moesia, soon repented of their actions, and a swift change of heart brought them laudatory epithets from Claudius; both became *legio Claudia Pia Fidelis* i.e. 'Claudian, Loyal and Faithful'. The size of the legionary garrisons of a province might change, in response to shifting pressures along the frontiers, but a general balance was maintained.

DEFENCE OF THE EMPIRE

The task of the legions and the auxiliaries under the Empire was the defence of its frontiers, and the maintenance of security in the provinces themselves. The concept of the army acting as a frontier defence force would have been incomprehensible and anathema to the Romans of the Republic. The reign of Augustus had witnessed each year the traditional concentration of troops into a summer camp, as a preparation for active campaigning, and in the autumn a fragmentation of the army to winter billets.

However a pause in the active expansion of the Empire under Tiberius and the gradual pacification of areas already overrun meant that the legions no longer needed to adopt an aggressive posture; when active campaigning became the exception rather than the rule, troops seem to have stayed put more often than not in their *hiberna*, unless some specific project was in hand.[21] We can sense too a shift in emphasis to the maintenance of the Empire's borders and their defence against attack and intrusion. Under Augustus substantial lengths of the 'frontier' were protected by client kingdoms which acted as buffers against more hostile forces beyond. But these client states were gradually eliminated, and Roman forces became directly responsible for the defence of a growing proportion of the Empire's boundaries, against threats whose intensity and direction they were increasingly unable to influence. But the fact that the army was changing to a static defence-force positioned on or near the borders of the Empire was not at first admitted. Theoretically the legions remained poised for further advance. In the preceding pages I have avoided the words 'fort' or 'fortress' as implying permanence of occupation, preferring 'winter-camp' or 'winter-base'. Certainly the transition from 'winter-camp' to permanent base could be quickly accomplished. Already under the Republic, the winter-camps contained stone-built accommodation, and we should not suppose that the legionaries had ever spent the colder winter months in their leather tents. Even at Numantia the internal buildings of the siege-camps encircling the hill-fort were of stone. Under Augustus the *legio IIII Macedonica* at Aguilar was sufficiently sedentary for its *prata* (the legion's pasture-grounds) to be defined by stone markers (above, p. 157). We have before the Empire no clear examples of en-campments—temporary or permanent—built or used by auxiliary regiments. It is clear that they often shared a camp with the legions, when an army was on campaign, and might be brigaded with legionaries in semi-permanent bases. At Dangstetten under Augustus men of *legio XIX* seem to have shared the site with a unit of

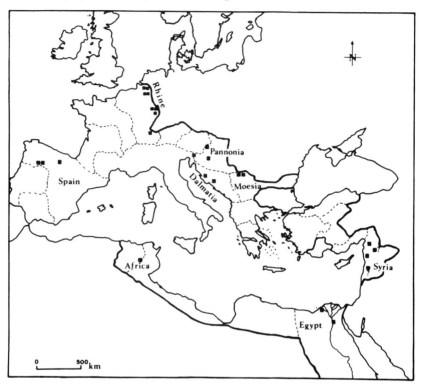

50 The Roman Empire, AD 14, showing distribution of legions

eastern archers, whose distinctive equipment has been found there. But under the Early Empire, when garrisons came to be more and more spread out along the frontiers, forts began to be constructed for individual auxiliary regiments. The earliest fort for which we have a comprehensive plan is Valkenburg in southern Holland (fig. 48), built soon after AD 40.

In the layout of forts and fortresses under the Empire the main features of the Polybian plan can easily be made out. By the Augustan age, and probably earlier, the term *principia* (see above, p. 37) had come to refer to a specific building, the 'headquarters', quite distinct from the *praetorium*, the name now given to the private house of the officer in command. The *principia* now occupies the central position, at the crossroads, with the *praetorium* to one side or behind (see figs 44, 48, 52).

In the western provinces the *hiberna* of the legions can often be identified without difficulty; often two legions were brigaded together. In AD 14 the winter bases of the Lower German legions were at

Vetera (where *V Alaudae* and *XXI Rapax* had been placed together) and at Cologne (*I Germanica* and *XX*); in the Upper province, two or even three legions were at Mainz (*XIV Gemina*, *XVI Gallica* and perhaps *II Augusta*), and the other (*XIII Gemina*) lay to the south, probably at Vindonissa (Windisch). The three Pannonian legions had their winter bases at Poetovio (Ptuj), Siscia (Sisak) and probably Emona. Elsewhere the picture is less clear. Tacitus provides the useful information that in AD 19, of the legions of the Syrian garrison, *X Fretensis* was at Cyrrhus (Kuros), and *VI Ferrata* not far from Laodicea-by-the-Sea (Latakia). Much later, under Nero, we know that *XII Fulminata* was at Raphanaea. No record preserves the location of the winter base of the other legion, *III Gallica*; it may well have shared a base with one of the others. In Egypt the two legions forming the garrison were from the reign of Claudius in a single base at Nicopolis, just to the east of Alexandria. In Africa the single legion (*III Augusta*) was at Ammaedara (Haidra). In Spain the three legions lay in the north-west, with *IIII Macedonica* still at Aguilar and *X Gemina* in a newly identified base at Rosinos de Vidriales south of Astorga, where a site of some 45–50 acres (18–20 hectares) has been detected from the air, and the garrison established by the discovery nearby of a boundary stone of Claudian date naming the legion (I owe this information to the kindness of Dr Patrick Le Roux). This may have been its base from Augustus onwards. The siting of the third legion, *VI Hispaniensis*, remains unknown; the old view, that it probably shared a two-legion camp with *X Gemina*, can no longer be maintained, as the Rosinos site is too small to have housed both. In Dalmatia *VII Macedonica* was at Tilurium (Gardun) and *XI* at Burnum.[22] Tacitus and modern commentators have deprecated the fact that the legions of Syria were seemingly billeted in major towns, to the detriment of discipline, fitness and general morale.[23] We should remember however that it had always been common to billet troops for the winter in towns where they existed. Caesar's troops in Gaul could be found wintering in or beside small towns.[24] Such towns provided facilities and services for the soldiers, especially welcome in winter. The arrival of an army to spend the winter in a town had always been considered a major calamity by provincial communities.[25] Only in the non-urbanised west are winter-camps found in isolated terrain.

A CHANGING ROLE

Even in winter the legions were often grouped in double camps, and in general their disposition represented a concentration of striking

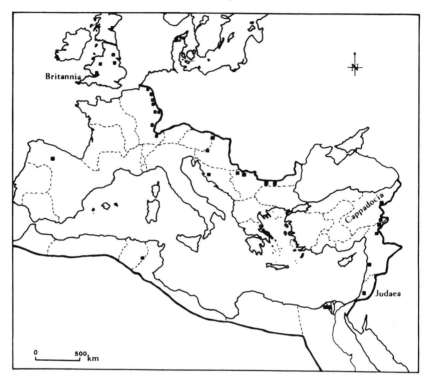

51 The Roman Empire, AD 73, showing distribution of legions

power. Of course there were long gaps between these bases, but this was initially unimportant. But as the army began to adopt a primarily defensive role, surveillance of the frontier line itself began to assume greater importance. In the course of the first century AD, the main groups of legions were split up, and the long river or land borders more regularly patrolled. Similarly, the regiments of auxiliaries were gradually spaced out, between the legionary bases, producing a more continuous cordon. This fragmentation had a political as well as military dimension, in that the number of troops instantly available to a disaffected legate was much reduced. So on the Rhine, the two-legion base at Cologne was abandoned about AD 30 in favour of single bases at Bonn and Neuss; a legion was placed at Strasbourg at much the same time. The two-legion base at Vetera, reconstructed in stone under Nero (fig. 52), was replaced after the battle there during the civil war of AD 69 by a new fortress for just one legion. Finally in 89, after the attempted revolt of the legate of Upper Germany, Antonius Saturninus, the two legions at Mainz were

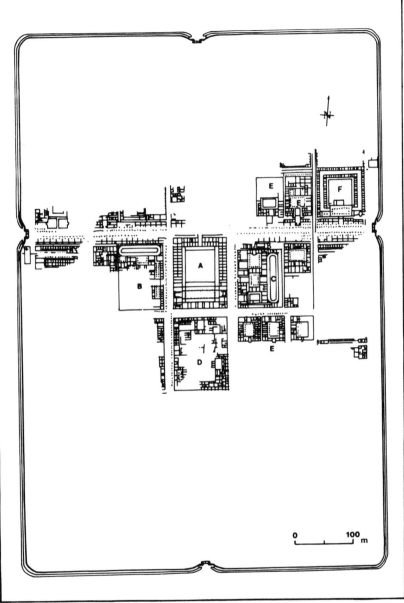

52 Fortress for two legions at Vetera (Xanten), Holland. (*After Bogaers* and *Rüger*). Built in Nero's reign; 138 acres (56 hectares). Note the headquarters building **a**, two legates' houses **b** and **c**, workshops **d**, tribunes' houses **e**, and hospital **f**

separated, and the fortress cut to one legion. Domitian is credited by his biographer with an official ban on double fortresses.[26] In fact the two legions in Egypt continued to occupy a single site at Nicopolis till early in the reign of Hadrian, when one was transferred to allow the reinforcement of the garrison of troublesome Judaea.

In the East we can observe a move away from the cities of northern Syria to the river barrier of the Euphrates; already before the middle of the first century *legio X Fretensis* had moved forward from Cyrrhus to the Euphrates crossing at Zeugma. By AD 72–3, with the establishment of garrisons in Cappadocia and in Judaea, the legions formed a line stretching from Satala in the highlands of eastern Turkey to Jerusalem; later, with the annexation of Arabia under Trajan and the placing of a legion at Bostra, the line between the Black Sea and the Nile Delta could be deemed complete. In Spain and Dalmatia the legionary garrisons were reduced in the course of the century, as the provinces became more settled, and the troops were needed on the northern frontiers. By AD 70 the garrison in Spain was down to one legion, *VII Gemina*, at Leon (which is derived from the word *legio*) among the Asturians; the last legion in Dalmatia (*IIII Flavia*) moved northwards to the Danube in 86. In Africa we can chart the progress of the single *legio III Augusta* to the south-west, from Ammaedara to Theveste (Tebessa), and to Lambaesis.

As the legions and auxiliaries became more static, and widely spaced, the problem of responding to particular threats became more acute. In the Republic, the Senate would levy additional troops. Under the Empire with its large standing army, a major war, or a decisive shift in the pressure along a frontier, could lead to the permanent transfer of one or more legions to new postings. We have already seen that the Varus disaster resulted in a major reorganisation of forces. Under Tiberius the *legio VIIII Hispana* went from Pannonia to Africa for four years to assist *III Augusta* in putting down a native rebellion. When a renewed bout of fighting against Parthia flared up in Nero's reign, and a strong military presence was politically as well as militarily desirable in the East, *IIII Scythica* and *V Macedonica* were moved there from Moesia and *XV Apollinaris* from Pannonia. All three remained in the East throughout the Jewish War of 66–73; *XV Apollinaris* never returned.

When a new province was added to the Empire, a garrison had to be put together to serve in its defence. New legions were sometimes formed—but normally these were not themselves intended for service in the new province. So when an invasion and permanent occupation of Britain became a hard possibility under Caligula, two new legions, *XV* and *XXII*, both entitled *Primigenia* ('First Born'), were formed in advance. Their intended role was as replacements for legions earmarked to join the invasion force: *XV* to release *XX* from Neuss, and *XXII* to replace *XIV Gemina* at Mainz. Both the new legions were put into double-fortresses along with experienced legions. The invasion force which sailed for Britain in the summer of AD 43 consisted of *XX* and *XIV*, along with *II Augusta* which had been at Strasbourg (this base was now left empty) and *VIIII Hispana* from Pannonia. The new legions were not temporary additions to the army list, to be disbanded after the campaign, but permanent accretions.

When a legion was transferred to a different province, the distance involved was usually kept to a minimum. One interesting exception is the movement of *XIV Gemina* from Britain in AD 67, to Italy, in preparation for a leading role in Nero's projected Caspian campaigns—evidently its high reputation for valour in the wake of the Boudican revolt (when it earned the chief credit for the defeat of the rebels) determined the choice. But such transfers could leave a long stretch of frontier virtually undefended, and wholesale transfers became unpopular as legions acquired local links. Therefore the custom developed, especially from the Flavian period, of sending not an entire legion to the flashpoint, but detachments drawn from the various legions of a province. These were termed 'vexillations' (from the *vexillum*, the flag under which such detached groups would be brigaded). Ancient authors often refer to such men as *delecti* or *selecti*; they had been specially 'chosen' to form the task-force. Vexillations from individual legions usually amounted to some 1000 or 2000 men each. It was obviously less disturbing, and quicker, to despatch 1000 or 2000 men from a legion rather than uproot the legion itself. Vexillations could remain detached from their parent legions for many years before finally returning. The use of vexillations to deal with emergencies points the way to the mobile field armies of the Late Empire, which supplemented the static garrison forces of the frontier zones.

CONCLUSION

By the Flavian period of the later first century AD, the imperial army had acquired most of its familiar features, and the great process of transition from Republic to Empire may be judged complete.

'If one looks at the Romans military system, one will recognise that the possession of a large Empire has come into their hands as the prize of their valour, not as a gift of fortune. For this people does not wait for the outbreak of war to practise with weapons nor do they sit idle in peacetime bestirring themselves only in time of need. Rather they seem to have been born with weapons in their hands; never do they take a break from their training or wait for emergencies to arise. Their manoeuvres fall no way short, in the amount of energy expended, of real warfare; but every day each soldier exercises with as much intensity as he would in war. This is the reason why the shock of war affects them so little. No confusion ruins their customary neat formations, nor are they paralysed by fear, or worn out with fatigue. Victory over enemies who have experienced none of this comes sure and certain. One would not be wrong in saying that their manoeuvres are like bloodless battles, and their battles bloodstained manoeuvres. With such splendid planning and organisation, no wonder that the boundaries of their Empire are in the east the Euphrates, in the west the Atlantic Ocean, in the south the new lands of Libya and in the north the Danube and the Rhine. One would easily say that the people who have won this Empire are greater than the Empire itself.'[27]

So wrote Joseph ben Matthias, better known to history as Josephus, who saw the powerful Roman army of Vespasian and his son Titus in action against his Jewish countrymen at the close of Nero's reign, and whose somewhat idealised account of its institutions and routine procedures may serve as a testimony of how much—and yet in a sense how little—the army had really changed in the two centuries or more since Polybius offered a Greek viewpoint on Rome's spectacular rise to pre-eminence in the Mediterranean world.

APPENDIX 1 The Civil War Legions

1a CAESAR'S CONSULAR SERIES

I–IV
  I
  II   in Macedonia, 44; later fighting at Forum Gallorum and Mutina
  III   (later *Gallica*)
  IIII *Macedonica*

1b PANSA'S CONSULAR SERIES

  I
  II   *Sabina* (? = later *II Augusta*)
  III
  IIII *Sorana*
  V   *Urbana*

Note: The later *I Germanica* should belong in one or other series. Pansa's *legio III* may be the future *III Augusta*, given that both *III Gallica* and *III Cyrenaica* were almost certainly with Antony.

2 CAESAR'S GALLIC LEGIONS

V–XIV
  V   *Alaudae*
  VI   *Ferrata*
  VII   (later *Claudia*)
  VIII (later *Augusta*)
  IX
  X   *Equestris* (later *Gemina*)
  XI
  XII   (? = later *Fulminata*)
  XIII
  XIV

Notes: The evidence for continuity into the Empire in the cases of *IX, XI, XIII* and *XIV* is insecure, and it remains possible that the legions we know as *IX*

Appendices

Hispana, XI Claudia, XIII Gemina and *XIV Gemina* were all formed by Octavian in 41–40, or by amalgamation after Actium. In 43 Ventidius formed a legion with the numeral *IX*, evidently recalling Caesar's legion, but its later history is not known, and it may not long have survived. Caesar raised a *legio XV*, but in 50 it was handed over to Pompey (above, p. 102).

3a CAESAR'S LEVY IN 49

XV–?XXXIII

XV	These were perhaps lost in Africa in 49.
XVI	Whether the numbers were re-used now, or later, is not known.
XVII	
XVIII	
XIX	Colonist at Nuceria, 41 (*AE* 1974, 283)
XX	
XXI	Spain, 49 (*B. Alex.* 53)
XXII	
XXIII	
XXIV	
XXV	Africa, 46 (*B. Afr.* 60)
XXVI	Africa, 46–43 (*B. Afr.* 60). Transported to Italy, 43; joined Octavian. Colonists at Luca, 41 (*ILS* 887)
XXVII	Pharsalus, 48 (Caesar BC iii.34); Alexandria, 47; Egypt, 47–42?; Philippi with Liberators?
XXVIII	Spain, 49; Thapsus, 46 (*B. Afr.* 60); Munda, 45?; Italy, 42; Philippi, 42. Colonist at Philippi (*AE* 1924, 55)
XXIX	Thapsus, 46; Africa, 46–43; transported to Rome, 43; joined Octavian, 43. Colonist at Hadria, 41? (*CVSI* 73); tribunes attested at Pola (*ILS* 2229 = *CVSI* 90) and Saturnia (*AE* 1931, 95)
XXX	Spain, 49 (*B. Alex.* 53.5); Thapsus, 46 (*B. Afr.* 60); ?Munda, 45; Colonist, Urso, 45 (*ILS* 2233); ?Philippi, 41. Colonists, Beneventum, 41 (*CVSI* 30, 32, 35, 37 etc.). Colonist, Locri, 36? (*CVSI* 76, with title *Classica* = *ILS* 2232).
XXXI	Crete, ?–41 (*AE* 1933, 199).
XXXII	
XXXIII	Veteran returns home to Terventum, central Italy (*ILS* 2234 = *CVSI* 57).

3b LEGIONS FORMED FROM POMPEY'S BEATEN ARMY, 48

XXXIV–XXXVII?

XXXIV	
XXXV	Macedonia, 44; transferred to Italy; Forum Gallorum and Mutina, 43.

XXXVI   Alexandria, 47 (*B. Alex*. 34.3); Egypt, 47–42? (Liberators)
XXXVII   Zela, 47 (*B. Alex*. 9.3); Egypt, 47–42? (Liberators)
Notes: The total number of Pompeian soldiers accepted into Caesar's army was 24,000; no source reports how many legions were formed. Scholars have argued for three or for four; the latter must be more likely—but even five would be possible.

3c RECRUIT LEGIONS OF 47–44

XXXVIII–?
  XXXVIII
  XXXIX
  XXXX
  XXXXI   Colonists at Tuder (Todi), 36 or 31 (*ILS* 2230–31 = *CVSI* 93–94).
Notes: If the total number of legions in service in 44 has been correctly estimated by scholars at 37, the numerical sequence must reach *XXXXVII*, and could go higher. Legions *XV–XXXVII* would, where they had survived the Civil Wars, be released in 41; those which fought for the Triumvirs received land in Italy. Legions numbered *XXXVIII* and over may have continued to serve, at least until 36, and perhaps until Actium.

3d LEGIO MARTIA

To be included in the above totals, probably in section 3a, is the *legio Martia* whose exploits are recorded by Appian, Dio, Valerius Maximus and Cicero. It was part of the Macedonian garrison in 44, and, on transfer to Italy to become part of Antony's force in the province of Cisalpina, it defected to Octavian, for whom it fought at Forum Gallorum and Mutina. Thereafter it must have returned with Octavian to Rome, and later appears to have been with him during operations in 42 against Sextus Pompeius around Rhegium (only this explains its non-arrival at Philippi). During a crossing of the Adriatic in November 42, the transports carrying the legion were intercepted and the soldiers mostly drowned or were killed. The legion is not heard of again. Its numeral is not reported, but Valerius Maximus (iii.2.19) notes an incident involving the legion, which we know took place in Africa in 46. Legions present in Africa, excluding the veterans, were *XXVI*, *XXVIII*, *XXIX*, *XXX* and another, perhaps *XXV*; hence *Martia* may have been the title attached to one of these five legions, but it has not been possible to establish which.

4 OCTAVIAN'S NEW ORDER OF BATTLE, 41–31

VII, VIII, IIII *Macedonica* brought back from Philippi.
Survivors from Pansa's consular series of 43, to include *II Sabina, IIII Sorana, V Urbana.*

Appendices

Legions left in the west, 42–41, including *XXXXI*
New formations, including:
V (= later *Macedonica*, unless the latter should be identified with *V Urbana* above)
VI (later *Hispaniensis*, afterwards *Victrix*)
IX (later *Hispaniensis*—if not Caesarian)
X *Fretensis*
XI (later *Claudia*—if not Caesarian). Colonists, Ateste (Este), 30.
XII *Victrix* (present at Perusia, 41)
XIII (later *Gemina*—if not Caesarian); S. Italy, 36.
XIV (later *Gemina*—if not Caesarian)
XV (later *Apollinaris*). Colonist, Ateste, 30 or 14?
XVI
XVII
XVIII Colonist, Ateste, 30 or 14?
XIX Colonist, Pisa, 30?
Notes: The numerical sequence may have gone higher, but no records survive.

5 ANTONY'S LEGIONS, 41–30

I–XXIII	reported on his coin series (above, p. 126)	
III	*Gallica*	Tacitus *Hist.* iii.24; Plutarch *Ant.* 42.
VI	*Ferrata*	Coin of Lucius Verus
X	*Equestris*	Colonists, Patrae, 30
V	*Alaudae*	Colonists, Beneventum, 30?
XII	*Antiqua*	Antony's coin series
XVII	*Classica*	do.
XVIII	*Libyca*	do.
VIII		With Pinarius Scarpus in Cyrenaica, 31–30
?IIII	(later *Scythica*)	(duplicate of *IIII Macedonica*)
III	*Cyrenaica*	With Pinarius Scarpus in Cyrenaica?

Notes: Colonists at Beirut (from legions *V* and *VIII Gallica*) and at Antiochia Pisidiae (*V* and *VII*) are conceivably Antonian. *Legio XII Fulminata* is presumably Antonian, and to be identified with *XII Antiqua*; its veterans were settled alongside men from *X Equestris* at Patrae. Notice an early inscription of a *legio VI* at the colony of Byllis in Macedonia (*AE* 1966, 419); perhaps an Antonian soldier.

6 TITLES USED BY THE LEGIONS DURING THE CIVIL WARS

Numeral and title of legion	Literal meaning	Implications of title	Later history of legion
II Sabina	Sabine	formed in the Sabine country, probably by Pansa, in 43	= II Augusta?
II Gallica	Gallic	after service in Gaul (before 35, when veterans were settled at Arausio)	= II Augusta?
IIII Sorana	Soran	formed at the town of Sora in Latium, probably by Pansa, in 43	?
V Gallica	Gallic	after service in Gaul	= V Alaudae?
V Urbana	Urban	formed by Pansa, in 43 and left to defend the city of Rome (*Urbs Roma*)	= V Macedonica?
VI Gemella	Twin	formed by amalgamation	?
VII Paterna	Paternal	after service with Caesar, one of whose titles was *Pater Patriae* (Father of the Nation)	= VII Claudia
VIII Gallica	Gallic	after service with Caesar in Gaul	= VIII Augusta?
VIII Mutinensis	Belonging to city of Mutina (Modena)	after participation in battle of Mutina, 43	= VIII Augusta?
VIIII Gemella	Twin	formed by amalgamation	?
VIIII Triumphalis	Triumphant	after participation in a Triumph at Rome, probably Caesar's in 47	?

Numeral and title of legion	Literal meaning	Implications of title	Later history of legion
X *Equestris*	Mounted or Knightly	after its members were mounted up as cavalry by Caesar, in 58	= X *Gemina*
X *Veneria*	Sacred to Venus	after service with Caesar who claimed descent from Venus	= X *Gemina?*
XII *Antiqua*	Ancient	a claim to descent from Caesar's *legio XII*	= XII *Fulminata?*
XII *Paterna*	Paternal	after service with Caesar	= XII *Fulminata?*
XII *Victrix*	Victorious	after a victory, before 41, when the title appears on a Perusine slingbullet	?
XVII *Classica*	Naval	after service with Antony's fleet, 41–31	disbanded, 31?
XVIII *Libyca*	Naval	after service in Libya under Antony, before 31	disbanded, 31?
XXX *Classica*	Naval	after service at sea	disbanded, 41?
legio Martia	Sacred to Mars	attesting its 'martial' qualities	lost at sea, 42

APPENDIX 2 The Origin and Early History of the Imperial Legions

I Germanica

Formed: ?48 (Caesar's consular series), or 43 (Pansa's consular series). Octavian, 41 onwards; operations against Sextus Pompeius, 36 (Appian. *BC* v.112). Colonists, Luceria, ?30 (*AE* 1969/1970, 158; *AE* 1976, 168, 169 = *CVSI* 82–84). Colonists, Acci, early Augustan ?. Spain, 30–c. 16 BC; Rhine frontier, c. 16 BC–AD 69; disbanded, AD 69.

Emblem: (not known)

Titles: *Germanica*, reflecting service on the Rhine, perhaps under the elder Drusus (or Germanicus, AD 14–16). First attested: *AE* 1976, 515 (Augustan date ?); *ILS* 2342 (Claudian); *AE* 1956, 169. Sir Ronald Syme has suggested that this was the legion deprived of its title *Augusta* in 19; see *JRS* xxiii (1933), 15. But no certain link has been demonstrated.

II Augusta

Formed: ?43 (Pansa's consular series; above, p. 115, 134). Note colonists of a *II Gallica* at Arausio, 36 (*CRAI* 1951, 367) and of a *II Sabina* at Venafrum (*ILS* 2227) which may easily be the same legion. In Spain, 30 BC–?AD 9; Rhine frontier. ?AD 9–43; Britain, AD 43 onwards.

Emblems: capricorn, which should indicate reconstitution by Augustus; pegasus (see above, p. 140).

Title: *Augusta*, reflecting reconstitution or a victory, 27 BC–AD 14. First attested: *ILS* 6948 (before AD 9); J. Roldan Hervas, *Hispania y el ejercito romano* (Salamanca 1974), no. 503 (before AD 9).

III Augusta

Formed: ?43 (Pansa's consular series); *or* Octavian, 41–40; Africa, 30 onwards (or even earlier?).

Emblem: perhaps pegasus (information from Prof. M. Euzennat and Dr Pol Trousset).

Title: *Augusta*, reflecting reconstitution or a victory, 27 BC–AD 14. First attested: *ILS* 6285, 9375 (both Tiberian date).

Appendices

III Cyrenaica

Formed: before 30, perhaps by Lepidus in Africa or Antony. Possibly with Pinarius Scarpus in Cyrenaica, 31–30. Egypt, 30 onwards.

Emblem: (not known)

Title: *Cyrenaica*, from service in province of that name, perhaps with Scarpus, or under Augustus. First attested: *EJ*² 368 (end of Augustus' reign).

III Gallica

Formed: ?48 (Caesar's consular series); Munda, 45 (*B. Hisp.* 30), Philippi, 42. Colonist at Aquinum, 41 (*CVSI* 1). With Antony, 40–31; Parthian War, 36 (Tacitus *Hist.* iii.24, Plutarch *Ant.* 42). Actium, 31?; Syria 30 onwards.

Emblem: bull, indicating Caesarian origin.

Title: *Gallica*, should reflect service in Gaul, 48–42. First attested: *CIL* III 217 (Augustan/Tiberian date).

IIII Macedonica

Formed: 48 (Caesar's consular series); Macedonia 47–44; transferred to Italy, 44; defected to Octavian; Forum Gallorum, 43; Mutina, 43; Philippi, 42 (Appian B.C. iv.117). Colonist: Firmum, 41 (*ILS* 2340 = *CVSI* 72). Siege of Perusia, 41, Actium ?, 31. Colonists: Ateste, 30 (or later; *CVSI* 22, 24, 25). Spain, 30 BC–AD 43; Rhine frontier, AD 43–69; disbanded, AD 69; reconstituted as *IIII Flavia Felix*, AD 70.

Emblem: bull and capricorn (indicating Caesarian origin, and reconstitution later by Augustus; see pl. 13).

Title: *Macedonica*, reflects service in Macedonia, 47–44. First attested: *ILS* 2340 = *CVSI* 72 (colonist at Firmum, 41).

IIII Scythica

Formed: before 30, perhaps by Antony (less convincingly the legion may be identifiable with *IIII Sorana*, one of Pansa's consular series, 43); Macedonia, 30 onwards, and later Moesia.

Emblem: capricorn (see pl. 14a and p. 229, below).

Title: *Scythica*, may reflect victories over Scythians of Dobrudja in 29–27 under M. Licinius Crassus. First attested: *Atti dell'Istituto Veneto* cxxviii (1969–70), 225, no.1, a veteran of mid-Augustan date (*veteranus lecione quartae Scuticae*); *CIL* X 680 (Augustan date).

V Alaudae

Formed: 52 (in Transalpina; see p. 98): with Caesar in Gaul 52–49; Spain 49; Pharsalus ?, 48, Thapsus, 46. Colonists: ? Thuburnica, 46 (*ILS* 2229). Munda, 45; Italy 44—disbanded ?; re-formed by Antony, 44; Forum Gallorum, 43; Mutina, 43; Philippi, 42; with Antony, 41–31; Actium?, 31; incorporated into Octavian's army, 30. Colonists: Beirut, 30 or later. Spain, 30–19?. Colonists: Emerita, 25; Rhine frontier, ?19 BC – AD 69; eagle lost in Gaul, 17 (Velleius ii.97); Balkans, AD 70 onwards?; destroyed, c. 86 ? (see Appendix 4).

Emblem: elephant, awarded 46, for success against charging elephants in battle of Thapsus (Appian B.C. ii.96 with *B. Afr.* 81, 84).

Title: *Alaudae,* plural noun of Celtic origin, meaning *Larks;* reflects formation in Transalpine province; also Celtic custom of wearing bird-crest or feathers attached to helmet (Pliny *NH* xi.121). Perhaps in origin merely a nickname. First attested: Cicero *Phil.* i.20, iv.12, xiii.3, 37 (44 BC); *CIL* IX 1460 = *CVSI* 55 (mid-Augustan).

V Macedonica

Formed: 43 (if identical to *V Urbana,* which seems to belong to Pansa's consular series) or 41–40 (Octavian); no record of movements, 40–31; Actium, 31. Note colonists of a *V Urbana* at Ateste, 30 (*ILS* 2236; *CIL* V 2515) and of a *V Gallica* at Antiochia Pisidiae (*CIL* III 6824, 6825, 6828, *JRS* vi, 1916, 90), 25. Stationed in Macedonia. 30 BC–AD 6; Moesia, AD 6 onwards.

Emblem: bull, but legion cannot have been a genuine Caesarian foundation (above, p. 134).

Title: *Macedonica,* from service in Macedonia in the generation after Actium. First attested: *ILS* 2281 (AD 33–34); 1349 (Claudian).

VI Ferrata

Formed: 52 in Cisalpina; with Caesar in Gaul 53–49; Spain, 49, Pharsalus, 48, Alexandria, 48–47; Zela, 47; released 47 and sent back to Italy; Munda, 45. Colonists Arelate (Arles), 45. Re-formed by Lepidus, 44; passed to Antony, 43; Philippi, 42. Colonists: Beneventum, 41; with Antony in East, 41–31; Parthian War, 36 (coin of L. Verus); Actium, 30. Colonists: Byllis, 30? (*AE* 1966, 419); Syria, 30 onwards.

Emblem: wolf and twins.

Title: *Ferrata,* 'Ironclad'. First attested: *CIL* IX 1613 = *CVSI* 36 (colonist at Beneventum, 41). Notice also a *legio VI Macedonica* recorded at Ephesus (*ILS* 8862), perhaps in the decade before Actium; if this is the same legion, the title could reflect a short-lived commemoration of Philippi, fought within the frontier of the Macedonian province.

VI Victrix

Formed: 41–40? (Octavian); Perusia, 41; movements not reported, 40–31; Spain, 30 BC onwards–AD 69.

Emblem: often stated to have a bull-emblem, suggesting (false) Caesarian antecedents, but the evidence is insecure.

Titles: *Hispaniensis,* 'stationed in Spain'. Attested: *AE* 1917/1918, 2 (Neronian); *CIL* V 4381 = *Sup.* 677; *PBSR* xli (1973), 12. *Victrix* (Victorious); first attested: *ILS* 2648 (Neronian)—that inscription notes a recent victory *contra Astures,* perhaps the occasion for the award; but *AE* 1968, 206 may be earlier.

VII Claudia

Formed: 59 or earlier; Caesar's campaigns, 58–49; Spain, 49, Pharsalus, 48; Africa, 46; disbanded 46. Colonists: Calatia, 45. Re-formed by Octavian, 44; Forum Gallorum, 43; Mutina, 43; Philippi, 42; Perusia siege, 41; with Octavian, 41–31. Colonists: Baeterrae, 36?. Actium?, 31. Colonists: Rusazus,

Tupusuctu, Saldae (all Mauretania), 30–25 (*AE* 1921, 16, *CIL* VIII 8837, 8933). Galatia, 30–20? Colonists: Antiochia Pisidiae, 25 (*CIL* III 6826, 6827). Balkans, ?–AD 9; Dalmatia, AD 9 onwards.

Emblem: bull, indicating Caesarian origin.

Titles: *Paterna* (*CIL* X 3880 = *CVSI* 60), commemorates link with Caesar as *pater patriae*. *Macedonica*, from service in Balkans under Augustus (*CIL* III 7386, X 1711, 4723, 8241, *AE* 1938, 141). *Claudia Pia Fidelis*, from loyalty to Claudius after revolt of Camillus Scribonianus in Dalmatia, AD 42 (Dio lv. 23.4); first attested: *CIL* V *Sup.* 474 (Claudian).

VIII Augusta

Formed: 59 or earlier; with Caesar in Gaul, 58–49; Italy, 49–48; Pharsalus, 48, Thapsus, 46; disbanded, 46–45. Colonists: Casilinum, 44; re-formed by Octavian, 44; Forum Gallorum, 43; Mutina, 43; Philippi, 42; with Octavian, 41–31. Colonists: Forum Julii, 36?; Actium, 30?; Balkans, 30 onwards. Colonists: Beirut and Heliopolis, 30/14 (but this could be an Antonian legion).

Emblem: bull.

Titles: *Mutinensis* (*ILS* 2239 = *CVSI* 92, colonist at Teanum, 41), seems to commemorate battle at Mutina, 43; *Gallica* (*CIL* III 14165[6], colonist at Beirut), reflects early service in Gaul with Caesar. *Augusta*, after some victory, 27 BC–AD 14; first attested: *ILS* 2466 (Augustan date).

IX Hispana

Formed: Uncertain. The legion may go back to Caesar's legion IX, already in Gaul by 58, but direct descent is not proved. Caesar's *IX* was disbanded in 46–45, and some men settled in Picenum, and perhaps Histria (*CIL* V 397 = *CVSI* 87 for *VIIII Triumphalis*); this legion was re-formed by Ventidius, but whether it long survived is not known. A new legion may have been formed by Octavian, 41–40, which served with him till Actium. Spain, 30 –19? Colonists: Cales, ?14 (*EE* VIII 530 = *CVSI* 59). Pannonia, AD 9–43, except for period 20–24 when the legion was sent to Africa; Britain, AD 43 onwards.

Emblem: (not known).

Titles: *Macedonica*, from service in Balkans under early Julio-Claudians (*ILS* 928 with *AE* 1919, 1). *Hispaniensis*, i.e. 'stationed in Spain'; first attested: *CIL* V 7443, *EE* VIII 530 (mid-Augustan), *AE* 1975, 446 (Augustan), *CIL* X 6098(?). Later, *Hispana*, i.e. 'Spanish'.

X Fretensis

Formed: Octavian, 41–40?; Mylae and Naulochus, 36? Colonists: Capua, 36? (*CIL* X 3890 = *CVSI* 63). Actium ?, 30. Macedonia, 30 onwards—? (*EJ*[2] 268); later, Syria (by AD 14, and probably much earlier).

Emblems: bull, dolphin, galley, boar.

Title: *Fretensis*, named after the *Fretum* or *Fretum Siculum*, the Channel between Italy and Sicily, which indicates participation in naval battles, 36. First attested: *CIL* X 3890 (colonist at Capua); *EJ*² 268 (mid-Augustan).

X Gemina

Formed: 59 or earlier; with Caesar in Gaul 58–49; Spain, 49; Pharsalus, 48; Thapsus, 46; disbanded 46–45, but fighting again at Munda, 45. Colonists: Narbo, 45–44. Re-formed by Lepidus, 44; passed to Antony, 43; Philippi, 42. Colonist at Cremona, 41 (or earlier?); with Antony in the East, 41–31; Actium, 31. Colonists, Patrae, 30. Stationed in Spain, 30? onwards. Colonists, Emerita, 25 (coins, see pl. 16a).

Emblem: bull.

Titles: *Equestris*, 'Mounted' or (better) 'Knightly' (above, p. 84). Attested: *CIL* III 508; *Athens Annals of Archaeology* iv (1971), 112; *AE* 1934, 152; R. Frei-Stolba, *Talanta* x–xi (1978–79), 44–61. *Gemina*, 'Twin' (above, p. 135); first attested: *AE* 1934, 152 (Augustan), *CIL* II 1176 (Augustan). Note that the inscription *AE* 1953, 268, which seemed to record a legion entitled *Gemina Victrix*, was misread.

XI Claudia

Formed: Uncertain. The legion may go back to Caesar's *XI*, formed in 58, but direct descent is not proved. Caesar's legion was disbanded in 46–45, and some colonists may have been settled at Bovianum (Boiano) in Samnium, which gained the appellation *Undecumanorum* ('Of the Eleventh'). More probably, a new legion was formed by Octavian in 41–40 and served with him in 41–31, and at Actium, 31 (see *ILS* 2243 = *CVSI* 6). Colonists: Ateste, 30 (including three men who style themselves *Actiacus*) Balkans, 30 BC–AD 9; Dalmatia, AD 9 onwards.

Emblem: Neptune.

Titles: *Claudia Pia Fidelis*, (Claudian, Loyal and Faithful) from loyalty to Claudius after revolt of Camillus Scribonianus in Dalmatia, AD 42 (Dio liv. 23.4). First attested: *CIL* V 3374–75 (Neronian). No earlier title, e.g. *Macedonica*, to match *legio VII*, is recorded.

XII Fulminata

Formed: probably in origin the legion *XII* formed by Caesar in 58 for the campaign against the Helvetii (above, p. 82). With Caesar in Gaul, 58–49; Italy, 49; Pharsalus, 48. Disbanded 46–45. The colonist of *XII Paterna* attested at Parma (*ILS* 2242) may belong now. Re-formed in 44–43 (by Lepidus?), and passed to Antony. With Antony in the East, 41–31 (his coinage reports a *XII Antiqua*); Greece, 41–31? (*CIL* III 6097), or briefly under Augustus. Colonists: Patrae, 30 (*CIL* III 504, 507 = 7261, 509); Sicily, date uncertain (*CIL* X 7349); Ateste (*CIL* V 2520), ? 14. Sent to Egypt under Augustus (above, p. 158)?; Syria, from late Augustan times onwards.

Emblem: Thunderbolt.

Titles: *Paterna*, after Caesar as *pater patriae*, *ILS* 2242 (colonist at Parma, 46–45, or later?); *Antiqua*, 'ancient' (Antony's legionary coinage); *Ful-*

minata, 'equipped with the thunderbolt' (the Greek version is κεραυνοφόρος (thunderbolt-carrier); first attested: colonists at Patrae (above); *CIL* X 7351 (Augustan). What happened to Octavian's *XII Victrix*, reported at Perusia in 41, is not clear. The title *Gall(ica)* reported for this legion on an inscription from Rome (*AE* 1964, 67 where the numeral is misread as *VII*) is in fact a late epithet, *Gallieniana* (from the emperor Gallienus).

XIII Gemina

Formed: Uncertain. The legion may go back to Caesar's *XIII*, formed in 57, but direct descent cannot be proved. Caesar's *XIII* was disbanded in 46–45, and colonists are known at or near Hispellum (Spello) (*ILS* 6619a; *CIL* XI 1933). The legion may be a fresh creation of Octavian in 41–40, with whom it served 40–31; at Puteoli (Pozzuoli), 36 (App. *BC* v.87); Actium?, 31; Balkans, 30 onwards; Rhine frontier after AD 9.

Emblem: lion (symbol of Jupiter).

Title: *Gemina*, 'Twin', perhaps indicating amalgamation after Actium. First attested: *CIL* V 1882 (Augustan).

XIV Gemina

Formed: Uncertain. The legion may go back to Caesar's *XIV*, formed in 53 (after an earlier legion with the same number had been destroyed; above, p. 87); Caesar's *XIV* was disbanded in 46–45. Alternatively it may be a fresh creation of Octavian, in 41–40, with whom it served until Actium. Balkans, 30 BC–AD 9; Rhine frontier, AD 9–43; Britain, AD 43–66; in transit, 67–68; Italy, AD 68; Britain, AD 68–70; Rhine frontier, AD 70 onwards.

Emblem: capricorn, indicating an origin, or some degree of reconstitution, under Augustus.

Titles: *Gemina*, 'Twin', perhaps indicating amalgamation after Actium. First attested: *ILS* 2649 (before AD 5); *Martia Victrix*, 'Martial and Victorious', after victory over Boudica's rebels, AD 60–61. First attested: *CIL* XI 395 = *ILS* 2648 (AD 66).

XV Apollinaris

Formed: Octavian, 41–40? (or earlier? Notice a colonist at Cremona, *CVSI* 68); with Octavian, 40–31; Actium, 31?; Colonist, Ateste, 30 or 14 (*CIL* V 2516 = *CVSI* 17); Balkans, 30 onwards; Pannonia, AD 9 onwards. Colonists: Emona, AD 14? (*CIL* III 3847, ILS 2264). Syria, AD 58–66; Judaea, AD 66–70; Cappadocia, AD 72 onwards.

Emblem: (not known).

Title: *Apollinaris*, sacred to the god Apollo, to whom Augustus was especially devoted. Augustus may have honoured the legion with this title after Actium, where victory had been attributed to the intervention of Apollo. But if the colonist at Cremona reached that town in 41, the title and the legion itself may have a longer pedigree. First attested: *CVSI* 68 (early/mid-Augustan).

XVI Gallica
Formed: Octavian, 41–40? Rhine frontier, 30 onwards (or even earlier). Colonist: Alexandria Troas (Troy), 30? (*AE* 1914, 204) (or an Antonian legion with same numeral?); disbanded, AD 69; reconstituted as *XVI Flavia Firma*; transferred to Cappadocia, by AD 72.

Emblem: ? lion (symbol of Jupiter).

Title: *Gallica*, from service in Gaul, but date of award not known. First attested: *ILS* 2695 (Claudian); *ILS* 2034 (Neronian)

XVII
Formed: Octavian, 41–40?; probably Rhine frontier from 30 onwards; presumed to have been lost with *XVIII* and *XIX* in Varus disaster, but no source, literary or epigraphic, mentions it.

Emblem: (not known).

Title: none known (no link with Antony's *XVII Classica* is likely).

XVIII
Formed: Octavian, 41–40?; no record during Civil War; Colonist: Ateste, 30 or 14 (*CIL* V 2499 = *ILS* 2268). Rhine frontier, 30 BC–AD 9; destroyed with Varus, AD 9.

Emblem: (not known).

Title: none known (no link with Antony's *XVIII Libyca* is likely). (epigraphic records: *ILS* 1314 = Pl. 18; *ILS* 2268; *CIL* XIV 2950).

XIX
Formed: Octavian, 41–40?; no record during Civil War. Notice a colonist at Pisa (*CIL* XI 1524 = *CVSI* 89) but this could refer to an earlier legion of the 49–48 levies. Stationed on the Rhine frontier, 30 BC–AD 9, when destroyed in Varus disaster.

Emblem: (not known).

Title: none known. (epigraphic records: *ILS* 2269, *AE* 1969/1970, 444 = *AE* 1975, 626; *CIL* XI 5218, 6058, V 5126a, XII 259; cf. Tacitus *Ann.* i.60.3).

XX Valeria Victrix
Formed: Octavian, 41–40 or after Actium? Spain, 30–?20. Colonists: Emerita, 25 or later (*CIL* II 22*, 662, 719), Balkans, ?20 BC–AD 9; Rhine frontier, AD 9–43; Britain, AD 43 onwards.

Emblem: boar.

Titles: *Valeria Victrix* (Valiant and Victorious), from victory over Boudican rebels, AD 60–61 (see above, p. 138). First attested: *AE* 1980, 445; *RIB* 508, *ILS* 9200 (Flavian date).

XXI Rapax
Formed: Octavian, 41–40, or after Actium? Vindelicia and Rhine frontier, 30 onwards; Pannonia, AD 70 onwards; destroyed, c. AD 92?

Emblem: capricorn, indicating Augustan origin or reconstruction.

Title: *Rapax*, 'Grasping', of a bird of prey descending on its victim. First attested: *CIL* V 4858, 4892, 5033 (all Augustan date).

XXII Deiotariana

Formed: by transfer from forces of Galatian Kingdom, 25 at latest (above, p. 141). Stationed in Egypt, ?25 onwards.

Emblem: (not known).

Title: *Deiotariana*, from the name of Deiotarus, king of Galatia who died in 40. First attested: *ILP* 86 (early Flavian date); *Michigan Papyri* VII 432 (AD 95). One inscription, of Tiberian date (*ILS* 2690) gives the legion the title *Cyrenaica*, perhaps in commemoration of a campaign on Egypt's western border, but the stonecutter may have confused *legio XXII* with the *III Cyrenaica*, the other of the two legions then in Egypt.

APPENDIX 3 New Legions Raised During the Early Empire

XV Primigenia, XXII Primigenia: by Caligula, AD 39 or (less probably) Claudius, AD 42, in preparation for projected invasion of Britain. Numbers chosen to fit sequence of garrisons in two German provinces. Title: *Primigenia*, 'First Born', of a new breed of legions.

I Italica: by Nero, AD 66 or 67, for projected Caspian expedition (Suetonius *Nero* 19.2). Title: *Italica*, recruited from Italians (see above, p. 181).

I Adiutrix: by Nero from sailors at Misenum, AD 68; taken over by Galba. Title: *Adiutrix*—'Supportive'.

II Adiutrix: during Civil War, AD 69, at time of Flavian advance on Italy, from sailors at Ravenna; accepted as a legion by Vespasian.

VII Hispana: by Galba in Spain, AD 68, after being proclaimed Emperor. The number was chosen to continue sequence from *VI Hispaniensis* (above, p. 207). Titles: *Hispana* (see A. Garzetti, in *Legio VII Gemina*, Leon 1970, p. 334 = *AE* 1972, 203); afterwards *Gemina*, from reconstitution, AD 70. Tacitus describes the legion as *Galbiana* (*Hist.* ii. 86, iii. 7, 21) but this seems to have been a distinguishing nickname rather than the legion's formal title.

I Minervia: by Domitian, AD 83. Title: *Minervia*, sacred to Minerva, who was Domitian's favourite goddess.

II Traiana, XXX Ulpia: by Trajan for Dacian Wars, AD 101? Numerals indicate that latter was the 30th legion of the army (there already being in total 29), and that the former was the second legion which Trajan himself raised. The titles of both are drawn from the names of Trajan (Marcus Ulpius Traianus).

APPENDIX 4 Legions Destroyed or Disbanded

XVIII and *XIX* (and presumably also *XVII*): lost with Varus in Teutoburg Forest, AD 9.

I Germanica, XV Primigenia: seemingly disbanded in AD 70, after collaborating with the rebel leader Civilis. Meanwhile, *IIII Macedonica* and *XVI Gallica*, which had not been so deeply compromised, were reconstituted as *IIII Flavia Felix* and *XVI Flavia Firma*. *Legio VII Gemina*, the former *Hispana*, may have received some men from one or both disbanded legions.

V Alaudae: perhaps on Danube, under Domitian, AD 85–86? The legion was once thought to have been disbanded in AD 70, along with *I Germanica* and *XV Primigenia*, and for the same reason, but an inscription reports a colonist at Scupi (mod. Skopje) seemingly under Domitian, which could indicate that it was transferred to the Balkans after AD 70, and lost somewhat later. (See A. Mócsy, *Gesellschaft und Romanisation in der römischen Provinz Moesia Superior* (Budapest–Amsterdam 1970) 68); but it would be hard to argue that the survival of the legion into the Flavian period has yet been decisively proved.

XXI Rapax: probably on Danube, under Domitian, c. AD 92?

IX Hispana: perhaps in Judaea under Hadrian, AD 132–135, or later under Marcus Aurelius, in Armenia, AD 161. No longer thought to have been destroyed in Britain, but to have been transferred, first to Germany, and then to the East.

XXII Deiotariana: probably under Hadrian, in Judaea, AD 132–35.

Note: Roman historians under the Empire are reticent about mentioning the loss of Roman legions. Apart from the catastrophe under Varus, no legion is specifically reported as destroyed by an ancient author (but see Dio lxxxi.2 on a disaster in AD 161). A sudden break in the epigraphic evidence, or the arrival of another legion to occupy a frontier fortress, may offer the best available clues. The loss of an eagle was traditionally held as the supreme disgrace for a legion, leading to its disbandment, but the only direct references to such losses—by *legio V Alaudae* in Gaul, 17 (Velleius ii.97) and *XII Fulminata* in Judaea, AD 66 (Suetonius *Vesp.* 4) did not lead to the legion being disbanded.

APPENDIX 5 Glossary of Military and Technical Terms

Accensi	Light-armed troops of the middle Republic, described by Livy (viii.8). Later the term denoted soldiers' servants and, generally, non-combatant personnel.
Aedile (*aedilis*)	One of the annually elected junior magistrates at Rome charged with the upkeep of public buildings and streets in the city.
Ala	A division of Latin or Allied troops equivalent in size to a legion. Later, a regiment of auxiliary cavalry (lit. 'a wing').
Aquilifer	Standard-bearer who carried the *aquila* of the legion.
As	Small copper coin, of which four equalled a *sestertius* and 16 a *denarius*.
Aureus	Gold coin, equivalent to 25 *denarii*.
Capite censi	Those citizens owning insufficient property to be eligible for military service, and who were registered at the census by a head-count only.
Centurion (*centurio*)	Commander of a company (*centuria*) of legionaries, originally of 100 men, but later 80 or fewer.
Cohort (*cohors*)	Initially a contingent of Latin or Allied troops, about 500 men strong. From the period of the Second Punic War groupings of single maniples from the *hastati*, *principes* and *triarii* of a legion were given this title; from the time of Marius the cohort became the chief sub-unit of the legion, and under the Empire also designated a battalion of auxiliary infantry.

Conquisitor	Recruiting officer appointed by a magistrate to hold a levy of troops.
Consul	Supreme magistrate at Rome, one of two elected annually, who took charge of the army on campaign.
Denarius	Silver coin, equivalent to four *sestertii*; $\frac{1}{25}$ of an *aureus*.
Dictator	Magistrate appointed by the Senate to deal with an emergency military situation; the man appointed, usually an ex-consul, held office for six months at the most. Modern connotations of the word should be resisted.
Dilectus	A levying of troops (lit. 'choosing') at the start of the campaigning season.
Dupondius	Brass coin, equivalent to two *asses*.
Equestrian Order (*Ordo Equester*)	Originally the richer elements in Roman society who could be called on for military service as *equites*. Later the term encompassed the members of the business or middle class, with no commitment to military service.
Gladius	Short two-edged thrusting sword, of Spanish origin, which became the legionary's chief weapon for close-range fighting from the second century BC onwards.
Hastati	Young soldiers forming the front line of the manipular army of the Middle Republic (lit. 'spearmen').
Hoplite	Armed soldier of the Greek, and (later) Etruscan and Roman armies, who was equipped with a short thrusting spear and a round shield, and who formed line of battle in a *phalanx* (p. 17).
Legate (*legatus*)	Officer to whom a magistrate on campaign delegated some part of his administrative, juridical or military duties.
Legion (*legio*)	Originally the 'levy' of all men eligible for military service. By the middle Republic the term meant a 'division' of soldiers, some 4000 to 6000 men strong.
Maniple (*Manipulus*)	Formation of two centuries, the chief sub-unit of the legion in the middle Republic, containing up to 160 men (p. 19).

Peltast	Lightly-armed infantryman of Thracian origin, named after his distinctive crescent-shaped wicker shield (*pelta*).
Phalanx	Line of battle formed by *hoplites* (lit. 'roller').
Plebeian Tribune (*tribunus plebis*)	One of 10 magistrates elected annually to represent the interests of the common people (the *plebs*).
Praetor	One of the annually elected magistrates (8 in number by the Late Republic) whose principal responsibility in the city was the judging of legal cases; second only to the consuls in the hierarchy of office-holding.
Praetorian Cohort	Originally the bodyguard of a magistrate on campaign. During the Civil Wars of the Late Republic the number of cohorts multiplied, and after Actium Augustus retained nine cohorts to form a peacetime bodyguard for himself alone p. 153).
Pilani	Another name (from the second century BC onwards) for the *triarii*, the soldiers of the third line; the word appears to derive from *pilus* (a file of soldiers) rather than *pilum* (a javelin).
Pilum	Socketed javelin, the principal throwing weapon of the legionary.
Primus Pilus (or *centurio primi pili*)	The chief centurion of the legion, who commanded the first century of the *triarii* (or *pilani*), and later the first century of the First Cohort.
Principes	Soldiers in the prime of life who served in the second line of the manipular legion of the Middle Republic (lit. 'chief men').
Procurator	Senior official charged with the administration of finance or the emperor's own property in a province of the Roman Empire.
Proconsul	A consul whose command of an army was prolonged beyond his own year of elected office.
Propraetor	A praetor whose command of an army was prolonged beyond his year of elected office.
Pugio	A short dagger, a cut-down version of the *gladius*, carried by all legionaries.
Quaestor	One of the annually elected junior magistrates (20 in number by the late Republic), principally concerned with financial matters.

Quincunx	A modern term, used to describe the diagonal placing of maniples or cohorts in the legion's battle-order, from the positioning of dots for the number five (*quinque*) on a dice-cube.
Rorarii	Lightly armed troops of the Middle Republic, described by Livy (viii.8).
Scutum	Oblong or oval shield made of sheets of wood covered by ox-hide. Under the Empire a rectangular shape became the norm.
Senate (*senatus*)	Council of ex-magistrates who acted as the chief policy-making body of the Roman Republic, and offered advice to current office-holders.
Sestertius	Brass coin, equivalent to 4 *asses*; $\frac{1}{4}$ of a *denarius*.
Stipendium	Payment made to a soldier to help meet his living expenses on campaign. By the Late Republic the term was synonymous with 'pay'.
Triarii	The older soldiers forming the third (reserve) line of the manipular legion in the middle Republic (lit. 'third rankers').
Tribune (*tribunus* or *tribunus militum*)	One of the six middle-ranking officers in a legion. Their tasks were administrative and protective of the soldiers' interests, and they exercised no definite military command over any sub-unit within the legion. (lit. 'tribal officer').
Velites	Lightly equipped skirmishers who operated in front of the three main lines of the manipular legion (lit. 'cloak-wearers'—they wore no defensive armour).

APPENDIX 6 List of Dates

149	Macedonia made a province
146	Carthage destroyed; Africa made a province
133	Capture of Numantia; Asia made a province; Ti. Gracchus Plebeian Tribune
123	C. Gracchus Plebeian Tribune
121	Southern Gaul (Transalpina) made a province
112	War against Jugurtha
109	Metellus in command against Jugurtha
107	Marius consul
106	Jugurtha captured; end of war
102	Marius defeats Teutones
101	Marius defeats Cimbri
90	Social War
88–83	Sulla in the East against Mithridates
82	Sulla dictator
80–72	Sertorius in Spain
74–66	Lucullus in the East
73–71	Rebellion of Spartacus
67	Pompey voted command against pirates
66	Pompey succeeds Lucullus in war against Mithridates
63	Victory in the East; Syria made a province; Cicero consul; conspiracy of Catiline
60	First Triumvirate (Pompey, Crassus, Caesar)
59	Caesar consul
58–49	Caesar proconsul of Gaul and Illyricum
53	Crassus defeated by Parthians at Carrhae
49	Caesar crosses Rubicon; Civil War with Pompey
48	Battles at Dyrrhachium and Pharsalus
47	Caesar at Alexandria; battle of Zela
46	Battle of Thapsus
45	Battle of Munda
44	Caesar assassinated
43	Battles at Forum Gallorum and Mutina; Second Triumvirate (Antony, Lepidus and Octavian)
42	Battle of Philippi
41	Siege of Perusia
36	Defeat of Sextus Pompeius
31	Antony and Cleopatra defeated at Actium. End of the Civil War
30	Egypt becomes a province
27	Octavian receives the title *Augustus*; provinces divided between Emperor and Senate; his visits to Gaul and Spain
20	Standards recovered from Parthians
16	Tiberius and Drusus campaign north of the Alps; new provinces of Raetia and Noricum

Appendices

APPENDIX 7 Notes on the Plates

1 Italian Hoplites

Two bone plaques, probably decorating a small wooden box, from a cemetery at Praeneste (Palestrina); now in the Villa Giulia Museum, Rome. The plaques show hoplites dressed in moulded cuirass, tunic and cloak, wearing crested helmets and greaves. Each holds a spear and rests one hand on a circular shield. Similar warriors decorate other plaques from Palestrina.

Presumably such soldiers served in the army of Praeneste itself, 23 miles south-east of Rome. The plaques should form good evidence for the arms and equipment in use in Italy before the adoption of the long shield (*scutum*) and javelin (*pilum*) of the manipular army.

Photo: Mansell Collection

Bibliography: F. Coarelli, in *Roma Medio Repubblicana* (Roma 1973) no. 435, tav. xcvi.

2 Scene from the frieze of the victory monument of Aemilius Paullus at Delphi

One of a series of battle-scenes depicting incidents in the Battle of Pydna (168 BC) which ended in a victory for the legionaries over the Macedonian phalanx (above, p. 43). In this scene two Roman infantrymen equipped with the oblong *scutum*, and an *eques* (right) engage the Macedonians. At the lower right corner lies a wounded Macedonian hoplite, who covers his body with a richly ornamented circular shield.

Photo: École Française, Athens

Bibliography: *Fouilles de Delphes*, vol. iv (Paris 1927), pp. 40–41; pl. lxxviii.1; H. Kähler, *Der Freis vom Reiterdenkmal des Aemilius Paullus in Delphi =* *Monumenta Artis Romanae* v (Berlin 1965); A. Jacquemin et P. Laroche, 'Notes sur trois piliers delphiques', *BCH* cvi (1982), 191–218.

3 Detail from the 'Altar of Domitius Ahenobarbus'

The so-called Altar of Domitius Ahenobarbus is a large rectangular base believed to have once stood outside a temple to Neptune in the Campus Martius at Rome, and decorated with elaborate scenes. The temple itself was built at the expense of Cn. Domitius Ahenobarbus, a senator who commanded naval squadrons for Brutus and subsequently for Antony. Three sides of the base (now in Munich) show sea-deities, and the fourth (now in the Musée du Louvre, Paris) shows a scene of purification. The centre of this scene (see fig. 19) is dominated by a sacrifice, the *suovetaurilia*, in which a sheep, pig and bull are killed in honour of Mars. To the left is a tall handsome figure in military dress, in a crested helmet and moulded cuirass, resting on a circular shield and carrying a spear. Most probably he is a military tribune. Two other soldiers, in crested helmets and mail shirts, seem to keep guard while citizens are registered at a census, or for military service. To the right of the central scene, two other infantrymen (*Ill.*) similarly equipped, stand relaxed at ease, along with a cavalryman, also in a mail shirt, who prepares to mount his horse.

There has been much discussion on the significance of the Altar, its original location, and most important, the date. For the present purpose the arms, and equipment of the soldiers attract special notice. The most convincing modern view (Coarelli) places the monument in the later decades of the second century BC, when an ancestor of Domitius Ahenobarbus was *censor*. The presence of an *eques* by itself could suggest a date before the time of Marius. The interesting detail that one of the infantrymen wears a different style of helmet from the others may point to a period before the standardisation of equipment, perhaps when the *hastati*, *principes* and *triarii* retained separate identities.

Photo: Bildarchiv Foto Marburg

Bibliography: I.S. Ryberg, *The Rites of the State Religion in Roman Art* (=*MAAR* xxi) (Roma 1955); F. Coarelli, 'L' "ara di Domizio Enobarbo" e la cultura artistica in Roma nel II secolo a.C.', *Dialoghi di Archeologia* ii (1968), 302–68; H. Kähler, *Seethiasos und Census: Die Reliefe aus dem Palazzo Santa Croce in Rom* = *Monumenta Artis Romanae* vi (Berlin 1966).

4 The army on the coinage

a *Denarius*, issued at Massilia, 82 BC, by C. Valerius Flaccus, proconsul of Gallia Transalpina in the Marian interest. The reverse shows a legionary *aquila* flanked by military standards. The standard on the left bears a plaque or flag bearing the letter H (for *Hastati* or *Hastatorum*), that on the right bears a plaque or flag bearing the letter P (for *Principes* or *Principum*). Below: *ex s(enatus) c(onsulto)* ('by decree of the Senate'). On left: *C(aius) Val(erius) Fla(ccus)*. On right: *imperat(or)*.

Bibliography: M.H. Crawford, *Roman Republican Coinage* (Cambridge 1974) no. 365/4.

b *Denarius*, issued at Rome, 49 BC, by Cn. Nerius as Urban Quaestor. The reverse is identical to 4(a). Around: *L(ucio) Lent(ulo) C(aio) Marc(ello) co(n)s(ulibus)* ('in the consulship of Lucius Lentulus and Gaius Marcellus'). Issued by the Pompeians at the onset of civil war against Caesar, emphasising legitimate government.

Bibliography: Crawford, *op. cit.* no. 441/1.

c *Denarius*, issued at Rome, c.40 BC by Ti. Sempronius Gracchus, quaestor designate. The reverse shows a legionary *aquila*. On the left is a military standard with a plaque or flag bearing a letter (probably P, but the coin is worn). On the right are a plough and a surveyor's measuring-pole. Around: *Ti(berius) Sempronius Gracc(h)us q(uaestor) desig(natus) s(enatus) c(onsulto)*. The plough and surveyor's pole indicate an allusion to the land settlement schemes currently under way in Italy, in the aftermath of the Philippi battle. Gracchus' forebears, as Plebeian Tribunes in 133 and 123–22, had also carried through land settlement schemes.
Bibliography: Crawford, *op. cit.* no. 525/4b.

d *Denarius*, issued in the East by Caesar, 48–47. The reverse shows a trophy with Gallic arms including shields and a war-trumpet (*carnyx*); on the right, an axe. Below: *Caesar*.
Bibliography: Crawford, *op. cit.* no. 452/2.

e *Denarius*, issued by Caesar in the East, 48–47. The reverse shows a trophy with Gallic arms and a war-trumpet. Below is a bearded captive, sitting with hands tied. On either side: *Caesar*.
Bibliography: Crawford, *op. cit.* no. 452/4.
Photos: **a, b, e** British Museum; **c, d** Hunter Coin Cabinet.

5 Soldiers of the Late Republic

a Monument commemorating an *eques* L. Septumius and his parents. Found, c.1939, at Casale delle Cappellette, on Via Prenestina, 4 miles outside Rome (*ILLRP* 697; *NS* 1939, 83). The full inscription reads: *mag(ister) Capitolinus quinq(uennalis). L(ucius) Septumius L(uci) f(ilius) Arn(ensi) eques. Hirtuleia L(uci) f(ilia)* '. . . Capitoline Master in the census year; Lucius Septumius, son of Lucius, of the Arnensian voting-tribe, member of the Equestrian Order; Hirtuleia, daughter of Lucius'. Above are busts of the three deceased, Lucius Septumius (centre) and his parents. Young Septumius is shown in heroic pose, in a tunic with the draperies of a cloak over his left shoulder, and holding the pommel of a *gladius* in his left hand. (Cf. nos. 5(b), (c), (d), below). Date 75–50?
Photo: L. Keppie
Bibliography: C. Nicolet, *L'ordre équestre à l'époque républicaine* (Paris 1966), 244. D.E.E. Kleiner, *Roman Group Portraiture: the Funerary Reliefs of the Late Republic and Early Empire* (New York—London 1977), p. 218, no. 39. D.E.E. and F.S. Kleiner, 'A Heroic funerary relief on the Via Appia' *Arch. Anz.* XC (1975), 258–60.

b Monument commemorating the tribune L. Appuleius and his (?) parents. Provenance unknown. Now built up on the outside wall of a building in the Piazza Garibaldi, Mentana (ancient Nomentum), Lazio. (*CIL* XIV 3948). The full inscription reads: *L(ucius) Appuleius L(uci) l(ibertus)/Asclepiades. L(ucius) Appuleius L(uci) f(ilius)/trib(unus) mil(itum). Appuleia L(uci) l(iberta)/Sophanuba/de suo fecit.* 'Lucius Appuleius As-

clepiades, freedman of Lucius. Lucius Appuleius, son of Lucius, military tribune. Appuleia Sophanuba, freedwoman of Lucius, set (this) up at her own expense'. The tribune Appuleius is shown in heroic pose, naked to the waist, except for the fold of a cloak over his left shoulder. In his left hand he holds a *gladius*, whose pommel is shown horizontally and its scabbard vertically. The tribune, it seems, is the son of a freedman and freedwoman of a family Appuleius. His rise to the rank of tribune provides a parallel for the young poet Horace, and would only have been possible in the civil-war context of the Late Republic. His mother's slave-name Sophanuba may indicate a North African origin. It remains possible, but perhaps less likely, that Asclepiades and Sophanuba are freed slaves of the tribune himself.
Photo: L. Keppie
Bibliography: Kleiner and Kleiner, *loc. cit.*: Kleiner, *op. cit.*, p. 227, no. 55.

   c Part of a tomb monument commemorating C. Raius Perulla. Built into a farm building at Altilia (ancient Saepinum), Molise, Italy. *CIL* IX 2532. The inscription reads: *C(ai) Rai N(umerii) f(ilii) Volt(inia)/Perullae ex testamen(to)*. 'Of Gaius Raius Perulla, son of Numerius, of the Voltinian voting-tribe, in accordance with his will'. Raius is shown facing the front, in military dress with cloak over his left shoulder, holding a *gladius* with both hands, at his left side. The surviving block evidently formed the end of a more substantial monument, flanked by fluted pilasters and topped by an architrave. Interestingly, the inscription makes no mention of military service.
Photo: J. Patterson
Bibliography: *Sepino: archeologia e continuita* (Campobasso 1979), 25.

   d Monument commemorating P. Gessius and two members of his household. *ILLRP* 503. Found near Viterbo, Italy; now in the Museum of Fine Arts, Boston. The full inscription reads: *Gessia P(ubli) l(iberta) Fausta. P(ublius) Gessius P(ubli) f(ilius) Rom(ilia). P(ublius) Gessius P(ubli) l(iberta) Primus.* To the left: *ex testamento (ubli) Gessi P(ubli) l(iberti) Primi.* To the right: *arbit[ratu] Gessia[e P(ubli) l(ibertae)] Fausta[e].* 'Gessia Fausta, freedwoman of Publius. Publius Gessius, son of Publius, of the Romilian voting-tribe. Publius Gessius Primus, freedman of Publius. (Set up) in accordance with the will of Publius Gessius Primus, freedman of Publius. Under the supervision of Gessia Fausta, freedwoman of Publius'. Gessius himself is clad in a (?) mail shirt with a cloak at his left shoulder, and holds a *gladius* by its pommel. Here too (as in 7(c)) there is no specification of military service. Gessius' features are hard-bitten and sour; he is clearly a long-serving soldier, but no rank is indicated. The voting-tribe *Romilia* shows that he came from or was settled at either Sora or Ateste (Este), both colonies for Civil War veterans. Date: usually placed c. 50. Photo: Museum of Fine Arts, Boston.
Bibliography: M.B. Comstock and C.C. Vermeule, *Sculpture in Stone* (Boston 1976), 200–1, no. 319 with fig.

6 Bust of Julius Caesar

Vatican Museums

Photo: Mansell Collection

Bibliography: W. Amelung, *Die Sculpturen des vaticanisches Museum* (Berlin 1908), II, 473.

7 Caesar's bridge across the Rhine, 55.

End-elevation, plan and elevation, following Caesar, *BG* iv.17ff.

Photo: Glasgow University Photographic Unit. Reproduced from Napoléon III, *Histoire de Jules César* (Paris 1865–66), Planche 15.

8 Alesia: general views of the hilltop.

Seen from the north-west, north-east, east and south.

Photo: Glasgow University Photographic Unit. Reproduced from Napoléon III, *Histoire de Jules César* (Paris 1865–66), Planche 26.

9 Alesia: details of the Roman fortifications.

Described by Caesar, *BG* vii.72ff.

Photo: Glasgow University Photographic Unit. Reproduced from Napoléon III, *Histoire de Jules César* (Paris 1865–66), Planche 27.

10 Soldiers of Caesar

Graveslab commemorating the brothers Canuleius, a soldier and a veteran of Caesar's *legio VII*. Capua, Museo Campano (*CIL* X 3886 = *ILS* 2225 = *ILLRP* 497 = *CVSI* 61). The inscription reads: *C(aius) Canulei[u]s/ Q(uinti) f(ilius) leg(ione) VII evo/cat(us) mort(uus) est ann(os) nat(us)/ XXXV donat(us) torq(uibus) armil(lis)/p(h)aler(is) coron(a)/Q(uintus) Canu-leius Q(uinti) f(ilius)/leg(ione) VII occeis(us in Gall(ia)/ annor(um) nat(us) XVIII/duo fratr(es)/ieis monum(entum) pat(er) fec(it)*. 'Gaius Canuleius, the son of Quintus, a soldier in *legio VII*, called out for additional service, died aged 35, awarded torcs, bangles, medals and a crown. Quintus Canuleius, the son of Quintus, a soldier in *legio VII*, killed in Gaul, aged 18. Two brothers. Their father erected (this) monument to them.'

Photo: Museo Campano, Capua

Bibliography: V.A. Maxfield, *Roman Military Decorations* (London 1981), 64; L. Keppie, *Colonisation and Veteran Settlement in Italy* (London 1983), 144.

11 Warship of the Late Republic

Marble relief found in the eighteenth century in the ruins of the Temple of Fortuna Primigenia at Praeneste (Palestrina). Now in the Vatican Museum. Part of a larger monument of uncertain nature, the relief shows a warship with two banks of oars (and perhaps a third bank of shipped oars). The upper works are protected by a line of shields. At the prow, close to the water-line, is a crocodile-emblem, and, above, a box containing a head, presumably that of the gorgon Medusa. On the deck a group of helmeted legionaries, carrying javelins and oval shields, await the order to engage or board. One of the soldiers, in elaborate corslet and apron, may represent the admiral of a naval squadron. Another soldier carries a shield on which a hand is shown grasping a trident. Towards the high prow is a tower. In front, standing on the outrigger, are two soldiers, of whom the right-hand figure, in a breastplate, may be a tribune. From the presence of the crocodile it is generally thought that the relief shows one of Antony's warships at Actium. The soldiers may well belong to a *legio classica* (above, p. 152). Other representations of similar warships with crocodiles are known, so that the theme was perhaps more familiar in Roman art than we suppose.

Photo: Mansell Collection

Bibliography: W. Amelung, *Die Sculpturen des vaticanisches Museum* (Berlin 1908), II, 65–72; R. Heidenreich, 'Zum Biremenrelief aus Praeneste', *Röm. Mitt.* li (1935–36), 337–46; L. Casson, *Ancient Ships and Seamanship* (Princeton 1971), 144; H. Williams, 'A ship of Actium on a Roman lamp', *International Journal of Nautical Archaeology* x.i. (1981), 23–27.

12 Antony's military coinage

a *Denarius* issued 32–31 BC, in the East. The obverses of all the coins in this series show a galley. Above: *Ant(onius) aug(ur)*. Below: *IIIvir r(ei) p(ublicae) c(onstituendae)*.

b *Denarius* honouring *legio XII Antiqua*. The reverse shows a legionary *aquila* between two standards. Around: *leg(ionis) XII Antiquae*.

c *Denarius* honouring Antony's Praetorian Cohorts. The reverse shows a legionary *aquila* between two standards. Around: *c(o)hortium praetoriarum*.

d *Denarius* honouring the *cohors speculatorum*. The reverse shows three identical standards, each showing a ship's prow and topped by floral decoration. Around: *c(o)hortis speculatorum*.

Photos: Hunter Coin Cabinet

Bibliography: C. Kirkpatrick, 'The Legionary Coinage of Mark Antony', *Seaby's Coin and Medal Bulletin* (March 1967), 102–5. L. Keppie, *Colonisation and Veteran Settlement in Italy* (London 1983), 27.

13 Catapult-shield of the legio IIII Macedonica

Embossed bronze sheet from the site of the Second Battle of Cremona, AD 69. Found 1887; now in the Museo Civico, Cremona. For attachment to the front of a catapult. To either side are standards of the legion, topped by medallions bearing (left) a leaping bull and (right) a capricorn. (See above, p. 139.) Each standard has a handle near the base of the pole, to facilitate its removal from the ground. The inscription (*ILS* 2283) reads: *leg(ionis) IIII Mac(edonicae)/M(arco) Vinicio II Tauro Stat[ili]o Corvino [co(n)]s(ulibus) C(aio) Vibio Rufino leg(ato)/C(aio) Horatio [.......]o princ(ipe) p[r(aetorii)]*. '(Property) of *legio IIII Macedonica*. (Made) in the consulship of Marcus Vinicius (for the second time) and Taurus Statilius Corvinus; during the legateship of Gaius Vibius Rufinus and while Gaius Horatius . . . was the centurion-overseer of legionary headquarters'. The inscription informs us that the catapult was constructed in AD 45, presumably in the Upper

German province of which the legion (based at Mainz) formed part of the garrison. Vibius Rufinus was the *legatus pro praetore* of that province. The centurion Horatius was *princeps* of the legion, i.e. the centurion second in seniority to the *primus pilus*. The *princeps* had charge of the day-to-day administration of the legion. The catapult was evidently brought to Italy by the detachment of the legion which fought for Vitellius in the civil war of AD 69, and was disabled or captured during the fighting around Cremona against the Flavian forces in October of that year.

Photo: D. Baatz

Bibliography: D. Baatz, 'Ein Katapult der Legio IV Macedonica aus Cremona', *Röm. Mitt.* lxxxvii (1980), 283–99.

14 Emblems and symbols

a Sculptured slab from a tomb monument, now built into the 12th century bell-tower of the monastery of S. Gulielmo al Goleto, near S. Angelo dei Lombardi, southern Italy. The slab shows three military standards. The left standard is topped by a hand (presumably symbolising a maniple), with a *vexillum*-flag suspended from the cross-bar, and a gorgon-head medallion decorating the pole. The middle standard is formed by a spear whose shaft is decorated with a shield-roundel and a globe encircled by a crescent. Set on the cross-bar are three busts. The standard on the right is topped by a capricorn perched on a globe with a crescent and roundel below.

Also built into the bell-tower are other sculptured panels, one showing an eagle, and also an inscription commemorating M. Paccius Marcellus, former *primus pilus* of the *legio IIII Scythica* (*CIL* IX 1005 = *ILS* 2639). The various sculptures have been described by Filippo Coarelli, who identified the animal on the right-hand standard as a dragon, especially appropriate to a legion with the title *Scythica*, and who dated the assemblage to the beginning of the Empire. Coarelli saw the three busts as showing Augustus and his two ill-fated grandsons, Gaius and Lucius Caesar. But the inscription itself could date to the mid first century AD or even later, and the busts may therefore represent Vespasian and his sons Titus and Domitian (The chubby features suggest the Flavian family). *Legio IIII Scythica* fought for the Flavians in the Civil War of AD 68–69. The animal emblem is clearly a capricorn, which is shown surmounting a globe on many Augustan coin issues. There is no other evidence for the standards of the *legio IIII Scythica*, which is usually considered to have fought in the Civil War with Antony. The capricorn should indicate some degree of reconstitution within Augustus's reign.

Photo: J. Patterson

Bibliography: F. Coarelli, 'Su un monumento funerario romano nell'abbazia di San Gulielmo al Goleto', *Dialoghi di Archeologia* i (1967), 46–71.

b Sculptured block from a funerary monument, built into a doorway at Venafrum (Venafro), Campania. The front face of the slab shows an *aquila* flanked by military standards. The eagle, grasping a thunderbolt in its talons, sits on a column topped by a mock Corinthian capital. The two flanking standards are ornamented with roundels. The left-hand standard is topped by a *vexillum*-flag, whose tassels are just visible. Motifs within the roundels include two heads in profile and (second from top) a winged victory. Coarelli (*op. cit.* p. 54) identified the two heads as Augustus and his wife Livia, and associated the slab with the funerary inscription of a *primus pilus* (*CIL* X 4868) of the Augustan period, but it must be doubtful whether any close dating is possible within the early Empire.

Photo: M.H. Crawford

Bibliography: F. Coarelli, *loc. cit.* (above); S. Diebner, *Aesernia-Venafrum* (Roma, 1979), no. 32.

15 Statue of Augustus

Found in 1863 in the ruins of his wife Livia's villa at Prima Porta just outside Rome. Now in the Vatican Museum. Augustus stands with his weight on his right leg, clad in a muscle cuirass, and a cloak which he supports with his left forearm. In his left hand he holds a sceptre. He is shown in the act of addressing his victorious troops. The breastplate is highly ornamented. In the centre a Roman officer with a hound at his feet prepares to accept an *aquila* from a bearded barbarian, evidently a Parthian. The pole of the *aquila* is ornamented with discs, as on pl. 4a–b. There is substantial if not unanimous agreement that the Roman is the young Tiberius, and the occasion is the recovery in 20 of the eagles lost by Crassus at the Carrhae disaster in 53. The event was widely trumpeted across the Roman world, and Augustus regarded it as the pinnacle of his successful foreign policy. Below is a personification of Earth, and above the Heaven, with the sun in his chariot.

Photo: Mansell Collection

Bibliography: H. Kähler, *Die Augustus-Statue von Prima Porta* = *Monumenta Artis Romanae* i (Köln 1959); E. Simon, 'Zur Augustusstatue von Prima Porta', *Röm. Mitt.* lxiv (1957), 46–68.

16 Augustan colonies on the coinage

a *Denarius*, issued c. 25–23 at Emerita. The reverse shows a bird's eye view of the town with, in the foreground, a double gate flanked by towers. Above: *Emerita*. Around: *P(ublius) Carisius leg(atus) pro pr(aetore)*. The town is Merida (*colonia Augusta Emerita*) which became a colony for veterans of the army in Spain in 25, when P. Carisius was the legate of Further Spain.

b *Sestertius*, issued AD 31–32 at Caesarea Augusta. The reverse shows a *vexillum* flanked by two standards each topped by a large circular disc. Above: *c(olonia) C(aesarea) A(ugusta)*; around: *M(arcus) Cato M(arcus) Vettiacus IIvir(i)*. In field: *leg(ionis) IV, leg(ionis) VI, leg(ionis) X*. Cato and Vettiacus were the joint mayors of the town when this coin was issued. Zaragoza (*colonia Caesarea Augusta*) was founded about 19 as a colony for veterans of three legions of the garrison in Spain, *IV Macedonica, VI Hispaniensis* and *X Gemina*.

c *Sestertius*, issued under Augustus, at Philippi. The reverse shows three standards, with, around, *cohor(tium)* [*praetoriarum*] *Phil(ippi)*. The coin issue shows that veterans of the Praetorian Cohorts were settled at Philippi, probably in 41.

d *Sestertius*, issued under Claudius, at Patrae. The reverse shows a legionary *aquila* flanked by standards. Around: *col(onia) A(ugusta) A(roe) Pat(rensis) X XII*. Legions *X Equestris* and *XII Fulminata*, both of which had probably fought in the Civil War under Antony, were settled at Patrae in 30. Photos: Hunter Coin Cabinet.

17 Imperial propaganda on the coinage

a *Denarius*, issued at Rome, c.18. The reverse shows a Parthian, kneeling, in breeches and a skin cloak, about to hand over a standard, with an attached flag bearing the letter or numeral X. If a numeral, it may represent the total number of standards recovered. Around: *Caesar Augustus sign(is) rece(ptis)*. The issue commemorates the recovery of standards from the Parthians in 20 BC (above, pl. 15).

b *Dupondius*, issued at Rome AD 37–41. The obverse (not illustrated) shows Germanicus riding in a chariot. The reverse shows Germanicus standing, with a legionary *aquila* over the crook of his left arm. Left and right: *signis recept(is)*. *Devictis Germ(anis)*. 'Standards recovered. Germans beaten'. The issue, struck during the reign of Germanicus' son Caligula, commemorates the recovery of one of the eagles lost with Varus, in AD 15–16.

c *Sestertius*, issued at Rome AD 40–41. The reverse shows Caligula addressing a file of five legionaries, each carrying a sword and a rectangular shield. Above are four *aquilae*. Above: *adlocut(io) coh(ortium)*. 'Addressing the troops'. The issue commemorates Caligula's visit to the army of Upper Germany in AD 39, when he put down an attempted revolt. The *aquilae* represent the four legions of the Upper German garrison.

d *Sestertius*, issued at Rome, c. AD 64–66. The reverse shows Nero standing on a low platform, addressing three soldiers in pointed cloaks, who carry two standards. Behind Nero is a second figure, perhaps an officer. In exergue: *adlocut(io) coh(ortium)*. 'Addressing the troops'. The soldiers, with their distinctive cloaks, long swords and lack of defensive armour, may be identified as *Germani corporis custodes* (above, p. 154). Photos: Hunter Coin Cabinet.

18 Cenotaph of Marcus Caelius

Found near the Roman legionary fortress at Vetera (Xanten), Holland. Now in the Rheinisches Landesmuseum, Bonn (*CIL* XIII 8648 = *ILS* 2244). The inscription reads: *M(arco) Caelio T(iti) f(ilio) Lem(onia) Bon(onia)/(primo) o(rdini) leg(ionis) XIIX. Ann(orum) LIII/[ce]cidit bello Variano ossa/inferre licebit. P(ublius) Caelius T(iti) f(ilius)/Lem(onia) frater fecit.* 'To Marcus Caelius, son of Titus, of the Lemonian voting-tribe, from Bologna, a centurion in the First Order of *legio XVIII*, aged 53; he fell in the Varian War.

His bones—if found—may be placed in this monument. Publius Caelius, son of Titus, of the Lemonian voting-tribe, his brother, set this up.'

Above is a frontal portrait of Caelius in full uniform, carrying the vine-stick denoting his rank as centurion, and wearing his military decorations: an oak-leaved *corona civica* (for saving the life of a fellow citizen) on his head, torcs suspended from shoulder straps, four medallions (*phalerae*) on a harness (other medallions are hidden behind his arm), and bracelets on each wrist. The awards are appropriate to a centurion. Caelius' precise rank is indicated by the designation I⁻O (i.e. *primo ordini*). To either side are busts of his freedmen *M(arcus) Caelius M(arci) l(ibertus) Privatus* and *M(arcus) Caelius M(arci) l(ibertus) Thiaminus*. It is not made clear whether they too fell with the army in the Teutoburg Forest.

Photo: Rheinisches Landesmuseum, Bonn

Bibliography: H. von Petrikovits, 'Zu CIL XIII 8648 aus Vetera (Caeliusstein)', *BJ* cl/cli (1950–1951), 116–18; *Corpus Signorum Imperii Romani*, Deutschland III.i (Bonn 1978), p. 18ff, no. 1; V.A. Maxfield, *Roman Military Decorations* (London 1981), 186ff.

19 The army of the Early Roman Empire

a Gravestone found at Mainz, 1804; now in Mittelrheinishes Museum, Mainz. *CIL* XIII 6898 = *ILS* 2341. The inscription reads: *Cn(aeus) Musius T(iti) f(ilius) Gal(eria) Veleias an(norum) XXXII stip(endiorum) XV aquilif(er) leg(ionis) XIIII Gem(inae) M(arcus) Musius (centurio) frater posuit.* 'Cnaeus Musius, son of Titus, of the Galerian voting-tribe, from Velleia (in northern Italy), aged 32, served 15 years, eagle-bearer of the *legio XIIII Gemina*. Marcus Musius, centurion, his brother, set (this) up.' The deceased, in a tunic and mail shirt, stands within a niche. Over his chest is a harness supporting nine medallions; at his shoulders are two torcs, and on his wrists two bangles. His sword (*gladius*) is secured by a belt at the waist. In his right hand he carries an eagle-standard, with a metal butt and a handle two-thirds of the way up the shaft. The eagle has its wings erect and encircled by a laurel wreath. Musius supports a small oval shield with his left hand. The gravestone belongs before AD 43, when the legion was transferred to Britain.

Photo: Mittelrheinisches Museum, Mainz.

b Gravestone found at Mainz, 1804; now in the Mittelrheinisches Museum, Mainz. *CIL* XIII 7029. The inscription reads: *C(aius) Romanius eq(ues) alae Norico(rum) Claud(ia) Capito Celeia an(norum) XL stip(endiorum) XIX, h(ic) s(itus) e(st). h(eres) ex te(stamento) f(aciundum) c(uravit).* 'Caius Romanius Capito, of the Claudian voting-tribe, from Celeia, cavalryman of the *Ala Noricorum*, aged 40, served 19 years, lies here. His heir saw to the erection of the monument, in accordance with the will'. Romanius is shown on horseback riding down a native warrior. He wears a mail shirt, with shoulder-pieces, a helmet and a long sword suspended from a belt over his left shoulder. He carries an oblong shield and raises a spear to strike at the barbarian. Behind is a servant or slave with two extra spears. Romanius is a citizen, from Celeia in Noricum. His regiment was based in the later Julio-Claudian period at or near Mainz.

Photo: Mittelrheinisches Museum, Mainz.

c Gravestone found at Mainz 1795. Now in Mittelrheinisches Museum, Mainz. *CIL* XIII 7041 = *ILS* 2562. The inscription reads: *Monimus Ierombali f(ilius) mil(es) c(o)hor(tis) I Ituraeor(um) ann(orum) L stip(endiorum) XXI h(ic) s(itus) e(st)*. 'Monimus, son of Ierombalus, soldier of the First Cohort of Ituraeans, aged 50, served 21 years, lies here'. Above, is a representation of Monimus, in a heavy cloak, holding a bow and a sheaf of arrows. The soldier's name and that of his father are Semitic, and the unit derives from the kingdom of Ituraea in southern Syria. Archers from Ituraea are found serving with the Roman army from the time of Pompey's eastern campaigns. The stone is probably pre-Claudian. The unit was stationed at or near Mainz in the early Julio-Claudian period; its later movements are not known.

Photo: Mittelrheinisches Museum, Mainz.

d Gravestone found at Mainz, 1851; now in the Mittelrheinisches Museum, Mainz. *CIL* XIII 7255. The inscription reads: *P(ublius) Flavoleius P(ublii) f(ilius) Pol(lia) Mutina Cordus mil(es) leg(ionis) XIIII Gem(inae) h(ic) s(itus) e(st) ann(orum) XLIII stip(endiorum) XXIII. C(aius) Vibennius T(iti) f(ilius) ex t(estamento) fec(it)*. 'Publius Flavoleius Cordus, son of Publius, of the Pollian voting-tribe, from Mutina, a soldier of the *legio XIIII Gemina*, lies here. Aged 43, served 23 years. Gaius Vibennius, son of Titus, set this up, in accordance with the will'. Above is a full-length representation of Flavoleius in high relief. He wears a tunic and cloak. At his right side is a *gladius*, and at his left a short dagger (*pugio*). In his left hand he holds a scroll and in his right a javelin. Suspended from a strap over his left shoulder is an oval shield. This stone, like pl. 19(a) should predate AD 43, when the legion was transferred from Upper Germany to Britain.

Photo: Mittelrheinisches Museum, Mainz.

Bibliography: *Germania Romana* III: *Die Grabendenkmäler* (Bamberg 1926), Taf. I.3, III.3, V.3, VII.3.

20 The Praetorian Guard
Relief once in the Villa Mattei at Rome, but since 1824 in the Musée du Louvre, Paris. The relief, presumably part of a larger scene, shows a group of soldiers in richly decorated equipment, standing on guard or on parade. The central figure, with a gorgon-head on his breastplate, must be a tribune. He and the figure to the left once held metal weapons, long since lost. The heads of the front row of figures are restored. Above is a large *aquila*-standard, with an eagle grasping a thunderbolt in its talons. The relief appears to date to the Trajanic-Hadrianic period. The presence of the *aquila* has prompted some scholars to suppose that legionaries are represented here, but the richness of the apparel, especially the helmets and oval shields, mark out these soldiers

as belonging to the Guard, in their ceremonial dress. Guardsmen can be shown with the *aquila*, e.g. on Trajan's Column, where the eagle is usually enclosed within a laurel wreath. Alternatively we could suppose that another panel to the left (now lost) contained some legionaries.

Photo: Mansell Collection

Bibliography: E. Michon, 'Les reliefs historiques romains du Musée du Louvre', *Monuments Piot* xvii (1909), 64; M. Durry, *Les cohortes prétoriennes* (Paris 1938), 223ff.

Postscript

A recent study of the above relief (Pl. 20) suggests rather that it could once have formed part of an Arch of Claudius in Rome, erected in AD 52, which commemorated the successful invasion of Britain in 43; see G.H. Koeppel, *Röm. Mitt.* 90 (1983), 103–9.

Notes and References

1 The Army of the Roman Republic *(pages 14–56)*

1 Livy i.43; Dionysius of Halicarnassus iv.16

2 Later the term *classis navalis* denoted that part of the citizenry called up for service at sea; by the time of the Second Punic War *classis* meant 'a fleet'. The noun *classicum* means a military trumpet-call to arms

3 An alternative explanation, favoured in antiquity, saw the word as derived from 'sheaves' of corn-stalks, suspended from a pole as a military standard (see Ovid *Fasti* iii.117)

4 Livy viii.8–10

5 The earliest reference to the *pilum* belongs to 295 (Livy x.39.12) during the Third Samnite War. Pyrrhus in the battle of Ausculum was wounded by a *pilum* (Plutarch *Pyrrh.* 21.9). But much earlier Camillus, when *dictator* in 367, ordered the soldiers to use their 'heavy javelins' as thrusting spears to ward off a Gallic attack (Plutarch. *Cam.* 40.4)

6 There was doubt in antiquity as to the meaning of *rorarius*: Varro derived the word from *ros* (dew), adding as his explanation the view that, just as dew often falls before a proper downpour, so the *rorarii* acted as skirmishers before the onset of a formal battle (*de Ling. Lat.* vii.58)

7 It appears to be linked to *hortus* (a garden), and to mean an area of farmyard, and thus of a military encampment

8 Plutarch *Pyrrh.* 21.9. The phrase 'Pyrrhic victory' is a later development; its first appearance in English was in the *Daily Telegraph* in 1885

9 Polybius x.20; cf. Livy xxvi.51

10 Word of the discovery of a quantity of slingbullets bearing the inscription L XIII (i.e. *legio XIII*) at Gandul near Seville has been received from the Societat Catalana d'Estudis Numismàtics. The slingbullets are associated with Punic coins of the period of the Second Punic War. We happen to know from Livy (xxix.2.9) that a *legio XIII* was in Spain in 205. This evidence, if confirmed, forms the earliest non-literary record of a specific legion. I owe this information to the kindness of Mr M.H. Crawford

11 Livy xxvi.4

12 Polybius vi.19.1

13 Under the Empire the term *evocatus* denoted a soldier, most often from the ranks of the Praetorian Guard at Rome, who willingly stayed on after completion of his due service, or was invited to remain. But in the Republic the term describes a soldier 'called out' (the literal meaning) for further service, and some measure of compulsion or obligation seems implied

14 At some undefined date, probably during the second century, the *triarii* also became known as *pilani*; the obvious derivation (which ancient authors preferred) would be from *pilum* and could reflect the adoption of that distinctive weapon by the *triarii*. But modern scholars prefer a derivation from *pilus* (a file of soldiers), hence the name *centurio primi pili*, the centurion of the 'first file'

15 Plutarch *Pyrrh.* 16.5

16 Livy xxxv.14.8; Frontinus *Strat.* iv.1.14

17 Polybius xviii.29–32

18 Pliny *NH* v.25 with *AE* 1894, 65 etc

19 Appian *Iberica* 90

20 Appian *Iberica* 86

21 See Schulten, *Numantia* IV, figs xxx, xxxi, xxxiii. It would be unwise to accept uncritically every claim by Schulten to have identified Republican camps in Spain and Portugal; see *Arch. Anz.* xlviii (1933), 522ff. Not every site investigated need belong within the Roman period

22 Livy xlii.34.5–11

2 Marius' Mules *(pages 57–79)*

1 Sallust *Jug.* 86.2

2 Plutarch *Mar.* 20.5–6

3 Livy i.43.8; Polybius vi.19.2; Cicero *Rep.* ii.40.

4 Polybius xi. 23.1

5 Sallust *Jug.* 49.6

6 Sallust *Jug.* 46.7

7 Plutarch *Mar.* 25

8 Festus 149M; Frontinus *Strat.* iv.1.7

9 Pliny *NH* x.16

10 Polybius vi.24.6

11 *ILLRP* 1089–1102; E. Zangemeister, *Ephemeris Epigraphica* VI (1885), 5ff

12 Plutarch *Sull.* 21.3

13 Numismatic evidence could indicate that Camps IV and V belong, like nos. I–III, to the mid-second century, so conflicting with Schulten's interpretation and ground-plan; see H.J. Hildebrandt, *Madrider Mitteilungen* xx (1979), 238–71. But M.H. Crawford rejects this view (pers. comm.)

14 R.E. Smith, *Service in the Post-Marian Roman Army* (Manchester 1958), 38–40

15 Smith, *op. cit.* (n. 14), 11ff
16 *ILLRP* 502
17 A. Von Domaszewski, *NHJ* 1894, 158. For a somewhat earlier era Livy records that Legions *V* and *VIII* formed the garrison of Spain in 185 (xxxix.30.12), and that *V* and *VII* were there in 181. The army fighting in Cisalpina in 203 included legions numbered *XI*, *XII* and *XIII* (Livy xxx.18.9)
18 Sallust *Jug.* 95
19 Polybius vi.19.1 with *Tabula Heracleensis* (= *ILS* 6085), 91

3 Caesar's Conquest of Gaul *(pages 80–102)*
 1 Napoléon III, *Histoire de Jules César* (Paris 1865–66), planche 3
 2 Caesar *BG* i.24ff
 3 Caesar *BG* i.42
 4 Some have doubted that Mauchamp is correctly placed to be the scene of the encounter, and others would deny that any Roman camp with a *clavicula*-type entrance can belong before the first century AD; but Caesar's description is precise, and the fortifications at Mauchamp so unusual, that the two must surely relate to the same event
 5 Caesar *BG* v.37
 6 Some 10,000 Roman soldiers became prisoners, and were settled as colonists in Parthia's own frontier zone to the north-west of her territory (Pliny *NH* vi.47; cf. Horace *Odes* iii.55 and below, p. 158). For the possibility that some of these prisoners travelled even further, to China, see H.H. Dubs, *AJP* lxii (1941), 322–30
 7 Caesar *BG* vii.36ff
 8 Caesar *BG* vii.72–74
 9 Caesar *BG* vii.83
10 A selection of the weaponry is on display in the Musée National des Antiquités, at St Germain-en-Laye (Paris). Full publication is still awaited
11 J. Le Gall, *Alésia: archéologie et histoire* (Paris 1963), 84
12 Caesar *BG* i. 21–22
13 Cicero *de Prov. Cons.* 28; idem, *Balb.* 61
14 *ILS* 2225
15 *ILS* 2239, 2240, 2242 etc
16 Models of siegeworks and engineering works undertaken by Caesar's army can be seen in the Musée National des Antiquités, Paris, and in the Museo della Civiltà Romana, Rome
17 Caesar *BG* v.33
18 Suetonius *Caes.* 65
19 Caesar *BG* i.25, from which all this supposition derives
20 The Rubicon also served as the northern limit of the territory of the old colony of Ariminum (Rimini), and only acquired its special significance as a provincial boundary in Sulla's time

Notes and References

4 Civil War *(pages 103–131)*

1 He borrowed money from the tribunes and centurions, to hand out as a donative to the soldiers (Caesar *BC* i.39). The centurions each offered to pay for the upkeep of a cavalryman during the campaign (Suetonius *Caes.* 68)

2 Suetonius *Caes.* 26

3 *Notizie degli Scavi* 1879, 319–20. The ditch was trapezoidal in shape, 2.6 m wide and 1.25 m deep

4 Plutarch *Pomp.* 60; Appian *BC* ii.37

5 *AE* 1924, 55 (*legio XXVIII*); *ILS* 2232 (*legio XXX*)

6 *AE* 1931, 95

7 Caesar *BC* i.3. Note *ILLRP* 502 for a centurion who joined Pompey in 49, and died at Athens soon after. Also Suetonius *Vesp.* 1.2; Cicero *Ad Brut.* xv.1.2

8 Col. Stoffel, *Histoire de Jules César: Guerre civile* (Paris 1887), I, 249–50, *planche* 3.

9 G. Veith, *Der Feldzug von Dyrrhachium zwischen Caesar und Pompejus* (Wien 1920), 147ff

10 Caesar *BC* iii.53

11 Valerius Maximus iii.2.23

12 Caesar *BC* iii.89

13 Suetonius *Caes.* 37

14 *B.Afr.* 75

15 *B.Afr.* 16

16 *ILLRP* 1104 (slingbullets)

17 Cicero *Fam.* xi.20.1

18 An officer sent by Lepidus, who seems to have brought Lepidus' Praetorian Cohort to assist Antony

19 Cicero *Fam.* x.30

20 Appian *BC* iii.68

21 Appian *BC* iii.105ff

22 *AE* 1924, 55; coins: see p. 231

23 Appian *BC* iv. 115–116. This legion and the cohorts had been with Octavian in south-west Italy during operations against Sextus Pompeius, and when Antony summoned Octavian to join him quickly at Brundisium for the crossing of the Adriatic, they were left to follow. Hence the delay in joining the main army

24 Appian *BC* iv.3. The total of 18 colonies reflected the number of legions (excluding recalled veterans) presently under the Triumvirs' control

25 *ILS* 2239

26 Appian *BC* v.33

27 Appian *BC* v.33–38

28 *ILLRP* 1106–18; see fig. 36; E. Zangemeister, *Ephemeris Epigraphica* VI (1885), 52–78. I am grateful to Dr Anna-Eugenia Ferruglio, Super-

intendent of Antiquities for Umbria, for access to the collection, and for supplying photographs

29 Appian *BC* v.87, 112

30 Tacitus *Hist.* iii.24; Plutarch *Ant.* 42 (*III Gallica*); BM, *Coins of the Roman Empire* IV (London 1940), p. 456, no. 500 (*VI Ferrata*)

31 M.H. Crawford, *Roman Republican Coinage* (Cambridge 1974), 529, 552

32 *CIL* III 504, 507–509, *Athens Annals of Archaeology* iv (1971), 112 (Patrae); *CIL* III 14165⁶ (Beirut); *AE* 1914, 204 (Alexandria Troas); Pliny *NH* v.20 (Gunugu); Dio lii.43 (Carthage)

33 *ILS* 2336; *CIL* V, 890, 2389, 2839; *ILS* 2243; perhaps *CIL* V 8846

5 The Emergence of the Imperial Legions *(pages 132–144)*

1 H.M.D. Parker, in his standard work *The Roman Legions* (Oxford 1928) moves directly from discussing 'The Armies of Caesar and Pompey' to 'The Augustan System and Legions'; he devotes no space to the vital period between Caesar's death and Actium, presumably because of the scantiness of evidence available to him. Worthy of high recommendation is the unpublished thesis of Walter Schmitthenner, *The Armies of the Triumviral Period* (see Bibliography), which discusses the numbers of legions and auxiliary units in service between 44 and 31 and has been the source of great inspiration to the present writer over many years.

2 Suetonius *Aug.* 24.2

3 Dio liv. 23.7. In AD 70 legion *VII Hispana* newly raised by Galba, was reconstituted after the Civil War of AD 68–69 as *VII Gemina* (below, p. 213)

4 T. Mommsen, *Res Gestae Divi Augusti* (Berlin 1883), 70; E.G. Hardy, *Journ. Phil.* xxiii (1895), 29–44. The point that *XXII Deiotariana*, the highest numbered legion in the Augustan sequence, was probably formed in 25, or taken formally into the Roman army in that year, was made already by Parker, *Roman Legions* (Oxford 1928), 89

5 Cf. *ILS* 2288 for a list of the Empire's legions compiled in the mid-second century AD, which lists them in clockwise fashion, starting with Britain and ending in Spain

6 For possible titles borne by legions in the Social War, *CIL* IX 6086.xvii–xviii

7 Pliny *NH* xi.121

8 Valerius Maximus iii.2.19; below, p. 201

9 Cicero *Phil.* iii.6, 39, iv.5, v.53, xii.8, xiv.32; *fam.* x.30, 33

10 *CIL* IX 1613 (colonist at Beneventum in 41)

11 *ILS* 2340 (colonist at Firmum, 41)

12 Dio liv. 11.5

13 Velleius ii.112

14 *Britannia* xii (1981), 293. The titles are normally abbreviated to vv or VAL VIC; the expansion of VAL to VALERIA, reported on only a few inscriptions, is confirmed by Dio (lv. 23); a newly published stone appears

to give both titles in full, perhaps in the Flavian period. See *ZPE* 38 (1980), 173 no. 4 = *AE* 1980, 445; but some caution is advisable
15 Appian *BC* ii.96
16 *B. Afr.* 84
17 *ILS* 2243
18 Suetonius *Caesar* 24.2
19 Interestingly such records of members of the legion as survive from the Civil War era show only Italians or citizen provincials: note *ILS* 2249 (a soldier from Faenza in northern Italy); Cicero *Phil.* v.12, xiii.3,37 (soldiers who were eligible to serve on jury panels at Rome); *B. Afr.* 54 (two Spanish tribunes, and a centurion probably from Umbria)
20 Caesar *BC* ii.20; *B. Hisp.* 7.4, 10.3
21 *B. Alex.* 34
22 *B. Alex.* 34, 39–40
23 *B. Alex.* 62, *B. Afr.* 48
24 Caesar *BC* iii.110

6 The Age of Augustus *(pages 145–171)*
1 Appian *BC* v.3
2 Dio lii.1–40
3 See F. Millar, *A Study of Cassius Dio* (Oxford 1964), 102–118
4 Dio liv. 25.5
5 Polybius vi.19.2
6 Dio liv. 23.1
7 Suetonius *Aug.* 49.2; Tacitus *Ann.* i.78; M. Corbier, *l'aerarium Saturni et l'aerarium militare* (Roma 1974)
8 *EJ²* 269 (AD 19); Tacitus *Ann.* i.44 (AD 14)
9 *ILS* 2690
10 Suetonius *Aug.* 38.2
11 *Atlante aereofotografico delle sedi umane in Italia* (Firenze 1970), tav. cxxxv–vi
12 Pliny *NH* iii.119
13 Octavian had five cohorts at Actium (Orosius vi.19.8); Antony had three in his army during the Parthian War of 36 (Plutarch *Ant.* 39)
14 Suetonius *Aug.* 49.1
15 Appian *BC* v.3
16 Dio liii.11.5
17 *X Fretensis* spent some time in Macedonia (*AE* 1936, 18 = *EJ²*268); *XII Fulminata* was perhaps in Egypt (below, p. 158) and *VIII Augusta* perhaps in Africa (below, p. 159); for *legio XX* on the Lower Danube, *ILS* 2270; for *XV* in Spain, *AE* 1959, 111
18 For *XIV* in Aquitania, *ILS* 2263
19 P. Barocelli, *Augusta Praetoria*, in series *Forma Italiae* (Roma 1948), 92
20 For a serving soldier of a *legio XV* dying in Lusitania at an uncertain date, *AE* 1951, 111

21 Dio liv. 11.5
22 *ILS* 2321
23 Strabo iii.3.8
24 *ILS* 2454–2455, 5969–70; *AE* 1946, 11, 17–19
25 *AE* 1936, 18
26 Josephus, *Ant.J.* xvii.10.9; idem, *Bell. Jud.* ii.3.1
27 But see Tacitus *Ann.* ii.79.3, ii.57.2 for a slightly later period (below, p. 193)
28 Strabo xvii.1.12, xvii.1.30
29 *ILS* 2690; but see below, p. 212
30 Strabo xvi.4.22ff
31 *ILS* 151
32 *ILAfr.* 471, 472 (Thuburnica). This legion provided manpower for a colony at Thuburbo Minus, but the date of foundation is not known
33 Dio liv. 23.2ff
34 Velleius ii.97.1; Dio liv.20. Notice the 'Sword of Tiberius' found at Mainz in 1848, which has a scabbard richly decorated with scenes seemingly showing the young Tiberius being congratulated by Augustus after his victory over the Vindelici; see now S. Walker and A. Burnett, *Augustus* (handlist to the exhibition 'The Image of Augustus', and supplementary studies) = *British Museum Occasional Paper* 16 (1981), 49ff
35 *AE* 1963, 41 (*legio XVI*); *ILS* 2466 (Magdalensberg)
36 The site has produced three records of the legion, as Prof. R. Fellmann of Basel kindly informs me; see now the plan in *Führer zu römischen Militäranlagen in Süddeutschland* (Stuttgart 1983), 23
37 Velleius ii.105.3
38 Velleius ii.106.3
39 *AE* 1969/1970, 444
40 *Germania* xlix (1971), 132–36. A useful study of graffiti on pottery from Haltern allows the identification of many members of its garrison under Augustus; see B. Galsterer, *Die Graffiti auf der Gefässkeramik aus Haltern* (Münster 1983)
41 Dio liv. 33.4; Velleius ii.102.4
42 Dio lvi.18.2
43 Velleius ii.112.1–2
44 Velleius ii.113
45 Velleius ii.113.1
46 Tacitus *Ann.* i.61–62. All three eagles were eventually recovered, the last under Claudius (Tacitus *Ann.* i.60, ii.25; Dio lx.8.7)
47 *EJ²* 368
48 Suetonius *Aug.* 25.2
49 Frontinus *Strat.* iv.7.8 reports the ingenuity of Caedicius, the *praefectus castrorum* left behind in charge of the base camp at Aliso: 'When our men were besieged, he was afraid that the barbarians would bring up against the rampart the timber they had collected and set his camp on

fire. So he pretended that there was a shortage of firewood, and despatched men in all directions to acquire it. The result was that the Germans took away all the trees they had felled' (so saving the garrison from attack!) Cf Velleius ii.120.2

50 Tacitus *Ann.* i.16ff
51 Tacitus *Ann.* i.23
52 Tacitus *Ann.* i.41

7 The Army of the Early Roman Empire *(pages 172–198)*

1 Tacitus *Ann.* i.11; Suetonius *Aug.* 101.4
2 Tacitus *Ann.* xi.20
3 Tacitus *Ann.* i.20; Suetonius *Aug.* 24.2; *Otho* 10.1. A few epigraphic examples can be adduced of the word in its meaning 'comrades' (*ILS* 2161, 5462). Note also *CIL* X 3524 commemorating a *manipularis* (i.e. private soldier) of the fleet at Misenum; cf. *AE* 1896, 21
4 Notice Crastinus, who had held the rank of *primus pilus* in Caesar's army, and who dashed forward from the front rank at Pharsalus followed by '120 volunteers from his own century' (Caesar *BC* iii.91); see also fig. 23 and caption
5 Obsequens *Lib. Prod.* 72. Note *B. Hisp.* 32 for P. Caucilius 'who had formerly been in command of Pompey's camp'. The incident dates to 45 but the rank and status of Caucilius is not known.
6 R. Syme, *Germania* xvi (1932), 109–11
7 Suetonius *Claud.* 25.1
8 F. Coarelli, *Dialoghi di Archeologia* i (1967), 46–71
9 Men who had been through the three Rome tribunates usually returned to a legion for a second tour of duty as *primus pilus* (a post which inscriptions report as *primus pilus bis* or *p.p.II*), before their procuratorship
10 *ILS* 2483
11 Pliny *NH* vii.149; Suetonius *Aug.* 24.1
12 Tacitus *Ann.* iv.4
13 Tacitus *Hist.* ii.21
14 Tacitus *Hist.* iii.24
15 Tacitus *Hist.* iv.65
16 Tacitus *Hist.* ii.93
17 Tacitus *Ann.* iv.46
18 Pliny *Ep.* vi.16.4
19 See *AE* 1978, 286; previously the change was ascribed to Caligula
20 Suetonius indicates (*Vit.* 10) that the old cohorts were completely disbanded, but if Vitellius really formed 16 new cohorts each of 1000 men from the legions with him at Rome, the latter would have all but ceased to exist as fighting formations, which clearly was not the case
21 The word *hiberna* came in due course to mean the permanent base of a military unit of any size; *AE* 1915, 42; *AE* 1896, 21, line 27

22 Cf. Tacitus *Ann.* iv.5 for a convenient account of the disposition of the legions in AD 23
23 Tacitus *Ann.* xiii. 35–36
24 Caesar *BG* iii.1, viii.5
25 *ILS* 38 (*Lex Antonia de Termessibus*, 68 BC), col. 2, line 7; J.M. Reynolds, *Aphrodisias and Rome* (London 1982), 77f
26 Suetonius *Dom.* 7.3
27 Josephus *Bell. Jud.* iii. 70–107

List of Abbreviations

IEJ	*Israel Exploration Journal*, Jerusalem
ILAfr.	R. Cagnat, A. Merlin, L. Chatelain, *Inscriptions Latines d'Afrique* (Paris 1923)
ILLRP	E. Degrassi, *Inscriptiones Latinae Liberae Rei Publicae* (Firenze 1957–1963)
ILP	M. Mello and G. Voza, *Le Iscrizioni latine di Paestum* (Napoli 1968)
ILS	H. Dessau, *Inscriptiones Latinae Selectae* (Berlin 1892–1916)
JHS	*Journal of Hellenic Studies*, London
JOAI	*Jahreshefte des Österreichen Archäologischen Instituts*, Wien
JRS	*Journal of Roman Studies*, London
Journ. Phil.	*Journal of Philology*, London
MAAR	*Memoirs of the American Academy in Rome*, Rome
MEFR	*Mélanges d'Archéologie et d'Histoire de l'École Française de Rome*, Paris
NHJ	*Neue Heidelberger Jahrbücher*, Heidelberg
NS	*Notizie degli Scavi*, Roma
PBSR	*Papers of the British School at Rome*, London
PIR²	*Prosopographia Imperii Romani*, ed. 2 (Berlin and Leipzig 1933 onwards)
RE	A. Pauly, G. Wissowa, W. Kroll, *Real-encyclopädie des Classischen Altertumswissenschaft* (Berlin, 1894 onwards)
REA	*Revue des Études Anciennes*, Bordeaux
REL	*Revue des Études Latines*, Paris
Rev. Phil.	*Revue de Philologie*, Paris
RIB	R.G. Collingwood and R.P. Wright, *The Roman Inscriptions of Britain*, vol. i (Oxford 1965)
Röm. Mitt.	*Mitteilungen des Deutschen Archaeologischen Instituts, Römische Abteilung*, Heidelberg
SB Wien	*Sitzungsberichte der Österreichen Akademie der Wissenschaft*, Wien
SJ	*Saalburg-Jahrbuch*, Berlin
TAPA	*Transactions of the American Philological Association*, Cleveland, Ohio
ZPE	*Zeitschrift für Papyrologie und Epigrafik*, Bonn

Bibliography

The following list of books and published papers is designed to guide the reader towards previous work on the topics discussed in the foregoing pages. It is not proposed to cite here every work consulted, merely those which the author is happy to recommend as particularly sensible and reliable. The number of books on Caesar and his Gallic campaigns by French authors abounds, and the trickle of works on army units in general becomes a deluge under the Empire. More detailed bibliographies can be found in the works by Harmand (who alone cites 237 items for the period between Marius and Caesar), Webster and Parker (2nd ed.).

GENERAL

F.E. Adcock, *The Roman Art of War under the Republic* (Cambridge, Mass. 1940)

H.M.D. Parker, *The Roman Legions* (Oxford 1928); rev. by G.R. Watson, 1971

J. Harmand, *L'Armée et le soldat à Rome de 107 à 50 avant notre ère* (Paris 1967)

G. Webster, *The Roman Imperial Army* (2nd ed. London 1979)

M.J. Jones, *Roman Fort Defences to A.D. 117* (Oxford 1975)

H. Delbrück, *Geschichte der Kriegskunst im Rahmen der politischen Geschichte* (Berlin 1920–21); English translation, *History of the Art of War within the Framework of Political History* (Westport, Conn., 1975)

W. Kubitschek, article *Legio*, in *RE* xii (1925), 1186–1210

E. Ritterling, article *Legio*, in *RE* xii (1925), 1211–1829

A. Passerini, article *Legio*, in *Dizionario epigrafico* iv (1949), 549–627

P. Couissin, *Les armes romaines* (Paris 1926)

J. Marquardt, *De l'organisation militaire chez les romains* (Paris 1891)= *Manuel des antiquités romaines*, tome xi

J. Kromayer and G. Veith, *Heerwesen und Kriegführung der Griechen und Römer* (München 1928)

J.P. Brisson (ed.), *Problèmes de la guerre à Rome* (Paris 1969)

A. Passerini, *Le forze armate*, in V. Ussari and P. Arnaldi (eds.), *Guida allo studio della civiltà romana antica*, I (Napoli 1958)

G.R. Watson, *The Roman Soldier* (London 1983)
P. Connolly, *The Roman Army* (London 1975)
P. Connolly, *Greece and Rome at War* (London 1981)
J. Warry, *Warfare in the Classical World* (London 1980)
R. Humble, *Warfare in the Ancient World* (London 1980)
J. Keegan, *The Face of Battle* (London 1976)
V.A. Maxfield, *The Military Decorations of the Roman Army* (London 1981)
P.A. Brunt, *Italian Manpower, 225 BC–AD 14* (Oxford 1971)
L. Keppie, *Colonisation and Veteran Settlement in Italy, 47–14 B.C.* (London 1983)
J. Kromayer and G. Veith, *Schlachten-Atlas zur antiken Kriegsgeschichte* (Leipzig 1922)
A. Johnson, *Roman Forts* (London 1983)

CHAPTER 1

E. Rawson, 'The literary sources for the pre-Marian Army' *PBSR* xxxix (1971), 13–31
J. Suolahti, *The Junior Officers of the Roman Army in the Republican Period* (Helsinki 1955)
V. Ilari, *Gli italici nelle strutture militari romane* (Milano 1974)
W.S. Messer, 'Mutiny in the Roman Army. The Republic', *Class. Phil.* xv (1920), 158–75
P. Fraccaro, *Opuscula iv: della guerra presso i Romani* (Pavia 1975)

The earliest Roman army
R.M. Ogilvie, *Early Rome and the Etruscans* (Glasgow 1976)

The Servian Constitution
G.V. Sumner, 'The legion and the centuriate organization', *JRS* lx(1970), 61–78
R. Thomsen, *King Servius Tullius: a historical synthesis.* (Copenhagen 1980)

Hoplites and maniples
E.T. Salmon, *Samnium and the Samnites* (Cambridge 1967)
M.P. Nillson, 'The Introduction of hoplite tactics at Rome', *JRS* xix (1929), 1–11
A.D. Snodgrass, 'The Hoplite Reform and History', *JHS* lxxxv (1965), 110–122
E. Meyer, *Das römische Manipularheer*, in *Kleine Schriften* II (Halle 1924), 193–329

Carthage and Hannibal
B.H. Liddell Hart, *Scipio Africanus, A Greater than Napoleon* (Edinburgh & London 1926)
H.H. Scullard, *Scipio Africanus, Soldier and Politician* (London 1970)
J.F. Lazenby, *Hannibal's War* (Warminster 1978)

Bibliography

Numantia

A. Schulten, *Numantia: die Ergebnisse der Ausgrabungen 1905–1919* (München 1914–31)

A. Schulten, *Geschichte von Numantia* (München 1933)

A. Garcia y Bellido, *Numantia* (Zaragoza 1969)

H.J. Hildebrandt, 'Die Römerlager von Numantia: Datierung anhand der Münzfunde', *Madrider Mitteilungen* xx (1979), 238–71

Polybius

E. Fabricius, 'Some Notes on Polybius's Description of Roman Camps', *JRS* xxii(1932), 78–87

P. Fraccaro, 'Polibio e l'accampamento romano', *Athenaeum* xii (1934), 154–61

J. Bennett, 'The Great Chesters *"pilum murale"* ', *Archaeologia Aeliana*, ser. 5, x(1982), 200–4

Army service in the second century BC

C. Nicolet, *The World of the Citizen in Republican Rome* (London 1980)

E. Cavaignac, 'Les six ans de service et la guerre d'Espagne', *Rev. Phil.* xxv (1951), 169–77

T. Steinwender, 'Altersklassen und reguläre Dienstzeit des Legionars', *Philologus* xlviii (1889), 285–305

Y. Shokat, *Recruitment and the Programme of Tiberius Gracchus* (Bruxelles 1980)

CHAPTER 2

R.E. Smith, *Service in the post-Marian Roman Army* (Manchester 1958)

E.H. Erdmann, *Die Rolle des Heeres in der Zeit von Marius bis Caesar* (Neustadt 1972)

H. Aigner, *Die Soldaten als Machtfaktor in der ausgehenden römischen Republik* (Innsbruck 1974)

B. Schleussner, *Die Legaten der römischen Republik* (München 1978)

Marius' military reforms

T.F. Carney, *A Biography of C. Marius* (Chicago 1970)

E. Gabba, 'Le origini dell'esercito professionale in Roma: i proletari e la riforma di Mario', *Athenaeum* xxvii (1949), 173–209

E. Gabba, 'Ricerche sull' esercito professionale romano da Mario ad Augusto', *Athenaeum* xxix (1951), 171–272. (Both these papers are now available in English, in E. Gabba, *Republican Rome: The Army and the Allies* (Oxford 1976).)

H. Aigner, 'Gedanken zur sogenannten Heeresreform des Marius', in F. Hampl and I. Weiler (eds.) *Kritische und vergleichende Studien zur Alten Geschichte und Universalgeschichte* (Innsbruck 1974), 11–23

M.J.V. Bell, 'Tactical Reform in the Roman Republican Army', *Historia* xiv (1965), 404–22

W. Schmitthenner, 'Politik und Armee in den späten römischen Republik', *Historische Zeitschrift* 190 (1960), 1–17

Social War
A. Von Domaszewski, 'Bellum Marsicum', *SB Wien* cci (1924), 3–30

War in Spain: Cáceres
A. Schulten and R. Poulsen, 'Castra Caecilia', *Archäologische Anzeiger* xliii (1928), 1–30; xlv (1930), 37–87; xlvii (1932), 334–87

Auxiliaries
T. Yoshimura, 'Die Auxiliartruppen und die Provinzialklientel in der römischen Republik', Historia x (1961), 473–95
A. Balil, 'Un factor difusor de la romanización: las tropas hispánicas al servicio de Roma (Siglos III–I a. de J.C.)' *Emerita* xxiv (1956), 108–34
A Garcia y Bellido, 'Los auxiliares hispanos en los ejércitos romanos de ocupación (200 al 30 antes de J.C.)' *Emerita* xxxi (1963), 213–26

CHAPTER 3

Caesar's Career
J.F.C. Fuller, *Julius Caesar, Man, Soldier and Tyrant* (London 1965)
M. Gelzer, *Caesar, Politician and Statesman* (Eng. trans.) (Oxford 1968)

Caesar and his army in Gaul
A. and P. Wiseman, *Julius Caesar: The Battle for Gaul* (London 1980)
L.-A. Constans, *Guide illustré des campagnes de César en Gaule* (Paris 1929)
H.P. Eydoux, *La France Antique* (Paris 1962)
Napoléon III, *Historie de Jules César, II, Guerre des Gaules* (Paris 1865–66)
J. Vogt, 'Caesar und seine Soldaten', *Orbis* (Freiburg 1960), 89–109
M. Rambaud, 'L'ordre de bataille de l'armée des Gaules', *REA* lx (1958), 87–130
T. Rice Holmes, *Caesar's Conquest of Gaul* (Oxford 1911)
P. Groebe, 'Cäsars Legionen im gallischen Kriege'; in *Festschrift zu Otto Hirschfelds 60. Geburtstage* (Berlin 1903), 452–60
G. Veith, *Geschichte der Feldzüge C. Julius Caesar* (Wien 1906)
H.P. Judson, *Caesar's Army* (Boston 1888)
P.J. Cuff, 'Caesar the Soldier', *Greece & Rome* n.s. iv (1957), 29–35
E. Sander, 'Die Reform des römischen Heerwesens durch Julius Cäsar', *Historische Zeitschrift* 179 (1955), 225–54
P. Mackendrick, *Roman France* (London 1971)
E. Abramson, *Roman Legionaries at the Time of Julius Caesar* (London 1979)

Nervii and Belgae
C. Peyre, 'Le champs de bataille de l'Aisne', *REL* lvi (1978), 175–215
J. Beaujeu, 'Les souvelements de 54 dans le nord de la Gaul et la veracité de César', *Revue du Nord* 40 (1958), 459–66
M. Lenóir, 'Lager mit *Claviculae*', *MEFR* lxxxix (1977), 697–722

Bibliography

Britain and the Rhine

P. Berresford Ellis, *Caesar's Invasion of Britain* (London 1978)

Gergovia

O. Brogan and E. Desforges, 'Gergovia', *Arch. J.* xcvii (1940), 1–36

M. Gorce, *César devant Gergovie* (Tunis 1942)

M. Rambaud, 'La bataille de Gergovie', *REL* lii (1974), 35–41

Alesia

J. Harmand, *Une campagne césarienne: Alésia* (Paris 1967)

J. Carcopino, *Alésia et les ruses de César* (Paris 1958)

J. Le Gall, *Alésia: archéologie et histoire* (Paris 1963)

A. Noché, 'Alesia: Fouilles de Napoléon III et fouilles récentes', *Ogam* x (1958), 105–20

A. Noché and G. Dufour, 'Fossés romains d'Alésia et fossés récemment découverts sur Les Chatelets près de Breteuil-sur-Noye (Oise)', *Celticum* vi (1963), 201–4

Bellovaci

G. Matherat, 'La technique des retranchements de César', *Gallia* i (1943), 81–127

G. Matherat, *Les retranchements de César au Bois des Côtes* (Paris 1933)

J. Harmand, 'Une question césarienne non résolue: la campagne de 51 contre les Bellovacques et sa localisation', *BSNAF* 1959, 263–81

Caesar as an author

J.H. Collins, *Propaganda, Ethics and Psychological Assumptions in Caesar's Writings* (Frankfurt 1952)

Archaeological Evidence

R. Agache, *La Somme pré-romaine et romaine* (Amiens 1978)

A. Grisart, *'l'Atuatuca* césarienne au fort de Chaudfontaine', *Ant. Class.* 1 (1981), 367–81

A. Grenier, *Manuel d'archéologie gallo-romaine*, vol. i (Paris 1931)

R. Goguey, *De l'aviation à l'archéologie* (Paris 1968)

J. Le Gall, 'Le rôle tactique des camps étables autour d'Alesia par l'armée de César en 52 av. J.-C', in D.M. Pippidi (ed.), *Actes du IXième Congres international d'Études sur les Frontières romaines* (Bucharesti 1978), 468–72

CHAPTER 4

A. Von Domaszewski, 'Die Heere der Bürgerkriege in den Jahre 49 bis 42 vor Christus', *NHJ* iv (1894), 157–88

P.A. Brunt, 'The Army and the Land in the Roman Revolution', *JRS* lii (1962), 69–86

Caesar against Pompey

H.M. Ottmer, *Die Rubikon—Legende* (Boppard 1979)

Col. Stoffel, *Histoire de Jules César: guerre civile* (Paris 1887)

G. Veith, 'Corfinium', *Klio* xiii (1913), 1–26

Dyrrhachium

G. Veith, *Die Feldzug von Dyrrachium zwischen Caesar und Pompejus* (Wien 1920)

Pharsalus

F.L. Lucas, 'The Battlefield of Pharsalus', *ABSA* xxiv (1919–21), 34–53

C.B.R. Pelling, 'Pharsalus', *Historia* xxii (1973), 249–59

Munda

A. Engel and P. Paris, 'Une forteresse ibérique à Osuna', *Nouvelles archives des missions scientifiques et literaires* xiii.4 (1906), 357–470

Second Triumvirate

H. Botermann, *Die Soldaten und die römische Politik in der Zeit von Caesars Tod bis zur Begründung des Zweiten Triumvirats* (= *Zetemata* 46) (München 1968)

I. Hahn, 'Die Legionsorganisation des Zweiten Triumvirats', *Acta Antiqua* xvii (1969), 199–222

Siege of Perusia

M. Reinhold, 'The Perusine War', *Class. World* xxvi (1932–33), 180–182

E. Gabba, 'The Perusine War and Triumviral Italy', *HSCP* lxxv (1971), 139–60

J.P. Hallett, 'Perusinae Glandes and the changing image of Augustus', *American Journal of Ancient History* ii (1977), 151–71

Octavian in Illyricum

G. Veith, *Die Feldzüge des C. Julius Caesar Octavianus in Illyrien in den Jahren 35–33 v. Chr.* (Wien 1914)

The Actium Campaign

J. Carter, *The Battle of Actium: The Rise and Triumph of Augustus Caesar* (London 1970)

J.H. Oliver, 'Octavian's inscription at Nicopolis', *AJP* xc (1969), 178–82

L.J.F. Keppie, 'A Note on the Title *Actiacus*', *CR* lxxxv (1971), 329–30

Naval warfare

J. Kromayer, 'Die Entwicklung der römischen Flotte . . .'. *Philologus* lvi (1897), 426–91

A. Alföldi, 'Commandants de la flotte romaine stationée à Cyrène sous Pompée, César et Octavien' in *Mélanges offerts à Jérôme Carcopino* (Paris 1966), 25–43

CHAPTER 5

Legionary origins

W.C.G. Schmitthenner, *The Armies of the Triumviral Period: A Study of the*

Bibliography

Origins of the Roman Imperial Legions (D. Phil. Thesis, Oxford 1958)

H.A. Sanders, 'The Origin of the Third Cyrenaic Legion', *AJP* lxii (1941), 84–87

Titles

E.B. Birley, 'A Note on the title "*Gemina*"', *JRS* xviii (1928), 56–60

R. McPake, 'A note on the Cognomina of Legio XX', *Britannia* xii (1981), 293–95

B.H. Isaac, 'Colonia Munatia Triumphalis and Legio Nona Triumphalis?', *Talanta* iii (1971), 11–43

J.G.P. Best, 'Colonia Iulia Equestris and Legio Decima Equestris', *Talanta* iii (1971), 1–10

P. Castrén, 'About the Legio X Equestris', *Arctos* viii (1974), 5–7

R. Frei-Stolba, 'Legio X Equestris', *Talanta* x–xi (1978–79), 44–61

Emblems

F. Coarelli, 'Su un monumento funerario romano nell'abbazia di San Gulielmo al Goleto', *Dialoghi di Archeologia* i (1967), 46–71

A.J. Reinach, 'Signa Militaria' in Daremberg-Saglio, *Dictionnaire des Antiquités* iv.2 (1910), 1307–25

D. Barag, 'Brick Stamp-Impressions of the Legio X Fretensis', *BJ* clxvii (1967), 244–67

E.J. Dwyer, 'Augustus and the Capricorn', *Röm. Mitt.* lxxx (1973), 59–67

A. Von Domaszweski, *Die Fahnen im römischen Heere* (Wien 1885)

A. Von Domaszweski, 'Die Thierbilder der signa', *AEM aus Österreich-Ungarn* xv (1892), 182–93

K. Kraft, 'Zum Capricorn auf den Münzen des Augustus', *Jahrbuch für Numismatik und Geldgeschichte* xvii (1967), 17–27

Non-citizens in the legions

O. Cuntz, 'Legionäre des Antonius und Augustus aus dem Orient', *JOAI* xxv (1929), 70–81

T. Yoshimura, 'Über die legio vernacula des Pompeius', *Annuario di Istituto Giapponese di Cultura di Roma* i (1963–64), 101–6

CHAPTER 6

Augustan Reforms

P.A. Brunt, 'Pay and Superannuation in the Roman Army', *PBSR* xviii (1950), 50–71

E.G. Hardy, 'Augustus and his Legionaries', *CQ* xiv (1920), 187–94

B. Campbell, 'The Marriage of Soldiers under the Empire', *JRS* lxviii (1978), 153–66

K. Raaflaub, 'The political significance of Augustus' military reforms', in W.S. Hanson and L.J.F. Keppie (eds.), *Roman Frontier Studies 1979* (Oxford 1980), 1005–26

A. Momigliano, 'I problemi delle istituzioni militari di Augusto, in *Augustus: studi in occasione del bimillenario augusteo* (Roma 1938), 195–216

M. Corbier, *L'aerarium Saturni et l'aerarium militare* (Roma 1974)

The legions

E. Cavaignac, 'Les effectifs de l'armée d'Auguste', *REL* xxx (1952), 285–96

L.J.F. Keppie, 'Vexilla Veteranorum', *PBSR* xli (1973), 8–17

C. Nicolet, 'Tribuni militum a populo', *Mélanges d'Archéologie et d'histoire* lxxix (1967), 29–76

The auxiliaries

M.P. Speidel, 'Citizen cohorts in the Roman Imperial Army', *TAPA* cvi (1976), 339–48

E. Birley, '*Alae* named after their commanders', *Anc. Soc.* ix (1978), 257–74

M. Le Glay, 'Le commandement des *cohortes voluntariorum* de l'armée romaine', *Anc. Soc.* iii (1972), 209–22

D.B. Saddington, 'Prefects and Lesser Officers in the Auxilia at the Beginning of the Roman Empire', *Proceedings of the African Classical Associations* xv (1980), 20–58

D.B. Saddington, *The Development of the Roman Auxiliary Forces from Caesar to Vespasian (49 B.C.–A.D. 79)* (Harare 1982)

The fleet

A. Donnadieu, *Fréjus, le port militaire du Forum Iulii* (Paris 1935)

Rome garrisons (see under Chapter 7)

Wars and campaigns

R. Syme, 'Some notes on the Legions under Augustus', *JRS* xxiii (1933), 14–33

R. Syme, 'The northern frontiers under Augustus', *Cambridge Ancient History*, vol. X (Cambridge 1934), 340–81

Gaul

E. Ritterling, 'Zur Geschichte des römischen Heeres in Gallien unter Augustus', *BJ* cxiv/cxv (1906), 159–88

E.M. Wightman, 'Military arrangements, native settlements and related developments in early Roman Gaul', *Helinium* xvii (1977), 105–26

E.M. Wightman, 'La Gaule chevelue entre César et Auguste', in D.M. Pippidi ed.) *Actes du IXième Congr. int. d'Études sur les Frontières romaines* (Bucharesti 1974), 474–83

Spain

A. Garcia y Bellido, 'L. Terentius, figlinarius en Hispania de la legio IIII Macedonica', in *Hommages à Léon Herrmann* (Bruxelles 1960), 374–82

A. Garcia y Bellido, 'Terminos Augustales de la legio IIII Macedonica', *Arch. Esp. Arq.* xxix (1956), 184–94

Bibliography

R. Syme, 'The Conquest of North-West Spain', in *Legio VII Gemina* (Leon 1970), 83–107

R.F.J. Jones, 'The Roman Military Occupation of North-West Spain', *JRS* lxvi (1976), 45–66

Africa

F.G. de Pachtère, 'Les camps de la troisième légion en Afrique au premier siècle de l'Empire', *CRAI* 1916, 273–84

J. Lassère, *Ubique Populus* (Paris 1977)

The East

S. Mitchell, 'Legio VII and the garrison of Augustan Galatia', *CQ* lxx (1976), 298–308

B.M. Levick, *Roman Colonies in Southern Asia Minor* (Oxford 1967)

M.P. Speidel, 'Legionaries from Asia Minor', in *ANRW* VII.2 (1980), 730–46

M.P. Speidel, 'Augustus' Deployment of the Legions in Egypt', *Chronique d'Égypte* lviii (1982), 120–24

Advance to the Danube

J.J. Wilkes, *Dalmatia* (London 1969)

R. Syme, 'Lentulus and the Origins of Moesia' (with addenda), in his *Danubian Papers* (Bucharest 1971), 40–72

Rhine and Elbe

C.M. Wells, *The German Policy of Augustus* (Oxford 1972)

C. Schönberger, 'The Roman Frontier in Germany: an Archaeological Survey', *JRS* lix (1969), 144–97

H. Von Petrikovits, *Die Rheinlande in römischer Zeit* (Düsseldorf 1980)

S. Von Schnurbein, 'Ein Bleibarren der XIX. Legion aus dem Hauptlager von Haltern', *Germania* xlix (1971), 132–36

S. Von Schnurbein, *Die römischen Militäranlagen bei Haltern* (Münster 1974).

C.M. Wells, 'The supposed Augustan base at Augsburg-Oberhausen: a new Look at the Evidence', *SJ* xxvii (1970), 63–72

H. Schönberger and H.-G. Simon, *Römerlager Rödgen* (Berlin 1976)

J.E. Bogaers and C.B. Rüger, *Der Niedergermanische Limes* (Köln 1974)

The Varian disaster and the Pannonian Revolt

E.G. Hardy, 'Did Augustus create eight new Legions during the Pannonian rising of 6–9 A.D.?', *Journ. Phil.* xxiii (1895), 29–44

P.A. Brunt, 'C. Fabricius Tuscus and an Augustan Dilectus', *ZPE* xiii (1974), 161–85

The mutinies of AD 14

J.J. Wilkes, 'A Note on the Mutiny of the Pannonian Legions in A.D. 14', *CQ* lvi (1963), 268–71

Bibliography

CHAPTER 7

Recruitment and terms of service

P.A. Brunt, 'Conscription and Volunteering in the Roman Imperial Army', *Scripta Classica Israelica* i (1974), 90–115

G. Forni, *Il reclutamento delle legioni da Augusto a Diocleziano* (Milano-Roma 1953)

G. Forni, 'Estrazione etnica e sociale dei soldati delle legioni nei primi tre secoli dell'impero', in *ANRW* II.i (1974), 339–91

J.C. Mann, *Legionary recruitment and veteran settlement during the Principate* (London, 1983)

R.W. Davies, 'Joining the Roman Army', *BJ* clxix (1969), 208–32

A.R. Burn, 'Hic breve vivitur: a study of the expectation of life in the Roman Empire', *Past & Present* iv (1953), 2–31

M. Grant, *The Army of the Caesars* (London 1974)

G.R. Watson, *The Roman Soldier* (London 1983)

G. Webster, *The Roman Imperial Army* (London 1979)

The legions: organisation and command structure

S.S. Frere, 'Hyginus and the First Cohort', *Britannia* xi (1980), 51–60

D.J. Breeze, 'The Organisation of the Legion: the First Cohort and the Equites Legionis', *JRS* lix (1969), 50–55

B. Dobson, 'The *Praefectus Fabrum* in the Early Principate', in *Britain and Rome*, ed. M.G. Jarrett and B. Dobson (Kendal 1966), 61–84

A. Von Domaszewski, *Die Rangordnung des römischen Heeres*, rev. by B. Dobson (Köln 1967)

B. Dobson, *Die Primipilares* (Köln-Bonn 1978)

R. Syme, 'Die Zahl der praefecti castrorum im Heere des Varus', *Germania* xvi (1932), 109–111

H. Von Petrikovits, *Die Innenbauten römischer Legionslager während der Prinzipatszeit* (Opladen 1975)

B. Dobson, 'Legionary centurion or equestrian officer? A comparison of pay and prospects', *Anc. Soc.* iii (1972), 193–208

B. Dobson, 'Praefectus Castrorum Aegypti—a Reconsideration', *Chronique d'Égypte* lvii (1982), 322–37.

D.J. Breeze, 'The Career Structure below the Centurionate during the Principate', *ANRW* II.i (1975), 435–51

D.C. Shotter, 'Irregular legionary commands', *CQ* lxiii (1969), 371–73

H.M.D. Parker, 'A Note on the Promotion of the Centurions', *JRS* xvi (1926), 45–52

The Auxiliaries

G.L. Cheesman, *The Auxilia of the Roman Imperial Army* (Oxford 1914)

D.B. Saddington, 'The development of the Roman Auxiliary Forces from Augustus to Trajan', in *ANRW* II.3 (1975), 176–201

Bibliography

E.B. Birley, 'Alae and cohortes milliariae', in *Corolla memoriae Erich Swobodae dedicata* (Graz 1966), 54–67

R.W. Davies, 'Cohortes Equitatae', *Historia* xx (1971), 751–63

M.P. Speidel, 'The Pay of the Auxilia', *JRS* lxiii (1973), 141–47

K. Kraft, *Zur Rekrutierung der Alen und Kohorten an Rhein und Donau* (Bern 1951)

H. Devijver, 'Suétone, Claude 25 et les milices équestres', *Anc. Soc.* i (1970), 69–81

H. Devijver, 'The Career of M. Porcius Narbonensis: new evidence for the reorganisation of the Militiae Equestres by the Emperor Claudius', *Anc. Soc.* iii (1972), 165–91

G. Alföldy, *Die Hilfstruppen der römischen Provinz Germania Inferior* = *Epigraphische Studien* vi (Düsseldorf 1968)

P.A. Holder, *Studies in the Auxilia of the Roman Army from Augustus to Trajan* (Oxford 1980)

W. Wagner, *Die Dislokation der römischen Auxiliarformationen in den Provinzen Noricum, Pannonien, Moesien, und Dakien von Augustus bis Gallienus* (Berlin 1938)

M.M. Roxan, 'The auxilia of the Roman Army raised in the Iberian Peninsula (Ph.D. London 1973, unpublished)

D.L. Kennedy, *The auxilia and numeri raised in the Roman Province of Syria* (D. Phil. Oxford 1981, unpublished)

M.G. Jarrett, 'Thracian Units in the Roman Army', *IEJ* xix (1969), 215–24

M.P. Speidel, 'The eastern desert garrisons under Augustus and Tiberius', in *Studien zu den Militärgrenzen Roms* II (Köln–Bonn 1977), 511–15

W. Glasbergen and W. Groenman-van Waateringe, *The Pre-Flavian Garrisons of Valkenburg Z.H.* (Amsterdam–London 1974)

Praetorian Guard

M. Durry, *Les cohortes prétoriennes* (Paris 1938)

A. Passerini, *Le coorti pretorie* (Roma 1939)

D.L. Kennedy, 'Some Observations on the Praetorian Guard', *Anc. Soc.* ix (1978), 275–301

C. Letta, 'Le imagines Caesarum di un praefectus castrorum Aegypti e l'XI coorte pretoria', *Athenaeum* lvi (1978), 3–19

Urban Cohorts

H. Freis, *Die Cohortes Urbanae* = *Epigraphische Studien* II (Köln–Bonn 1967)

Vigiles

P.K. Baillie Reynolds, *The Vigiles of Imperial Rome* (Oxford 1926)

J.S. Rainbird, *The Vigiles of Rome* (Ph.D Thesis, Durham 1976, unpublished)

Equites Singulares

M.P. Speidel, *Die Equites Singulares Augusti* (Bonn 1965)

Fleets

C.G. Starr, *The Roman Imperial Navy* (New York 1941)

D. Kienast, *Untersuchungen zu den Kriegsflotten der römischen Kaiserzeit* (Bonn 1966)

New legions

J.C. Mann, 'The Raising of New Legions during the Principate', *Hermes* xci (1963), 483–89

G.L. Cheesman, 'The Date of the Disappearance of legio XXI Rapax', *CR* xxii (1909), 155

J.P.V.D. Balsdon, 'Notes concerning the Principate of Gaius', *JRS* xxiv (1934), 13–24

Movements of Legions

R. Saxer, *Untersuchungen zu den Vexillationen des römischen Kaiserheeres von Augustus bis Diokletian = Epigraphische Studien* i (Köln–Graz 1967)

A. Betz, 'Zur Dislokation der Legionen in der Zeit von Tode des Augustus bis zum Ende der Prinzipatsepoche', *Carnuntina* (Graz–Köln 1966), 17–24

J. Szilagyi, 'Les variations des centres de prépondérance militaire dans les provinces frontières de l'empire romain', *Acta Ant. Hung.* ii (1953–54), 118–223

Spain

A. Garcia y Bellido, 'El "exercitus hispanicus" desde Augusto a Vespasiano', *Arch. Esp. Arq.* xxxiv (1961), 114–60.

J.M. Roldan Hervas, *Hispania y el ejercito romano* (Salamanca 1974)

P. Le Roux, *L'armée romaine et l'organisation des provinces ibériques d'Auguste à l'invasion de 409* (Paris 1982)

Africa

R. Cagnat, *L'armée romaine d'Afrique et l'occupation militaire de l'Afrique sous les empereurs* (Paris 1913)

M. Fentress, *Numidia and the Roman Army* (Oxford 1979)

Egypt

M. Lesquier, *L'armée romaine d'Égypte d'Auguste à Dioclétian* (Le Caire 1918)

The East

R.K. McElderry, 'The Legions of the Euphrates Frontier', *CQ* iii (1909), 44–53

J. Wagner, 'Legion IIII Scythica in Zeugma am Euphrat', in *Studien zu den Militärgrenzen Roms* II, ed. D. Haupt and H.G. Horn (Köln–Bonn 1978), 517–39

The Danubian Provinces

A. Mócsy, *Pannonia and Upper Moesia* (London 1974)

The Army in Politics

G.E.F. Chilver, 'The Army in Politics, AD 68–70', *JRS* xlvii (1957), 29–36

Frontiers

J.C. Mann, 'The Frontiers of the Principate', in *ANRW* II.i (1974), 508–33

Bibliography

E. Luttwak, *The Grand Strategy of the Roman Empire* (Baltimore 1976)

D.J. Breeze (ed.), *The Frontiers of the Roman Empire* (London, forthcoming)

The Army of Roman Britain

G. Webster, *The Roman Invasion of Britain* (London 1980)

M.G. Jarrett, 'Legio II Augusta in Britain', *Arch. Cambr.* cxiii (1964), 47–63.

M.G. Jarrett, 'Legio XX Valeria Victrix in Britain', *Arch. Cambr.* cxvii (1968), 77–91

E.B. Birley, 'The fate of the Ninth Legion', in *Soldier and Civilian in Roman Yorkshire*, ed. R.M. Butler (Leicester 1971), 71–80

A.R. Birley, 'VI Victrix in Britain', *ibid.*, 81–96

M.G. Jarrett, 'The Garrison of Maryport and the Roman Army in Britain', in M.G. Jarrett and B. Dobson (eds.), *Britain and Rome* (Kendal 1966), 27–40

P.A. Holder, *The Roman Army in Britain* (London 1982)

Index

Index

artillery, 94, 99, 112, 177, 189, 228f
Arverni, 88
as, 216
Asculum (Ascoli Piceno), 68f, 122
Asia Minor, 43, 106
Asprenas, L., 168f
Assisium (Assisi), 122
Astorga, 193
Asturians, 156, 196, 207
Ateste (Este), 129f, 202, 206f, 209ff, 226
Athens, 17, 119
Augsburg-Oberhausen, 159
Augusta Praetoria (Aosta), 156
Augustus, 11, 20, 44, 46, 78, 132,
    142f, 145ff, 154ff, 169f, 172ff, 180,
    182, 185f, 191, 205ff, 218, 221,
    229ff, pl. 15; military reforms,
    145ff; foreign policy, 154ff; *see
    also* Octavian
aureus, 216
Aurunculeius Cotta, L., 87, 101
Ausculum (Ascoli Satriano), 24, 235
Auzon (river), 58, 88
auxiliaries, 68f, 78, 100, 105f, 112,
    150ff, 166, 168, 182ff, 190f, 194;
    length of service, 151, 185f;
    rewards of service, 151f, 185;
    commanders, 150ff, 184; *see also
    ala, cohors, praefectus*, forts.
Avaricum, 88, 99, 137
Avernus, Lake, 153

Babylon (Cairo), 158
Baecula, 29
Baeterrae (Béziers), 207
baggage train, 66, 100
Balbus, L. Cornelius, 158
Balearic slingers, 78, 100
ballistae, 99
barracks, 173
Basel, 156, 159
Bassus, P. Ventidius, 118, 122f, 125,
    133, 208
Bastarnae, 159
Bateson, Dr. J.D., 13
Beauvais, 95
Belgae, 84
Bellovaci, 95
Beneventum, battle of, 24
Beneventum (Benevento), 13, 122f,
    200, 202, 207, 239

Berytus (Beirut), 130, 202, 206, 208
Bibracte (Mt. Beuvray), 82
Billienus, M., fig. 38
Bituriges, 88
Blaesus, Q. Junius, 169
boar (military standard), 67, 139
boar-emblem, 140, 143, 208, 211
Boii, 82
Bonn, 194
Bononia (Bologna), 115, 119, 122,
    169, 231
booty, 54f, 100f
Boudica, 139, 197, 210f, 222
Bovianum (Boiano), 209
Bostra, 196
Breche (river), 95
Brenne (river), 93
Britain, 11, 86, 96, 99, 137, 139, 155,
    172, 190, 197, 232f,
Brittany, 85
Brixia (Brescia), 129, 167
Brundisium (Brindisi), 70, 105, 114,
    238
Brutus, Dec. Junius, 115, 118
Brutus, M. Junius, 113f, 119ff, 141,
    150, 224
bull-emblem, 134, 139f, 142f, 206ff,
    228
Burnett, Mr. A., 13
Burnum, 193
Bussy, 94
Byllis, 202, 207

Cabilenus, Q., 99
Cáceres, 71ff; fig. 21
Caedicius, 241
Caelius, M., 169, 231; pl. 18
Caelius, P., 231
Caerleon, 190
Caesar, C. Julius, 11f, 63, 76f, 79,
    103ff, 118ff, 125, 132ff, 141ff, 145,
    149f, 153, 155, 168, 182, 193,
    199ff, 203f, 205ff, 208ff, 224f, 227;
    pl. 6; in Gaul, 80ff; his army, 80ff,
    97ff, fig. 29; as author 96; bridge
    across Rhine, 85, 99, pl. 7
Caesar, C. (grandson of Augustus),
    229
Caesar, L. (grandson of Augustus),
    229
Caesar, L. Julius, (*cos.* 90 BC), 68

Index

Index

Index

Index

Index

DATE DUE

JAN 10			
FEB 6			
MS 24 06			
NOV 1 8 2009			
DEC 2 4 2008			
GAYLORD			PRINTED IN U.S.A.